LORRA

MEDIT

GARDEN
PLANTS

Dedicated to these special people.

Firstly, to the two great ladies in my life – my mother and my grandmother. You have both always shown me the way forward, with love and tenacity. I hope I can always follow your example.

In memory of my dearest grandfather, a great man, who instilled in me a love of plants, gardens, books and reading – thank you for leading me down that particular garden path! I know you would have loved this.

To Merv for your patient and guiding hand on the mouse – proving to me that sea creatures, mice and Irishmen can be, surprisingly, compatible! The book germinated but would never have flourished without your continual help and encouragement. Thank you.

And lastly, but most importantly, to my two darling daughters – Madeleine and Grace – for your total lack of faith in the entire project, but then, what else are daughters for? Apologies for missed meals, chaotic timetables, lack of maternal attention etc. etc. – I admit to it all! I love you both. And thanks for your help in compiling the photos.

And a kiss for my very lovely grand-daughter, Ainhoa.

Agradacimientos - Acknowledgments

Primero a Damian, mi socio en nuestra compañía, Verdisimo, de montaje de jardines. Gracias, de corazon, por todo tu apoyo y por dejarme tiempo para seguir adelante con el libro.

Gracias a Pepe y Mari de Viveros Amberes, Torrox Costa y a Toni y MariLo de la floristeria en Cómpeta por ayudarme a conseguir la perfecta strelitzia de la portada.

Gracias a amigos y clientes que durante muchos años me han convencido para escribir este libro – teniais razon!

Thanks to all friends, clients and customers over the years who have nagged me into writing this book – you were all right! Special thanks to Margaret for your efforts to provide me with a perfect strelitzia flower.

And to all the staff at Baker-Pickard Printers who must be glad to see my book out on the street at last! You've all been great, but special hugs to Jo and Mike who have steered me through this.

And, finally, thanks to all you green-fingered, green-minded and some just simply green gardeners out there for buying this book. I hope it will be endlessly useful to you all.

CONTENTS

INTRODUCTION

Having lived in Spain for almost 20 years, owned a plant nursery for some seven of those and now running a garden landscape business with a Spanish partner, I have been constantly asked by friends, customers and clients to recommend a book on Mediterranean garden plants. There are, of course, some excellent books on the topic in general, but I believe this is something different. I listened to what you wanted - your queries over the years, your frustration at garden centres, lack of knowledge of indigenous and suitable plants – and this is my answer and, I hope yours too!

Firstly, a **POCKET-SIZED BOOK** but **BIG** on **FACTS AND INFORMATION**, easy to tuck into the car or carry around for use at the garden centre.

A **WIPE-CLEAN COVER** for gardeners mucky hands!

A **CLEAR AND SIMPLE DESIGN** with plants listed in **A-Z FORMAT** by their **LATIN NAMES**.

THREE INDEXES – LATIN, COMMON ENGLISH and **COMMON SPANISH NAMES** to help you identify and ask for your plant.

A CROSS REFERENCE SYSTEM which categorises plants into groundcover, annuals, biennials, perennials, bulbs, grasses and bamboo, succulents, water lovers, shrubs, hedging, climbers, and trees - weeping, conifers and palms. This is further divided into sun and shade lovers, with an indication of height and flower colour. Simply look up what you require and several options will be listed.

A **DOUBLE-PAGE DESCRIPTION** of each plant with a **HALF-PAGE COLOUR PHOTOGRAPH**. The **HABIT AND CULTIVATION** box gives all the necessary basic information. Further **CULTURAL AND HISTORICAL DETAILS** are given on the opposite page. And, below that, advice on **PROPAGATION**, **PRUNING** and **PROBLEMS**.

No confusing symbols
– it's all set out there in plain language.

Although the book has been written and totally compiled in Spain, it is, of course, entirely relevant to many other areas of the world – the entire Mediterranean basin, parts of Australia, South Africa, South America, California and milder areas of Great Britain and Ireland. Check through the origins of the plant, and you'll see that the majority of them are indigenous to these countries. Inner city areas of cooler climes can often have strange climatic quirks too, making possible the cultivation of many. The plants featured are generally adaptable to a winter rain/hot, dry summer pattern, unless otherwise indicated. Soil preferences are neutral to alkaline, as prevalent in the Mediterranean area; any exceptions to this are noted.

These are, in general, plants meant for this climate that will give you few problems – that has been my first priority in the shortlist. Then I have selected for beauty, for scent, for leaf and bark colour, stunning silhouettes, sheer flower power – the huge gamut that the plant world brings to us.

Ever more Northern Europeans are being enticed to the Mediterranean lifestyle. We all arrive somewhat green – to the culture and way of life, expectations high and generally with time on our hands. And nearly all our properties have gardens, roof terraces, or balconies to be planted. Keen and experienced gardeners are unaccustomed to many of the plants here; beginners are totally lost and bewildered. A great deal of time and money can be wasted buying and planting unsuitably. Heartbreak and frustration can be enormous when a plant curls up and dies despite all your best efforts. Disillusionment sets in and many would-be gardeners fall by the wayside. I'd like to bring you all back, restore your faith and make you dream again.

I believe this book will inspire and help all new and existing Mediterranean gardeners to select well, plant well and enjoy!

ABELIA FLORIBUNDA The Mexican Abelia, (Spanish : Abelia).

HABIT AND CULTIVATION

Category	Shrub
Family	Caprifoliaceae
Origin	Mexico
Size, height x spread	3 x 4 metres
Situation	Full sun/half shade.
Irrigation	Water until established, then drought tolerant.
Temperature	Down to –5°C
Evergreen/Deciduous	Generally evergreen
Flowering	Pink/purple. Spring and autumn.
Special Features	Flowers scented.

An attractive arching shrub, found in the wild on mountainsides and open woodland. Very neat small, dark green, glossy leaves with reddish- bronze new growth. Pendant bell flowers with long lasting green calyces are produced in great abundance over a long season. Once established and producing basal growth, it is drought tolerant. Grows in most soil types and stands up well to wind. In extremely hot areas, best with a little afternoon shade. Can also be wall trained or used as a hedging plant.

Propagation
Cuttings in late summer. Will also transplant quite readily if hard pruned first.

Pruning
Best selectively pruned by hand, not with shears, in winter. Prune out old branches to the ground to retain good shape. Bear in mind that it flowers on the previous season's wood, so only prune out, say, one branch in four. Old bushes can be rejuvenated by pruning to the ground and waiting for new basal growth.

Problems
Occasional powdery mildew.

Also **ABELIA GRANDIFLORA** from China. Similar, but smaller growing. Mid summer to autumn flowering, white tinged pink.

ABUTILON X HYBRIDUM Flowering Maple, (Spanish : Flor de Linternas).

HABIT AND CULTIVATION

Category	Shrub
Family	Malvaceae
Origin	Brazil
Size, height x spread	2 x 2 metres
Situation	Full sun or dappled shade, out of a cold wind.
Irrigation	Moderate
Temperature	Generally frost tender.
Evergreen/deciduous	Semi-evergreen
Flowering	White, cream, yellow, orange, pink and red. Spring and summer.
Special features	-

The abutilon is grown for its elegant form, both in foliage and flower. They have mid-green heart-shaped leaves, softly furry and the form is an open shrub, sometimes somewhat lax. May benefit from some light support or can be grown against trellising etc. The bell shaped flowers hang like lanterns in the branches and, apart from their wide range of colours, many are veined in a contrasting colour or with a central eye. It can also be trained as a standard, when it will form a slightly weeping mini tree, delicate and delightful. Also very pretty in pots with the advantage that root restriction induces prolific flowering.

Propagation
Easy and quick from seed, flowering within twelve months of sowing, but not always true to parent. Also from summer cuttings.

Pruning
Tip prune through the growing season to encourage bushy growth. Mature plants can have previous years growth cut back hard.

Problems
Watch out for aphids and red spider mite.

Acacia (Mimosa, Wattle)

The acacia group is extremely large and diverse with some 1000 family members of deciduous, semi-evergreen and evergreen shrubs and trees. 660 of these originate from Australia, with the rest native to either Africa or North America. We tend to call them all mimosa because they all bear the typical scented yellow powder puff flowers. The Australians call them wattle because early settlers used them to build simple wattle and daub huts.

For many years popularly regarded as Australia's national flower, on 1st. September 1988 the Golden Wattle (A. pycnantha) was officially proclaimed as such in celebration of Australia's bicentennial year. The word 'acacia' is derived from the Greek 'akakia' meaning sharp and pointed, a reference to the sharp spines many of the family bear. And 'pycnantha' is again from the Greek 'pycnos' meaning 'close, thick or crowded' and 'anthos' flower, alluding to the densely packed flower heads that many of the acacias characteristically carry.

Wattle Day is celebrated yearly on 1st. August, a huge party with guests wearing sprigs of wattle, green and gold bunting (being the predominant colours of the tree) and symbolic planting of wattle trees. There is also Wattle Town, Wattle Valley, etc. etc. There are a great many myths and legends attached to these plants, most with roots in Aborigine beliefs. For instance, if the Queen Wattles flower heavily this is a sure sign that bushfires are to come. And, in fact, the last 2 years of severe bushfires in and around Sydney were foretold by the Aborigines using exactly this technique. Local bush lore credits many of the wattles with all kinds of medicinal powers and culinary delights. A couple of rather nice examples of this are A. aneura, commonly called Mulga, which exudes a sweet, sticky substance when the branches are damaged. These are broken off and sucked upon as 'bush lollies'. And A. kempeana, commonly called the Witchetty Bush, houses in its roots the Witchetty Grub, one of the most famous – if not the most delightful – of bush tucker.

Ranging from about 4m up to 20m high, the wattles are extremely quick growers and immensely useful as screening and pioneer plantings. Their somewhat brittle branches can break off completely during heavy winds. Over watering and fertilising agravates this problem, as it makes for very rapid but weak growth. Best to water occasionally through the first summer but then leave them alone.

Acacias generally are short lived with a lifespan of perhaps 20 to 30 years. As they are easily replaced from seed, this is not generally looked upon as a problem. The seeds have great viability and have been known to germinate after 50 years. Generally give them hot water treatment and they will shoot easily. They are much admired and planted for their spectacular flowering, which, by using different varieties, can be spread over several months. Whilst their roots are not generally destructive, the plants themselves can be invasive because of their ability to self seed and in parts of Australia the wattles have almost reached weed proportions and are often considered as undesirables!

ACACIA DEALBATA Florist's Mimosa, (Spanish : Mimosa, hoja fina).

HABIT AND CULTIVATION

Category	Tree
Family	Leguminosae
Origin	Australia and Tasmania
Size, height x spread	12 x 12 metres
Situation	Full sun
Irrigation	Occasional deep soak until established, then drought resistant.
Temperature	Half hardy.
Evergreen/Deciduous	Evergreen
Flowering	Yellow. Late winter/early springtime
Special Features	Scented

A. dealbata is often sold as a young grafted tree, a guarantee of quality and quantity of leaf and flower. Even very young trees will be smothered in bloom. The grafting makes a more expensive tree, but for one specimen tree, it is worth it. For bulk plantings, ungrafted trees will suffice. This is an extremely quick and large grower, an excellent windbreak, shelter and privacy tree. It has very finely cut, greyish-green, feathery foliage and the typical yellow powder-puff flowers smother the branches and fill the air with their musky perfume. Cut armfuls of the flower laden branches for indoors. Quite a messy tree in terms of litter, but most people forgive it! Water deeply and occasionally throughout it's first summer, then leave it alone. Too much water and fertiliser encourages very rapid but weak growth and whole branches can be lost in storms.

Propagation
For ungrafted trees, by seed.

Pruning
In first year or two of growth, prune back side growths by half to strengthen. Later, top out to form a very large wide shrub or remove side growths to keep a clean trunk and spreading canopy. Prune out dieback. Thin out weaker growth, to minimise wind damage.

Problems
Mealy bug and scale insects.

See also **ACACIA VERTICILLATA** and **A. LONGIFOLIA**.

ACACIA LONGIFOLIA Sydney Golden Wattle, (Spanish : Mimosa, hoja gorda)

HABIT AND CULTIVATION

Category	Large shrub/small tree
Family	Leguminosea
Origin	Australia and Tasmania
Size, height x spread	5 x 5 metres
Situation	Best in full sun, though will accept some shade.
Irrigation	Occasional deep soak until established, then drought tolerant.
Temperature	To –5°C
Evergreen/deciduous	Evergreen
Flowering	Yellow. Springtime.
Special features	Scented.

An extremely quick grower and tolerant of very poor conditions. Its ability to withstand strong winds, coastal spray etc. and drought makes this a popular choice as a privacy/windbreak tree. Also excellent to stabilise ground and combat erosion. Narrow, oblong, dark green leaves grow very densely along the stems and the tree has a slightly weeping habit with a very large foliage canopy. Cylindrical clusters of yellow flowers smother the branches in springtime and fill the air with their musty perfume. As with most of the acacia family it is short lived, but the speed at which it can establish itself does not really make this a problem. Water and fertilize as A. dealbata.

Propagation
Easy and rapid by seed.

Pruning
As A. dealbata.

Problems
As A. dealbata.

Also **ACACIA VERTICILLATA**, Prickly Moses. A native of Australia and Tasmania. Shrub/tree to around 9 x 9 metres. Dark green needle-like leaves with lemon-yellow bottle brush flowers in springtime. Extremely tough.

See also **ACACIA DEALBATA**.

ACANTHUS MOLLIS Bear's Breeches, (Spanish : Acanto, Traseros del Oso, Hierba Giganta.)

HABIT AND CULTIVATION

Category	Perennial
Family	Acanthaceae
Origin	Mediterranean
Size, height x spread	1 x 1 metres
Situation	Best in dappled shade and deep soil, but quite tolerant.
Irrigation	None, unless very dry winter
Temperature	Fully hardy
Evergreen/Deciduous	Summer dormant
Flowering	Lilac-purple/white. Late spring/early summer.
Special Features	Flower stalks can be dried. Summer dormant.

This is a magnificent foliage plant, the huge, deeply serrated leaves emerging and unfurling with the first autumn rains. Then, in late spring the towering flower spikes, reaching up to 2m, add to the beauty of the plant with lipped white flowers set in purple bracts. Give it plenty of room to expand. Particularly good in a natural setting, but also, because of its architectural qualities, looks good set in paving, pots etc. where its tendency to spread and increase everywhere can be better controlled. Immortalised by the Ancient Greeks who used the leaf motif to decorate their Corinthian columns.

Propagation
Seed freely produced, which germinate easily. Self sows prolifically and young plantlets can be carefully lifted and transplanted. Can also be grown from root cuttings.

Pruning
Not necessary. Plant disappears underground during the summer months, to re-emerge with autumn rains.

Problems
Slugs and snails like the large juicy leaves and can cause considerable damage.

ACHILLEA MILLEFOLIUM Yarrow, (Spanish : Milenrama, Flor de Pluma, Milhoja).

HABIT AND CULTIVATION

Category	Perennial
Family	Compositae
Origin	Europe
Size, height x spread	0.75 x 0.50 metres
Situation	Full sun/dappled shade
Irrigation	Occasional deep soak in summer
Temperature	Fully hardy.
Evergreen/deciduous	Will stay evergreen above 0°C
Flowering	Yellow, but wide range of colours in species. Summer
Special features	Attractive to butterflies and bees.

An upright perennial with masses of dark green ferny leaves. In summer large flat plate-like heads of flowers rise above the basal foliage, lasting for many weeks. The flowers can also be cut and dried for use in the house. The non-woody parts of the plant have medicinal properties, and it is well recognised for helping stomach disorders, colds and fevers. Also, externally, for skin rashes and eczema and to help heal wounds. The ancient Greeks acknowledged the power of the plant and named it thus after their famous warrior heroe, Achilles. Millefolium, a thousand leaves, refers to its very cut and downy foliage. Tolerates most soils and conditions but does best in an open, sunny site. Can survive summer drought, though will look better with an occasional deep soaking.

Propagation
Softwood cuttings in summer, or, easier, by division in late autumn.

Pruning
Cut out dead flower stems.

Problems
Generally none.

ACTINIDIA CHINENSIS Kiwi Vine, (Spanish : Kiwi).

HABIT AND CULTIVATION

Category	Climber
Family	Actinidiaceae
Origin	China
Size, height x spread	10 metres high
Situation	Dappled shade.
Irrigation	Water well when fruits developing
Temperature	Withstands 0°C for short periods
Evergreen/deciduous	Deciduous
Flowering	Creamy-white/buff. Spring.
Special features	Fruits very vitamin rich. Flowers scented.

A very vigorous, woody-stemmed, twining climber, which needs strong supports. Has very pretty hairy heart shaped leaves and many cultivars have reddish stems and attractive red new growth. Both sexes are needed for fruit. One male plant to eight females, if the male is planted in the middle. Starts fruiting at 3years old. In summer, clusters of creamy white cup shaped flowers develop which, by early autumn, produce the egg sized hairy fruits. It is important, at this stage, to water generously. The kiwi vine has been grown commercially in New Zealand since the early 1900's when it was more commonly known as the Chinese gooseberry, but it had little recognition. It was only after changing the name to kiwi fruit in 1962 that great inroads were made into the world market. What's in a name!

Propagation
Seed in spring and autumn, softwood cuttings in summer or by layering during the winter months.

Pruning
Prune during the winter months to control growth.

Problems
Fruit fly, and occasional root rot .

ADENANTHOS DRUMMONDII
Woollybush, (Spanish : Adenanthus).

HABIT AND CULTIVATION

Category	Shrub
Family	Proteaceae
Origin	Australia
Size, height x spread	1 x 2.5 metres
Situation	Full sun.
Irrigation	Drought tolerant.
Temperature	To around –5°C
Evergreen/deciduous	Evergreen
Flowering	Red. Spring/summer/ autumn
Special features	-

A very attractive low shrub, but one little used. It forms a low sprawling mound of dense foliage which is extremely soft and silky to the touch – this is a very tactile plant. The downy tips are silver grey which combine with the fine red tubular flowers very prettily. It likes a hot sunny spot and, once established, is a very undemanding plant. An occasional deep soak in summer helps, but never leave it waterlogged. A useful addition to mixed plantings and also looks very good in a rockery situation or gravel garden.

Propagation
Semi hardwood cuttings in summer.

Pruning
Generally very little required. An occasional tidying up is best carried out during the winter months. Can be tip pruned if older branches start to get a bit leggy and bare at the base.

Problems
Generally none, though fluctuating daytime/ nightime temperatures can occasionally provoke a touch of mildew.

Aeonium Arboreum 'Schwarzkopf'

AEONIUM ARBOREUM
(Spanish : Aeonium).

HABIT AND CULTIVATION

Category	Succulent
Family	Crassulaceae
Origin	Canary Isles
Size, height x spread	1 x 0.5 metres
Situation	Full sun, tolerates some shade.
Irrigation	Drought resistant.
Temperature	Damaged below 0°C
Evergreen/deciduous	Evergreen
Flowering	Yellow. Spring.
Special features	Summer dormant.

A branching perennial succulent, extremely tolerant of drought. Bright green rosettes of leaves carried on the end of the woody looking stems. Branching and spreading to cover large areas. Particularly striking in springtime with it's domes of yellow star-shaped flowers. Easy to grow, demanding very little care. Plant in full sun or some shade. During drought, the rosettes shrink down and curl in on themselves, but with the first rains they fatten back out to original size.

Propagation
Easy from stem cuttings or branches that break off. Allow them to callous, then pot up or simply poke into ground.

Pruning
Not normally required apart from cutting down, to ground level, the dead flower stalks.

Problems
No pest problems. Over watering can produce soft floppy growth, rot and mildew.

Also **AEONIUM ARBOREUM ATROPURPUREUM**. As above but with very pretty purple/bronze foliage.

Also **AEONIUM ARBOREUM 'SCHWARZKOPF'**. Very dramatic foliage colour, a deep aubergine-black. Great contrast plant, combining wonderfully with all other colours.

Also **AEONIUM CANARIENSE**. A less branching habit but its giant sized rosettes and flower heads are stunning. Rarer but worth searching for.

AGAPANTHUS PRAECOX Nile Lily, (Spanish : Agapanto, Lirio del Nilo).

HABIT AND CULTIVATION

Category	Perennial
Family	Liliaceae
Origin	South Africa
Size, height x spread	1+ x 1 metres
Situation	Full sun or part shade
Irrigation	Drought tolerant once established
Temperature	To around –5°C
Evergreen/deciduous	Mainly evergreen, though some more unusual deciduous species exist.
Flowering	All shades of blue and white. Summer.
Special features	Poisonous

A very beautiful and strong growing plant which has a multitude of uses and is deservedly popular. The bright green strap shaped leaves are produced in clumps, with the very showy umbels of flowers held on erect stems through a long period. There is a blue to suit every mood, from a very pale ice blue through to a deep sapphire shade and pure white. A. praecox from the Cape area of South Africa is a real survivor often found growing in the most inhospitable places. They look excellent planted along the base of a wall, under deep green cypress trees, in large swathes amongst trees and shrubs and also make a very attractive pot plant. A stunning cut flower.

Propagation
Rootstocks can be lifted and split after flowering. This may delay flowering for 2 years. Also by seed, but much slower to flower.

Pruning
None. Cut out dead flower stalks.

Problems
None.

AGAVE AMERICANA Century Plant, (Spanish : Planta del siglo, Pita).

HABIT AND CULTIVATION

Category	Succulent
Family	Agavaceae
Origin	Mexico
Size, height x spread	3 x 2 metres
Situation	Full sun
Irrigation	None
Temperature	Below zero leaves are damaged by cold.
Evergreen/deciduous	Evergreen
Flowering	One of the most unusual of the plant kingdom, said to flower once every hundred years then die, hence the name, though flowering is actually much quicker.
Special features	Sap is extremely caustic and can cause a very severe reaction in many people, even blindness. Wicked spines along leaf edges and tips. Keep children well away.

The word 'agave' signifies, in Greek, 'marvellous' and indeed the large basal rosette of the agave forms a magnificent accent point and, where wisely used, it can make a very positive addition to a garden. It is an extreme survivor, often being the only plant remaining in neglected gardens. Its tough root will shoot up and form new plants in any crevice, breaking through poorly laid paving, concrete etc. It is very difficult to eradicate so site with much care. The flower stem can shoot up 8m and bears bell shaped creamy white flowers. The fibrous content of the leaves is traditionally used as hemp for sacking, ropes etc. and the South American Indians brew an alcoholic drink from the sap known as mescal..

Propagation
After flowering, the main plant dies back but only after producing multiple offshoots. Any baby plant, carefully separated out, or section of root will form a new plant.

Pruning
Cut back to base old outer leaves as they die back. Use extreme caution when handling.

Problems
None.

Also **AGAVE AMERICANA MEDIO PICTA**, (Spanish : Pita Matizada) has yellow striped leaves and **AGAVE AMERICANA MEDIO PICTA ALBA** has white striped leaves.

AGAVE ATTENUATA The Foxtail or Pearly Agave, (Spanish : Agave, Pita).

HABIT AND CULTIVATION

Category	Succulent
Family	Agavaceae
Origin	Mexico
Size, height x spread	1.5 x 2 metres
Situation	Full sun, though will accept some light or dappled shade.
Irrigation	Drought tolerant, though an occasional soaking is appreciated during long hot summers
Temperature	Can take down to 0°C for a short spell.
Evergreen/deciduous	Evergreen
Flowering	Yellow. Spring/summer
Special features	Poisonous sap

This agave is a much kinder family member than the americana. The wide, pearly grey/green leaves arch back gracefully resembling a huge opening flower. The leaves are smooth to the touch, bearing none of the teeth of its cousin. The 3m tall flower stalk, densely covered with yellow flowers, curves dramatically to the ground giving it the common name of foxtail. The attractive colouration of this agave blends happily into many planting schemes, and it also looks good in pots. Seaspray tolerant.

Propagation
Seeds develop into small bulbils and subsequently plants. Young plants at the base of the mother can also be carefully cut out and replanted.

Pruning
Removing the old outer leaves forms a stout woody trunk.

Problems
None if grown in open site.

See also **A. AMERICANA MEDIO PICTA** and **A. AMERICANA MEDIO PICTA ALBA**.

AILANTHUS ALTISSIMA The Tree of Heaven, (Spanish : Arbol del Cielo).

HABIT AND CULTIVATION

Category	Tree
Family	Simaroubaceae
Origin	China
Size, height x spread	20 x 8 metres
Situation	Full sun or light shade
Irrigation	Drought tolerant.
Temperature	Hardy but lusher growing in semi-tropics
Evergreen/deciduous	Deciduous
Flowering	Yellowish-green. Summer.
Special features	Very suckering habit.

The Tree of Heaven, as its name would suggest, is a very tall growing tree, elegant and beautiful. It has very lush and prolific fern-like foliage, each leaf around 60cm long and composed of up to 30 oval leaflets, in pairs. The inconspicuous greenish flowers are borne in summer and have a rather unpleasant smell. They are much more attractive later when they develop into rusty red winged seed pods. It is a very tolerant tree, surviving extremes of temperature, drought, smog etc. and is a very quick grower. Unfortunately, it also has some bad habits! It suckers at an incredible rate and can become very difficult to control and, because of this, in certain parts of the world it is classed as a noxious weed because of its invasive habit. However, used and sited with great care, it can become a valuable addition to the large garden, as a quick windbreak and shelter tree and to provide privacy.

Propagation
If you need to increase stocks! – easiest from suckers in winter or by seed sown in autumn.

Pruning
Can be severely pruned in spring to create shrubby growth.

Problems
None.

AJANIA PACIFICA
(Spanish : Planta de Plata).

HABIT AND CULTIVATION

Category	Perennial
Family	Compositae
Origin	Japan
Size, height x spread	0.30 x 0.30 metres
Situation	Full sun
Irrigation	Drought resistant.
Temperature	Hardy
Evergreen/deciduous	Generally evergreen, though below freezing will become deciduous.
Flowering	Yellow. Late summer through winter.
Special features	-

This neat little plant resembles a silvery-sheened chrysanthemum and was, in fact, first classified as such. A native of Japan, it grows wild there in particularly exposed spots, cliffs, rough shorelines etc. where it is exposed to fierce sun, wind, sea spray, drought and freezing winter conditions. The cut leaves, resembling those of chrysanthemum, are heavily lined with white felt on the undersides to prevent damage by the burning sand and this felting is painted along the margins of the leaves giving an extraordinary gilded appearance. The upper surface is also lightly covered with silver hairs to reflect strong sun, giving a totally satinised look. The effect is luminous, extremely eye-catching and neat. The leaves form overlapping rosettes to further protect themselves – a plant extremely well adapted to harsh conditions. Through autumn and winter it bears small yellow flowers.

Propagation
By summer cuttings or breaking off spreading rhizomes and replanting.

Pruning
None.

Problems
None.

AJUGA REPTANS Carpet Bugle,
(Spanish : Reptans de Ajuga).

HABIT AND CULTIVATION

Category	Perennial
Family	Labiatae
Origin	Europe
Size, height x spread	0.3 x 1 metres
Situation	Shade or dappled shade
Irrigation	Moderate
Temperature	Fully hardy
Evergreen/deciduous	Evergreen
Flowering	Blue. Spring.
Special features	-

A very showy small groundcovering plant, best suited with a coolish root run, under trees etc. The metallic crinkled leaves are very attractive and there are several cultivars with coloured leaves, though all bear the typical blue, conical, bugle flower.

'Jungle Beauty' is a very dark green tinged with bronze/purple, as is 'Atropurpurea'. 'Multicolor' is one of the most striking with pink, purple and cream markings. 'Burgundy Lace' has cream and dark raspberry coloured leaves. The variegated varieties show their colouration best in dappled shade. The plant was traditionally used to heal wounds.

Propagation
The mat forming plants spread by rooting runners. Rooted sections can be carefully cut out and lifted. Also by cuttings in springtime. Or, simply direct runners where you want them to go! Can be useful to pin runners down into soil with a section of wire until rooted.

Pruning
None necessary.

Problems
Watch out for fungal problems with variable daytime/nightime temperatures.

AKEBIA QUINATA The Chocolate Vine, (Spanish : Akebia, Parra de Chocolate).

HABIT AND CULTIVATION

Category	Perennial climber
Family	Lardizabalaceae
Origin	Central Asia
Size, height x spread	To around 10 metres
Situation	Dappled shade
Irrigation	Ensure it does not dry out during the summer
Temperature	To - 5°C
Evergreen/deciduous	Deciduous, though semi-evergreen in sheltered areas
Flowering	Purple/mauve, Late spring
Special features	Scented flowers and edible fruit.

The deliciously sounding common name of this plant is backed up by its beauty. It is a fast growing woody stemmed climber, pretty in habit, leaf and flower. Grey-green, delicate looking leaves are divided into 5 leaflets and the vanilla scented deep purple/ mauve flowers appear drooping along the fine stems in springtime. Male and female plants are needed to produce the interesting sausage shaped edible fruits, which are chocolate tasting. Dislikes root disturbance, but, given even moisture through the summer, it is otherwise surprisingly tolerant and belies its delicate airs! Will take a north or east facing position, but protect from cold winds.

Propagation
By seed in spring, semi-ripe cuttings in summer or layering in winter.

Pruning
Prune after flowering and can be cut to the base every 4 years or so if very tangled.

Problems
None

ALBIZIA JULIBRISSIN The Silk Tree,
(Spanish : Arbol de Seda).

HABIT AND CULTIVATION

Category	Tree
Family	Leguminosae
Origin	Area between Iran and Japan
Size, height x spread	8 x 6 metres
Situation	Full sun or dappled shade
Irrigation	Moderate in early years, gradually becoming drought tolerant.
Temperature	Down to –10°C
Evergreen/deciduous	Deciduous
Flowering	Pink. Summer.
Special features	-

The very beautiful Silk Tree was first discovered in 1759 by an Italian botanist named Albizi and it has since been highly valued as the only ferny leaved tree which will live in cool temperate climates. It has a very wide, spreading leaf canopy and is, therefore, a valuable shade tree. The leaflets have a tendency to close up at night or if lacking in water – an easy way to gauge watering. The exquisite bottlebrush type flowers are held upright on the branches like fluffy pink and cream powderpuffs.

Propagation
By seed in autumn

Pruning
Not generally needed. Dead wood and crossing branches can be pruned out during winter months.

Problems
None.

Also **ALBIZIA DYSTACHIA**. To around 6m, a very rapid grower, evergreen and native of Australia. Short lived, it is best used as a 'filler'. Attractive ferny foliage and yellow-green bottlebrush type flowers. Transplants easily, though damaged roots smell of goats!

ALCEA ROSEA syn. ALTHAEA ROSEA
Hollyhock, (Spanish : Malvavisco).

HABIT AND CULTIVATION

Category	Biennial/Perennial
Family	Malvaceae
Origin	Central Europe and China
Size, height x spread	2 x 0.5 metres
Situation	Full sun
Irrigation	Drought tolerant, but appreciates occasional summer soaking.
Temperature	Hardy
Evergreen/deciduous	Top growth will disappear in cold conditions.
Flowering	White, yellow, pinks to almost black. Summer.
Special features	-

The hollyhock has a very ancient history and was one of the first plants to be cultivated in Southern Europe. Today plantations are still maintained in middle Europe as a crop for the pharmaceutical industry. The name altheae comes from the Greek word althein, to heal. Dark flowering varieties are the best for medicinal extracts which are used in the treatment of coughs, asthma and respiratory illnesses. The foliage is rough and rounded and the tall flowering spike, to around 2m, bears many cup shaped flowers which open in succession. Many colours are now available, including swirled shades, and single and double forms. Although said to need water, they will self seed and establish themselves on any rough ground and, dry conditions seem to make stronger plants. Traditionally a biennial, here they are more likely to be perennial.

Propagation
Easy from seed in spring or late summer.

Pruning
None. Simply remove dead flower spike.

Problems
Prone to rust, though less if grown on the dry side.

ALLAMANDA CATHARTICA Golden Trumpet Vine, (Spanish : Alamanda).

HABIT AND CULTIVATION

Category	Shrubby climber
Family	Apocynaceae
Origin	South America
Size, height x spread	5 x 2 metres
Situation	Full sun or part shade
Irrigation	Water well during growing period
Temperature	Minimum 5°C
Evergreen/deciduous	Generally evergreen
Flowering	Yellow. Spring and summer
Special features	Poisonous. Soil, neutral to acid.

This vigorous and fast growing scrambling climber has whorls of shiny green leaves which will quickly carpet a fence, wall etc. Beautiful golden yellow trumpet shaped flowers, some 10cm. across, are produced through spring and summer. Provide some support and tie in growths. Also very pretty in a large pot, growing up a trellis etc. Prefers a fairly rich soil and favours neutral to acid. Find it a fairly protected spot, as cold winds are not appreciated and can cause yellowing of the leaves. Can also be pruned and kept shrubby.

Propagation
Softwood cuttings in spring and summer.

Pruning
Regular tip pruning is advisable to form good bushy plant. Prune previous sesaon's growth back to two nodes in winter or early spring.

Problems
Look out for aphids, especially greenfly and blackfly and occasionally red spider mite can be troublesome.

ALOCASIA MACRORRHIZOS
Elephant's Ear, Giant Taro,
(Spanish : Oreja de Elefante).

HABIT AND CULTIVATION

Category	Perennial
Family	Araceae
Origin	South East Asia, Sri Lanka
Size, height x spread	3 x 2 metres
Situation	Prefers humidity, filtered sun
Irrigation	Found naturally in wet, humid spots, but can survive on surprisingly little water.
Temperature	Will not tolerate frost, minimum 5°C
Evergreen/deciduous	Evergreen
Flowering	Mainly grown for foliage. Yellowish-green spathes. Summer.
Special features	Berries poisonous

When well sited, this plant produces huge lush leaves, in the shape of elephant's ears, giving an instant tropical effect. A native of humid jungles, it is particularly well suited to waterside plantings and protected from strong winds which will rip the leaves. Pamper it and it will reward you with giant sized leaves 1m long, constantly unfurling. However, it will also perform in much drier situations, even in pots, and, although it may not be quite so magnificent it is still worth growing as few plants have such large dramatic leaves. Yellow-green spathes produced in summer which later develop into red berries.

Propagation
By suckers which grow on easily and also by seed. Division of the fleshy rhizomes in spring is also possible.

Pruning
None. Simply removing dead leaves.

Problems
None

ALOE ARBORESCENS
Red Hot Poker Aloe, (Spanish : Aloe).

HABIT AND CULTIVATION

Category	Succulent
Family	Aloeaceae
Origin	South Africa
Size, height x spread	2 x 2 metres
Situation	Full sun.
Irrigation	Drought tolerant, though an occasional summer soaking is beneficial
Temperature	Down to –5°C
Evergreen/deciduous	Evergreen
Flowering	Orange-red. Winter
Special features	-

The aloe family, as a whole, is extremely tolerant of harsh conditions, particularly the bigger growing members. A.arborescens is a large branching succulent with wide-spreading toothed blue-grey-green leaves held in whorls on the tops of woody stems. In winter it is spectacular with its long lasting red hot poker flowers, particularly effective along a driveway or boundary with a dark backdrop of cypress - and equally good seen against a clear blue winter sky. Also perfectly happy in a windy coastal situation. Practically maintenance free, with just an occasional tidy up of dead flower stems and leaves.

Propagation
Can be grown by seed or stem cuttings, but the simplest is simply by breaking off offspring and replanting.

Pruning
None

Problems
None if grown in open situation

See also **ALOE FEROX**, **A.VARIEGATA** and **A. VERA**

ALOE FEROX
(Spanish : Aloe del Cabo).

HABIT AND CULTIVATION

Category	Succulent
Family	Aloeaceae
Origin	South Africa
Size, height x spread	3 x 2 metres
Situation	Full sun.
Irrigation	Drought tolerant
Temperature	Minimum 5°C
Evergreen/deciduous	Evergreen
Flowering	Orange. Winter.
Special features	-

As aloe arborescens, this is another survivor tolerating extreme conditions of heat and drought and windy coastal situations. It forms a succulent branching tree with woody stems and very dense juicy blue-green sword-shaped leaves in rosettes. The leaves bear stout spines all along the margins, and also erupting from the centre of the leaves, hence ferox = ferocious. A fabulously structural plant with stout poker flowering stems in winter/early spring stacked with orange tubular bell shaped flowers. A very slow grower.

Propagation
By seed and offsets.

Pruning
None. Tidy up withered flower stems and dead leaves.

Problems
None

Also **ALOE VARIEGATA**, Tiger Aloe or Partridge Aloe. Habit and cultivation as above but smaller growing, to 0.3 x 0.3 metres. This aloe has narrow dark green leaves, banded and spotted in white, hence the common names. A neat grower, perhaps better with some shade. Clusters of drooping pink or scarlet bell shaped flowers in late spring.

See also **ALOE ARBORESCENS** and **A. VERA**.

ALOE VERA syn. **ALOE BARBADENSIS** The Healing Plant, (Spanish : Aloe Vera).

HABIT AND CULTIVATION

Category	Succulent
Family	Aloeaceae
Origin	Tropical America
Size, height x spread	0.5 metres x indefinite
Situation	Full sun or part shade.
Irrigation	Drought tolerant, though better with occasional summer soaking.
Temperature	To around 5°C
Evergreen/deciduous	Evergreen
Flowering	Yellow. Summer.
Special features	Excellent healing properties.

Recently aloe vera has taken the world by storm, though its prowess as a healing plant was much recognised by the ancient Egyptians and Romans. It has excellent curative powers on all types of burns, sunburn and nuclear burns. Also highly useful in all types of skin disorders such as eczma, psoriasis etc. and a wonderful calmant for insect stings and bites. Many stomach complaints such as ulcers etc. can be eliminated with daily ingestion of aloe juice and, lately, there have even been some claims that it can help against cancer. Add to that it's supposed regenerative powers for damged skin and hair loss and here you have a miracle plant which has been taken up by the cosmetic and drug industries in a big way. Aloe vera is now available in all sorts of creams, shampoos, conditioners, sun lotions as well as many medications. Every home should have at least one plant! To use the leaf juice medicinally, always cut away either a section of, or an entire outer leaf, i.e. a mature leaf, as this is where the medical properties are strongest.

It is a clump forming succulent with juicy tapering leaves, often mottled in green. In full sun the leaves can change to a dusky pink colour, but will revert to green again in shade. Yellow bell shaped flowers are carried on stout flower stems.

Propagation
A. vera plants are sterile. To increase your stock, carefully break off young offspring and replant.

Pruning
None. Cut out dead flower stalk.

Problems
None. Never allow to waterlog.

See also **ALOE ARBORESCENS**, **A. FEROX** and **A. VARIEGATA**.

ALOGYNE HUEGELII Blue Hibiscus, (Spanish : Hibisco Azul).

HABIT AND CULTIVATION

Category	Shrub
Family	Malvaceae
Origin	Australia
Size, height x spread	3 x 2 metres
Situation	Full sun
Irrigation	Drought resistant
Temperature	To –5°C
Evergreen/deciduous	Semi-evergreen
Flowering	Lilac. Almost constantly.
Special features	-

This tough, semi-desert shrub always confuses with its delicate looks. It is, in fact, one of the toughest, thriving on total neglect! The dull green leaves are lobed and slightly serrated and covered in fine hairs, pretty enough, but it is the flowers that catch the eye. A shiny, glistening lilac resembling a hibiscus open-cup bloom. It was originally classified as one of the hibiscus family but has now been renamed, though its common name stays. They look impossibly delicate, but will withstand, and need, hot dry conditions and if it's windy too, no problem. Avoid summer watering as this will only induce soft floppy growth. Can also be grown in a pot.

Propagation
From seed in spring, or semi-hardwood cuttings in summer.

Pruning
Prune in late autumn or winter for compact growth.

Problems
None, if you leave it to struggle!

ALOYSIA TRIPHYLLA syn. **LIPPIA CITRIODORA** Lemon Verbena, (Spanish : Hierba Luisa).

HABIT AND CULTIVATION

Category	Shrub
Family	Verbenaceae
Origin	South America
Size, height x spread	3 x 3 metres
Situation	Full sun.
Irrigation	Low water requirements
Temperature	To – 5˚C
Evergreen/deciduous	Semi – evergreen
Flowering	White touched with lilac. Summer.
Special features	Lemon scented leaves.

A wonderfully fragrant shrub, its lemon scented leaves make a good tea and are also much used in pot pourri because the scent from the leaves can last 2 to 3 years. The leaves can be collected at any time, but are at their most potent just before flowering takes place. This is a commercially viable plant, extracts of the oil are much used in the cosmetic and perfume industries. A very bushy shrub with fresh green narrow leaves, it will not tolerate a cold position and, in cold areas, it is best grown with wall protection. Very small white flowers, sometimes tinged with pale lilac, are borne at the ends of the stem.

Propagation
Soft tip cuttings in spring or semi-hardwood in summer.

Pruning
Cut out any dead wood in early summer, and prune any drooping branches to encourage new strong growth. In late autumn, prune back to a low framework to maintain good shape.

Problems
None.

ALSTROEMERIA The Lily of the Incas, Peruvian Lily, (Spanish : Lirio de Peru).

HABIT AND CULTIVATION

Category	Perennial
Family	Liliaceae
Origin	South America
Size, height x spread	1 x 1 metres
Situation	Full sun or light shade
Irrigation	Moderate summer demands
Temperature	Down to around -5°C. If colder, provide some root protection
Evergreen/deciduous	Top growth dies down in winter.
Flowering	Yellow, orange, salmon, pinks, lilacs, red and purple. Spring and early summer.
Special features	-

Exquisite in flower, these tuberous plants are found in very inhospitable places – dry and windy coastlines and barren rocky hillsides. With kinder treatment, they perform wonderfully and summer irrigation, although not essential, provokes a stunning display of their showy flowers. Many are beautifully streaked, spotted and veined in a spectacular range of colours. They resemble dwarf trumpet lilies. The soft leaves soon build up into large clumps and, although disliking root disturbance, if carefully done, the clumps can be lifted and split. The fine thread like roots need to be handled with care, and initially the plants should be brought on in individual pots. They look well naturalised under trees. Good, long-lasting, cut flowers.

Propagation
From seed or by careful division in early spring.

Pruning
None

Problems
None

ANEMONE X HYBRIDA Japanese Anemone, Japanese Windflower, (Spanish : Anemona de Japon).

HABIT AND CULTIVATION

Category	Perennial
Family	Ranunculaceae
Origin	China
Size, height x spread	1.5 x 0.6 metres
Situation	Semi or full shade, though very adaptable.
Irrigation	Moderate watering in summer
Temperature	Fully hardy
Evergreen/deciduous	Semi-evergreen
Flowering	Pink and white. Late summer and autumn
Special features	Poisonous

The Japanese anemone, strangely enough, is a native of China. The conflict of names arose because of one (mistaken) early recording of a plant from Japan! It is one of our most elegant plants, stunningly beautiful in a natural setting, under trees etc. It is a vigorous and long-lived perennial, spreading by underground rhizomes. The basal leaves are dark green and deeply cut and covered in fine hairs. The tall, erect flower stalks bear many flowers on wiry stems that wave gently in the breeze. White and many shades of pink, the flowers are open cup-shaped, single or double, with a heavy boss of yellow stamens and very long lasting. Cut down dead flower stalks to promote further flowering. In colder climates, it is best to shear off all foliage at ground level, as it blackens with frost. Also excellent cut flower.

Propagation
Division of an established clump in very early spring, or by seeds in summer/autumn.

Pruning
None, only tidying.

Problems
Occasional mildew.

ANIGOZANTHOS Kangaroo Paw, (Spanish : Anigozantus).

HABIT AND CULTIVATION

Category	Perennial
Family	Haemodoraceae
Origin	Australia
Size, height x spread	2 x 0.5 metres
Situation	Full sun
Irrigation	Occasional water in summer, but avoid splashing leaves
Temperature	To 0°C
Evergreen/deciduous	Evergreen
Flowering	Greenish yellow, and shades of orange/ yellow/pink/red. Spring/summer
Special features	-

This plant is something of a curiousity. It came into vogue a few years back and it is perhaps mainly grown for its wierd looks rather than beauty. A native of Australia, it is usually found growing around eucalyptus trees. Long, sword-shaped leaves form in fan-shaped clumps, which can spread quite rapidly when suited. A very light, sandy soil is preferred. The tall flower stems emerge in spring, developing into rather strange looking fuzzy flowers, which are highly attractive to humming birds in their native country. Try a few flowers in a cut arrangement, they'll certainly cause comment.

Propagation
By division in spring or from fresh seed in late summer.

Pruning
None.

Problems
None.

Also **ANIGOZANTHOS FLAVIDUS**, yellow-green flowers sometimes tinged with red and **A. VIRIDIS**, lime green flowers.

ANISODONTEA CAPENSIS Cape Mallow, (Spanish : Malvaviscillo).

HABIT AND CULTIVATION

Category	Shrub
Family	Malvaceae
Origin	South Africa
Size, height x spread	1 x 1 metres
Situation	Full sun
Irrigation	Drought tolerant.
Temperature	To 0°C
Evergreen/deciduous	Evergreen
Flowering	Pink. Spring to autumn.
Special features	-

This is a very easy and tolerant plant for Mediterranean gardeners. It forms a neat, compact and bushy shrub with erect habit. Lots of small leaves fill out the twiggy framework. The flowers are like mini-hibiscus and, although small, are very prolifically produced during the warm months. They are tiny cup shapes, with a wide-eyed look, rose pink with darker veins in the centre. Apart from using it in mixed shrub plantings and general garden schemes, it also makes a useful informal hedge and is very attractive pruned to a standard or semi standard. Nor will it object to pot growth.

Propagation
By seed in spring or, easily, by semi-ripe cuttings in summer.

Pruning
Generally little required, but tip prune in summer to encourage bushy shape. Being small leafed and compact, it lends itself well to topiary and bonsai.

Problems
Occasionally a touch of green fly on flower tips.

APTENIA CORDIFOLIA Belly Button Plant, (Spanish : Aptenio).

HABIT AND CULTIVATION

Category	Succulent
Family	Aizoaceae
Origin	South Africa
Size, height x spread	0.05 x 1 metres
Situation	Full sun, though will also take some light shade
Irrigation	Drought tolerant
Temperature	To 0°C
Evergreen/deciduous	Evergreen
Flowering	Pink. Summer.
Special features	-

This little creeping and trailing succulent is immensely useful for covering sloping banks with greenery and can be used as a tough and easy lawn substitute, one that doesn't need cutting! Also useful for carpeting under palm trees, yuccas etc. as long as the shade is not too dense. It has oval, fleshy, mid-green leaves, shiny and attractive. It will very quickly carpet the ground with its prostrate, branching stems and help reduce water evaporation, soil erosion and weed growth. Throughout the summer it is studded with small, pretty pink daisies. It is also available in a variegated form.

Propagation
Easy by stem cuttings in spring or summer.

Pruning
None. Tips of plant can be pinched back to encourage bushiness. If the plant becomes very straggly, cut back hard and it will quickly regenerate.

Problems
None if grown in open position.

ARBUTUS UNEDO The Strawberry Tree, (Spanish : Madroño).

HABIT AND CULTIVATION

Category	Tree
Family	Ericaceae
Origin	Southern Europe and Ireland
Size, height x spread	6 x 3 metres
Situation	Full sun
Irrigation	Drought resistant but will tolerate a little summer water
Temperature	To –5°C
Evergreen/deciduous	Evergreen
Flowering	White. Autumn and winter.
Special features	Scented flowers. Edible fruit.

The strawberry tree is a native Mediterranean plant. It is a very beautiful and versatile small tree/large shrub, though removing lower foliage and allowing it to grow as a tree shows it to it's best. It has dark green, shiny leathery leaves and, although slow growing, the shrub has a nice compact habit. Clusters of white, honey-scented, bell-shaped flowers are produced in autumn when the fruit from the previous year is still on the tree; the combination of dark leaves, white flowers and red fruit is very attractive. The fruits resemble strawberries in looks and, although rather tasteless on their own, they are used to make a rich liqueur. As the tree matures, it develops deep toffee-coloured bark, beautifully shredding and peeling. It also makes an excellent specimen tree or second line windbreak.

Propagation
Objects to transplanting. Seed in autumn or semi-ripe cuttings in late summer.

Pruning
Little needed. Cut out any dead wood, thereafter prune by hand rather than with shears.

Problems
Can be prone to fungal infection if overcrowded.

ARCTOTIS ACAULIS African Daisy, (Spanish : Arctotis, Margarita Africana)

HABIT AND CULTIVATION

Category	Perennial
Family	Compositae
Origin	South Africa
Size, height x spread	0.5 x 1 metres
Situation	Full sun
Irrigation	Drought tolerant
Temperature	Frost tender.
Evergreen/deciduous	Evergreen
Flowering	Cream, yellow, orange, pink, russet. Spring and summer.
Special features	-

These extremely colourful and tough daisy plants have a multitude of uses in the garden. They are excellent as groundcover and for blanketing difficult, sloping banks. In a rock or scree garden they add wonderful colour and can also be used in pots or around the rims of larger containers. Their slightly furry rosettes of chrysanthemum like leaves, some silvery grey or grey-green, form large dense mats. The daisy flowers, some 8cm across, dance above the foliage in a dazzling array of colours, many with a contrasting black or golden eye. There are many shades to choose from – creamy-white, golden yellow, orange, copper, pinks, crimson and russet. The flowers close up in overcast conditions and late afternoon.

Propagation
Easiest from small offshoots which can be broken off and transplanted at any time of the year. Also by seed in spring or autumn.

Pruning
None. Deadhead.

Problems
Occasional touch of mildew under humid conditions.

ARGYRANTHEMUM FRUTESCENS
Marguerite, Paris Daisy,
(Spanish : Margarita).

HABIT AND CULTIVATION

Category	Perennial
Family	Compositae
Origin	Canary Islands
Size, height x spread	1 x 1 metres
Situation	Full sun. Will tolerate some light dappled shade.
Irrigation	Very little.
Temperature	To 0°C
Evergreen/deciduous	Evergreen
Flowering	White, yellows, pinks. Autumn, winter, spring.
Special features	-

The evergreen, perennial marguerite, much loved and respected in Mediterranean gardens, rapidly forms a billowing mound of attractively cut foliage and is a very useful planting in new gardens giving an almost instant look of maturity. It is now available in many shades of pinks and yellows as well as the original white, with single or double daisy flowers. Often the foliage is almost obscured by the mass of flowers. Relishing a dryish, sunny spot, which promotes compact growth. Do not plant in the shade as this induces weak, lanky growth, which is very prone to disease. It is also useful in pots.

Propagation
Cuttings in spring or summer.

Pruning
Pinch out tips frequently to maintain neat rounded shape. Dead-head regularly to promote further flowering. Hard pruning should be carried out in summer but never cut back into old wood as the plant may then refuse to regenerate.

Problems
Look out for greenfly, blackfly and, in adverse conditions, can suffer with mildew.

ARTEMISIA ARBORESCENS
Southernwood, Wormwood,
(Spanish : Artemisia de Olor).

HABIT AND CULTIVATION

Category	Shrub
Family	Compositae
Origin	Mediterranean
Size, height x spread	1 x 1 metres
Situation	Full sun.
Irrigation	Drought tolerant.
Temperature	To –5°C
Evergreen/deciduous	Evergreen
Flowering	Yellow. Spring.
Special features	Very aromatic foliage.

A quick growing shrub with wonderful, silvery-white foliage, feathery and extremely aromatic. The hotter and drier the growing conditions, the more silvery the leaves. Beautiful within its own right, it makes a superb contrast plant, highlighting dark colours and cooling down hot planting schemes. It produces small yellow flowers in spring, but we value it for its foliage and many people cut out the flowering stalks. The common name, wormwood, is from the anglo saxon wermod and the aperitive vermouth was thus named because, at one time, it contained traces of the herb. The plant also has fame as an antiseptic. On a hot day the air around the plant is heavy with its wonderful spicy aroma and brushing against the foliage is sheer delight!

Propagation
Soft or semi-ripe cuttings in summer.

Pruning
Occasional tip pruning, and can be cut back lightly in early spring. Do not prune back to old wood.

Problems
Constant irrigation will cause soft floppy growth and mildew and fungal problems.

ASTERISCUS MARITIMUS Gold Coin or Sea Daisy, (Spanish : Chuchera).

HABIT AND CULTIVATION

Category	Perennial
Family	Compositae
Origin	Mediterranean
Size, height x spread	0.30 x 1 metres
Situation	Full sun.
Irrigation	Drought tolerant.
Temperature	Down to –5°C
Evergreen/deciduous	Evergreen
Flowering	Yellow. Main flowering March to August, but nearly always an odd flower or two.
Special features	-

A grey-green leaved shrublet, found growing in crevices in rock faces in exposed coastal situations. Revels in an exposed, dry spot and is very tolerant of high summer temperatures. It will spread to around a metre across and is quite striking when in flower. The small narrow leaves are rough to the touch and through the summer months it will bear a constant array of dazzling yellow daisy flowers, some 5cm across.

Propagation
By seed in springtime.

Pruning
None.

Problems
None. The rough textured leaves seem to deter most insects.

Also **ASTERISCUS SERICEUS**, Canary Island Daisy. Larger growing than the above, reaching some 1 x 1 metres. A silvery foliaged shrub, densely mounded, with silky, soft hairs to the leaves. Summer flowering, yellow daisies up to 7.5cm across. A tendancy to be short lived, but easily replaced by seedlings. Cultivation as above.

ATRIPLEX CANESCENS Saltbush,
(Spanish : Atriplex, Arbusto de Sal).

HABIT AND CULTIVATION

Category	Shrub
Family	Chenopodiaceae
Origin	California
Size, height x spread	1.5 x 1.5 metres
Situation	Full sun
Irrigation	Drought tolerant
Temperature	To 0°C
Evergreen/deciduous	Evergreen
Flowering	Blue. Spring
Special features	Useful as fire retardant.

The saltbush is a useful silvery-grey leafed shrub, which is extremely tolerant of a very wide range of conditions. It is drought tolerant and will take a very high degree of exposure to wind, sun and salt-laden spray of coastal conditions without showing any undue signs of suffering. It is therefore a very useful planting in our Mediterranean gardens and associates well with herbs such as lavender, rosemary, thyme and sage, all liking similar conditions. Try it on difficult slopes and banks to counteract erosion. Another very useful asset is its use as a fire retardant, perhaps in front line to pine trees or eucalyptus, both notorious fire hazards. It has a quite pretty small blue flower in springtime.

Propagation
Softwood cuttings in summer or by seed in autumn.

Pruning
Occasional trim to keep tidy.

Problems
None in open, exposed situation.

AZARA MICROPHYLLA
(Spanish : Azara).

HABIT AND CULTIVATION

Category	Tree
Family	Flacourtiaceae
Origin	Chile, South America
Size, height x spread	8 x 3 metres
Situation	Sun or shade
Irrigation	Moderate
Temperature	To –10°C
Evergreen/deciduous	Evergreen
Flowering	Yellow. Spring.
Special features	Flowers scented of chocolate/vanilla

A very dainty large shrub or small tree with an erect form and arching branches. Very small, neat, dark green, shiny leaves, some 1cm. long. In spring the tree develops clusters of deep yellow flowers which are without petals and composed entirely of masses of fluffy stamens that exude a delicious hot spicy fragrance somewhere between chocolate and vanilla. Flowers are then often followed in autumn by orange-red berries. A very elegant and under planted tree, find it a special and sheltered position, where the rich aroma from the flowers can be best enjoyed on a warm day. Moderately fast growing. A variegated form is also available which has creamy white flowers.

Propagation
Semi-ripe cuttings in summer.

Pruning
Responds well to pruning and shaping, though it is naturally a very tidy grower.

Problems
None.

BAUHINIA PURPUREA The Orchid Tree, (Spanish : Arbol de las Orquideas).

HABIT AND CULTIVATION

Category	Tree
Family	Leguminosae
Origin	Tropical Asia
Size, height x spread	10 x 8 metres
Situation	Full sun or dappled shade
Irrigation	Occasional deep soak in spring and summer.
Temperature	To 0°C
Evergreen/deciduous	Deciduous
Flowering	Purple/pink. Spring.
Special features	Scented flowers

The Bauhinia makes a very beautiful specimen tree, with a wide, spreading head of foliage composed of two-lobed leaves. It was first discovered in the 16th. century and named after the Swiss botanist brothers, Bauhin. It is commonly confused with the Cercis or Judas Tree, which it closely resembles and is a near family member. It appreciates, and deserves, a warm and sheltered spot and it will then freely produce its stunning orchid-like flowers in early springtime, before the leaves unfurl. Flowers are softly scented. The seed pods are prolific and can create somewhat messy litter so take care with siting. Dislikes a cold wind.

Propagation
By seed or cuttings in spring.

Pruning
Thin out congested growth after flowering.

Problems
Occasionally attacked by mealy bugs.

Also **BAUHINIA VARIEGATA 'CANDIDA'**. A pure white flowering variety. Flowers up to 10cm across and particularly sweet scented.

BELAMCANDA CHINENSIS
The Leopard Lily, Blackberry Lily,
(Spanish : Lirio del Leopardo).

HABIT AND CULTIVATION

Category	Perennial
Family	Iridaceae
Origin	China and Japan
Size, height x spread	1 x 0.25 metres
Situation	Full sun or partial shade
Irrigation	Moderate
Temperature	Hardy, but appreciates some root protection in extremely cold spells
Evergreen/deciduous	Top growth dies down in cold conditions
Flowering	Orange/red. Summer.
Special features	-

The Leopard Lily is a little known and used summer flowering bulb. Fans of mid-green, sword-shaped leaves emerge, which arch elegantly as they grow. The loosely-branched stems bear a succession of orange-red spotted flowers through the summer, thus giving the plant its common name of Leopard Lily. The flowers are followed by clusters of shiny, black seeds, giving rise to its other common name of Blackberry Lily. Flowers and seeds are useful in cut arrangements. The plants look well in large drifts naturalised under trees and can also be used in summer pots. Plant the rhizomes in spring, just below the soil level in reasonably fertile soil and water regularly during active growth.

Propagation
By seed sown in springtime or splitting of rhizomes.

Pruning
None. Remove dead flower stems after seeding.

Problems
None.

BIGNONIA CAPREOLATA The Cross Vine, (Spanish : Bignonia de la Cruz).

HABIT AND CULTIVATION

Category	Perennial climber
Family	Bignoniaceae
Origin	North America
Size, height x spread	10 x 6 metres
Situation	Sun or shade
Irrigation	Moderate, becoming drought tolerant.
Temperature	To –10°C
Evergreen/deciduous	Evergreen, except under very harsh conditions.
Flowering	Tangerine colour. Late spring.
Special features	-

An easy to grow climber, a feature common of most of the bignonia family. A self-clinging vine, climbing by twisting tendrils, it is particularly at home over a pergola or some trellising. The leaves are composed of two slender leaflets with a tendril, in a mid-green shade. The trumpet-shaped flowers are around 5cm long and borne in clusters, a tangerine colour with a darker toffee-coloured backing and markings, a very unusual and pretty combination. They are produced in great numbers over several weeks. Long pea-pod type seed cases follow.

Propagation
Seed in spring, or semi or hardwood cuttings in autumn, or by layering during the winter months.

Pruning
Prune in early spring to control growth. A severely matted plant can be cut to the ground in very early spring and it will regenerate.

Problems
Occasional greenfly.

See also **BIGNONIA JASMINOIDES**, **B. RICOSOLEANA**, and **B. VENUSTA**.

BIGNONIA JASMINOIDES syn.
PANDOREA JASMINOIDES
The Bower Vine, (Spanish : Bignonia).

HABIT AND CULTIVATION

Category	Perennial climber
Family	Bignoniaceae
Origin	Australia
Size, height x spread	5 x 2 metres
Situation	Full sun or some partial shade.
Irrigation	Drought tolerant.
Temperature	To 0°C
Evergreen/deciduous	Evergreen
Flowering	White and pink. Almost constantly.
Special features	-

A beautiful twining climber which requires a minimum of attention. It has dark green, highly polished leaves, composed of seven to nine leaflets, on woody, twining stems. Spectacular and long-lasting in flower, it bears clusters of trumpet shaped flowers, some white with a deeper carmine throat and others a candy pink, again with deeper throat. The main flowering is through the springtime, when it looks magnificent, but some lesser flowering carries on almost right through the year. Dark green seed pods. It is a particularly healthy climber and loves to scramble over a pergola or up trellising. There is also a variegated form which has very prettily striped yellow and green leaves, with even the seed pods bearing the same markings.

Propagation
From fresh seed in spring or semi-ripe wood in summer. If layered, will root into mulch material.

Pruning
Generally none required, though a general tidying up can be carried out in winter.

Problems
None.

See also **BIGNONIA CAPREOLATA**, **B. RICOSOLEANA**, and **B. VENUSTA**.

BIGNONIA RICOSOLEANA
(Spanish : Bignonia Rosa).

HABIT AND CULTIVATION

Category	Perennial climber
Family	Bignoniaceae
Origin	South America
Size, height x spread	15 metres x indefinite
Situation	Full sun
Irrigation	Drought tolerant
Temperature	To –5°C
Evergreen/deciduous	Deciduous
Flowering	Pink. Summer and autumn.
Special features	-

Perhaps one of the biggest climbers in cultivation, this bignonia is not really suitable for normal gardens unless you like constant hacking back. However, it does have its place in a natural, wild garden. For speed of growth and sheer ability to smother, it probably has no match and can look stunning. Inside a very few years it can develop a tree trunk sized skeleton. Mid-green leaves, composed of leaflets, are attractive enough but the flowering is magnificent. Huge corymbs of candy-pink flowers, veined and throated in a deeper pink, open up and last for several months. It is at its best perhaps tumbling down a rough bank, or up into an old large tree – give it room.

Propagation
By seed in spring or semi-ripe summer cuttings. Often small plantlets can be detached that have rooted into the ground by natural layering.

Pruning
Carry out in winter when the plant is bare and you can see where you are going. Do not be afraid to massacre if necessary, it will re-grow and very rapidly. Try and establish a framework.

Problems
Occasional blackfly on flower tips.

See also **BIGNONIA CAPREOLATA, B. JASMINOIDES**, and **B. VENUSTA**.

BIGNONIA VENUSTA syn. PYROSTEGIA VENUSTA The Flame Vine, (Spanish : Bignonia de las Llamas).

HABIT AND CULTIVATION

Category	Perennial climber
Family	Bignoniaceae
Origin	South America
Size, height x spread	10 metres x indefinite
Situation	Full sun
Irrigation	Moderate and becoming drought tolerant.
Temperature	To 0˚C
Evergreen/deciduous	Evergreen
Flowering	Orange. Winter.
Special features	-

This is a magnificent, evergreen climber that is stunning in full flow. Although it will take temperatures down to 0C, it prefers a warm, protected position to give of its best. A little slow to establish, once settled it grows away at an amazing rate and looks wonderful draped over a warm wall. Mid-green leaves with tendrils, which twine themselves around any support given, but it will only flower well in full sun. The flowers are thin orange tubes held in great clusters that completely smother the plant during the winter months, creating a sheet of fire, hence the name. A real eye-catcher, developing into a large climber. It warrants space to flaunt its beauty.

Propagation
Semi ripe cuttings in summer or autumn. Also by summer layering.

Pruning
Prune out old and congested shoots and spent flowers.

Problems
None.

See also **BIGNONIA CAPREOLATA**, **B. JASMINOIDES**, and **B. RICOSOLEANA**.

Bougainvillea

A Brazilian beauty, the bougainvillea is much loved and admired for its sheer exuberance and unbeatable flower power. It generally features high on everyone's list of must-have plants for their Mediterranean gardens.

It is a native of the Amazon enclave, and grows throughout tropical and semi-tropical areas of, primarily, Brazil but also in Bolivia, Colombia, Ecuador, Peru and Venezuela. It lives in dense rainforest, with distinct dry and wet seasons, where its tough hooked spines help it to cling and climb up through trees to reach the light. The spines also largely protect it from insect attack and it is almost disease free. Surprisingly, it will tolerate high levels of rainfall, as long as it does not become waterlogged. Its leaves have special 'drip tips' to repel the water.

In the 1760's the French senator and Admiral, Louis de Bougainville, set out on a circumnavigation of the world arriving in Rio de Janeiro in 1767. His botanist on board, Commerson, first saw the stunning vine there and named it in honour of his expedition leader.

The plant he saw would have been b. glabra, which has since become the parent of many stunning varieties in jewel bright colours ranging through white, golden yellow and orange to all hues of pink, lilac, purple and red. There are even some with variegated foliage and two-tone pink and white flowers. What we loosely refer to as the 'flowers' are in fact papery bracts. The true flowers are small creamy-white tubes, grouped in threes, in the centre of 3-winged colourful bracts.

We most often grow them against the walls of a house, over a patio etc., but try it growing up into a large old cypress, the colour contrast is magnificent. On a wall you will need to provide support and it will need to be strong. Similarly, try it as a tall hedging plant, providing high-tensile wires to tie it into. Proving the versatility of the plant, it makes excellent groundcover, tumbling down a rough bank for example. And, if you've room, grow it as a specimen arching shrub' – train the leader up a strong stake, like a standard, to the desired height, then pinch it out and peg the subsequent growths down to the ground. A delightful, and little used, way of growing the plant. Whichever way you choose to grow it, the long shoots are best cut back to about 0.5m as it is on this part that they will bloom best.

Remember that bougainvillea is a tropical plant, they will perform much better in a warm and sheltered spot – they do not like a cold wind. Likewise, plant them during the warmer months for quicker establishment and take great care with the fragile roots, which never form a good rootball. They can be a little slow to establish but once settled in, they will grow away rapidly. Generally evergreen, in colder conditions they will lose their leaves and flowers to reshoot again with warmer temperatures.

BOUGAINVILLEA GLABRA
(Spanish : Buganvilla).

HABIT AND CULTIVATION

Category	Perennial climber
Family	Nyctaginaceae
Origin	South America
Size, height x spread	10 metres x indefinite
Situation	Full sun
Irrigation	Moderate water initially, later drought tolerant.
Temperature	To –5°C
Evergreen/deciduous	Semi evergreen
Flowering	Purple. Spring, summer, autumn.
Special features	-

Bougainvillea are magnificent and easy climbers, a little slow to establish but then growing away rapidly. They look wonderful tumbling over a wall or out of a big old tree. The true flower is white and insignificant; it is the wonderfully colourful bracts that draw the eye. Site carefully – they have vicious thorns and do create a lot of litter (most people forgive their vices) and they will not tolerate root disturbance, so cannot later be re-sited. They can also be grown in large containers, if regularly pruned. Do not over fertilise, as this encourages leaf growth and loss of flower. Glabra, the well-known purple, is the parent of several varieties and is the hardiest.

Propagation
Semi-hardwood cuttings in summer.

Pruning
Cut back previous season's lateral growths in early spring, leaving 3cm spurs. Flowering is on new wood.

Problems
Occasional whitefly and mealybug.

Also **BOUGAINVILLEA SPECTABILIS**. Several cultivars available in a large range of colours both single and double. White, gold, orange, pinks, lilacs and reds. Generally speaking, the paler colours tend to be less hardy and not so strong growing. Choose your colour when in flower as there are many variations. Flower tone can also change according to position – full sun or some shade – and soil type.

BRAHEA ARMATA The Mexican Blue Palm, (Spanish : Palmera Azul).

HABIT AND CULTIVATION

Category	Palm
Family	Palmae
Origin	California
Size, height x spread	12 x 2 metres
Situation	Full sun.
Irrigation	Occasional summer watering
Temperature	To –5°C
Evergreen/deciduous	Evergreen
Flowering	Cream inflorescences. Summer.
Special features	-

The steely blue-grey leaves of this fan palm are very attractive and a good colour foil for other plantings in the garden. It is a fairly slow grower, especially in cooler areas, but revels in a hot, dry spot and will tolerate wind better than a lot of palms. The creamy flower clusters are particularly attractive, arching out from the leaves and drooping pendulously and up to some 5m in length on mature trees.

Propagation
Erratic seed germination.

Pruning
Only removing dead leaves and flower stalks.

Problems
None

Also **BRAHEA EDULIS**, The Guadaloupe Palm. This is an endangered palm in its native habitat, the Guadaloupe Islands off the coast of Mexico, but it is now becoming quite a popular planting because of its lush green fan leaves and edible fruit. Faster growing than the armata, it is also more water demanding. Flowers are fairly insignificant.

BRUGMANSIA ARBOREA syn. **DATURA ARBOREA** Angel's Trumpets, (Spanish : Arbol de las Trompetas, Trompeta de Angel).

HABIT AND CULTIVATION

Category	Shrub
Family	Solanaceae
Origin	Andes, South America.
Size, height x spread	4 x 3 metres
Situation	Full sun or dappled shade.
Irrigation	Weekly watering in summer, more if containerised.
Temperature	To around – 5°C
Evergreen/deciduous	Semi-evergreen
Flowering	White, yellow and peach. Summer and autumn.
Special features	Sap is dangerously hallucinogenic and poisonous. Scented flowers.

Brugmansias form large shrubs or can be trained into small trees. They have an open structure with large, slightly felty, mid-green leaves. The long trumpet-shaped flowers droop down magnificently giving rise to their common name. Hauntingly scented, especially at night. Pot grown plants need regular watering.

Propagation
Easily propagated by cuttings in summer.

Pruning
Benefits from hard cutting back in early spring.

Problems
Whitefly.

Also **BRUGMANSIA X CANDIDA**. Beautiful white flowers with exquisite night-time perfume. 4 x 3 metres

Also **BRUGMANSIA METELOIDES**, syn. **DATURA METELOIDES**. Dark grey green foliage and to around 1 x 1 metres, this plant has open, cup-shaped, white flowers that look up at you and open at night. Prickly seed cases resembling chestnut cases. Scented and very beautiful.

Also **BRUGMANSIA SANGUINEA**, syn. **DATURA SANGUINEA**. Soft, hairy, dark green leaves and thinner trumpet flowers with are yellow shaded with red, some 20cm long but unscented. This is a more tender plant but very beautiful and under-used. To 4 metres.

Buddleja Davidii

BUDDLEJA ALTERNIFOLIA Weeping Butterfly Bush, (Spanish : Arbusto de la Mariposa).

HABIT AND CULTIVATION

Category	Shrub
Family	Buddlejaceae
Origin	China
Size, height x spread	3 x 2 metres
Situation	Full sun
Irrigation	Occasional summer watering.
Temperature	Hardy.
Evergreen/deciduous	Semi-evergreen
Flowering	Lilac. Late spring.
Special features	Attracts butterflies. Perfumed flowers.

This buddleja can grow into a rather large tangled bush. The prettiest way to admire its arching elegance is to train it into a small weeping tree. It bears slender, pendulous shoots decked out with typical leaves, dark green and narrow pointed with a silvery underside. The flowers are lilac with a deeper purple throat and very sweetly scented.

Propagation
Semi ripe summer cuttings.

Pruning
In winter prune out half of the older shoots to make way for new growth.

Problems
Occasional blackfly.

Also **BUDDLEJA DAVIDII**, Butterfly Bush. A very large arching shrub, 5 x 3 metres, with fragrant flowering spikes in white, pink, lilac and purple. Is an exceedingly tough shrub. Butterflies are greatly attracted to this shrub.

Also **BUDDLEJA GLOBOSA**. A larger, more erect shrub, 4 x 4 metres, which bears scented golden orange flower balls through spring and summer. Does not respond well to pruning.

BUTIA CAPITATA Jelly Palm or Yatay Palm, (Spanish : Butia).

HABIT AND CULTIVATION

Category	Palm
Family	Palmae
Origin	Brazil, South America.
Size, height x spread	7 x 5 metres
Situation	Full sun or some light shade.
Irrigation	Moderate water needs, can become drought tolerant.
Temperature	Hardy to around –10°C
Evergreen/deciduous	Evergreen
Flowering	Insignificant. Summer.
Special features	Edible fruit.

This palm has a stout, solitary trunk and arching, feathery, grey-green leaves, 2m long or more, which recurve dramatically back to the trunk, creating a very elegant look. The flowering is fairly insignificant but it is followed by 2.5cm edible, oval fruits coloured yellow and red. These are often used to make a jam or jelly, giving rise to its common name. It is one of the few hardy feather palms and is widely planted in temperate zones, withstanding a high degree of frost. Smaller trees can also be grown in containers.

Propagation
From seed, but erratic. Germination can vary from a few weeks to a year or more. A minimum temperature of 25°C will be needed for success.

Pruning
Cut out dead leaves and flower stalks.

Problems
Red spider mite can be a problem.

BUXUS SEMPERVIRENS 'SUFFRUTICOSA'
Common Box, (Spanish : Boj).

HABIT AND CULTIVATION

Category	Shrub
Family	Buxaceae
Origin	Mediterranean
Size, height x spread	1 x 1 metres
Situation	Full sun or semi-shade
Irrigation	Drought tolerant.
Temperature	Hardy
Evergreen/deciduous	Evergreen
Flowering	Greenish-white. Spring.
Special features	Poisonous. Excellent topiary plant.

The Latin buxus comes from the Greek word puxos. Traditionally small boxes were made from the wood, which is very hard, close-grained and does not warp. Because of this it was used for all sorts of carvings and engravings and also for making musical and navigational instruments. An extract from the plant was once used as a quinine substitute in the treatment of malaria. The plants have been used for centuries in formal garden design as mini hedging and are the first choice as topiary subjects. The suffruticosa is a dwarf variety, which is perfect for trimming and shaping, with its tiny glossy green leaves. The flowers are greenish white but fairly insignificant.

Propagation
Semi-ripe cuttings in summer.

Pruning
Promote new growth by cutting stems back hard in early spring. Trim and shear regularly to keep in good shape.

Problems
Will not tolerate a waterlogged soil.

CAESALPINIA GILLESII The Bird of Paradise Tree, (Spanish : Arbol de Ave de Paraiso).

HABIT AND CULTIVATION

Category	Tree
Family	Leguminosae
Origin	South America
Size, height x spread	4 x 6 metres
Situation	Full sun.
Irrigation	Regularly in summer months.
Temperature	To 0°C
Evergreen/deciduous	Deciduous
Flowering	Yellow and red. Summer.
Special features	-

Take care not to confuse common names here! The Bird of Paradise is the strelitzia reginae: the Bird of Paradise Tree is the caesalpinia gillesii. This delicate looking small tree, or large shrub, has very feathery, fine foliage and small spines on its branches. A rapid grower when suited and very airy looking, it is mainly grown for its striking flowers, which are bird-like and yellow with very prominent red stamens. They relish a warm spot with adequate summer irrigation and well protected from cold winds. In cooler areas they can be grown against a wall or even in a large container and look well with a dark background, say of cypress trees, where it's laciness is well highlighted. A sheltered courtyard situation suits them well.

Propagation
From seed in autumn. Also from softwood cuttings in summer.

Pruning
Very little needed. Maintain an open shape.

Problems
Mealy bug.

CALLISTEMON VIMINALIS The Bottle Brush, (Spanish : Calistemon).

HABIT AND CULTIVATION

Category	Shrub/Tree
Family	Myrtaceae
Origin	Australia
Size, height x spread	7 x 5 metres
Situation	Full sun.
Irrigation	Becoming drought tolerant, though also happy on an irrigation system.
Temperature	To around –5°C
Evergreen/deciduous	Evergreen
Flowering	Red. Spring, summer and autumn
Special features	Birds enjoy the seed cases.

C. viminalis forms a striking large shrub or an equally delightful small tree with weeping habit. The new growth is pinky-bronze and matures to a dark green, with tough narrow leaves. It is mainly grown for its extremely eye-catching, red, bottlebrush flowers, which are freely produced through spring, summer and autumn. The weight of the flowers tends to make the branches weep and the overall look is very pretty. New growth sprouts from the tips of the flowers leaving long-lasting woody seed capsules behind. Will make a wonderful informal hedge. This is a deservedly popular planting through many of the milder areas of Ireland, the Mediterranean, South Africa and the Far East.

Propagation
By seed in spring or autumn. Semi-ripe cuttings in summer.

Pruning
Prune out any wayward branches, dead wood etc., but generally little needed.

Problems
None.

CAMELLIA JAPONICA
(Spanish : Camelia).

HABIT AND CULTIVATION

Category	Shrub
Family	Theaceae
Origin	Eastern China, Korea and Japan
Size, height x spread	7 x 5 metres
Situation	Semi or full shade. Protect from strong sun.
Irrigation	Regular watering
Temperature	To 0°C
Evergreen/deciduous	Evergreen
Flowering	White, cream, pinks and red. Winter to spring.
Special features	Acid soil.

Legend has it that C. Japonica was introduced to England as a trick. British East India agents, because of the growing popularity through Europe for tea, tried to smuggle out some Camellia sinensis plants (whose leaves are used to make tea). But c. japonica plants were substituted, and hence one of our most beautiful flowering plants reached Europe. It may not have been as useful as c.sinensis, but its beauty was much appreciated and today there are over 30,000 varieties. Although closely associated with Japanese culture, most of the genus is actually from China and the Indo-China peninsula, where it grows naturally in shaded, mountainous, semi-tropical areas. Although not ideal for our Mediterranean climate, they can be grown in pots on shaded patios.

Propagation
Softwood cuttings in summer, hardwood in winter. Can also be grafted.

Pruning
Prune out inward growing shoots to increase air circulation.

Problems
The main problems are bud drop or buds failing to open, both of which are associated with faulty watering/humidity. Maintain moist compost; never allow to dry out, or to become waterlogged. Watering with cold tea is appreciated (no milk, no sugar!) and daily misting with soft water.

Campanula

CAMPANULA RAPUNCULOIDES
Bell Flower, (Spanish : Campanula, Farolillos)

HABIT AND CULTIVATION

Category	Perennial
Family	Campanulaceae
Origin	Europe
Size, height x spread	1 metre x indefinite
Situation	Dappled shade.
Irrigation	Occasional summer soaking.
Temperature	To 0°C
Evergreen/deciduous	Evergreen except under severe conditions when top growth will die down.
Flowering	Blue. Spring.
Special features	-

This is a large genus of around 250 species of perennials, biennials and annuals. Many rockery and scree type plants but some useful for pots and hanging baskets. Also looking good in gravel gardens. The one you are most likely to find is C. rapunculoides. It is a tough spreading perennial, useful in difficult stony ground. It colonises with basal rosettes of foliage and tall flower spikes in springtime. Flowers are useful for cutting. It will grow in full sun but often the flower colour becomes washed out, and it is better with some dappled shade. Do not be too kind with this one – forget the fertiliser - or it can become invasive.

Propagation
From seed in autumn, but quickest and easiest by division of plants in very early spring when growth is just beginning.

Pruning
None. Remove dead flower stalks.

Problems
None.

CAMPSIS GRANDIFLORA Trumpet Vine, (Spanish : Campsis Naranjo)

HABIT AND CULTIVATION

Category	Perennial climber
Family	Bignoniaceae
Origin	China
Size, height x spread	10 metres x indefinite
Situation	Full sun
Irrigation	Drought tolerant
Temperature	To 0°C
Evergreen/deciduous	Deciduous
Flowering	Orange, apricot-yellow. Summer, autumn.
Special features	-

A very large and magnificent self-clinging climber which grips surfaces with tiny aerial roots, similar to ivy. It is a very rapid grower and needs space, stunning when allowed its head to tumble over walls, large pergolas etc. The leaves are mid-green composed of nine leaflets, arranged in pairs. Huge drooping clusters of brilliant orange-red trumpet flowers, individually some 8cm. long, are produced all summer long, creating a very tropical, exotic look. There is also a very attractive apricot coloured variety with slightly smaller flowers and the two colours inter mingled look wonderful.

Propagation
In summer from semi-ripe cuttings, hardwood cuttings in winter and also by layering – they will easily root into mulch material. Also detach suckers and replant.

Pruning
Prune established plants hard to constrain growth. Can be cut back to main framework in winter, when plant is bare, and it will quickly regenerate when weather warms up.

Problems
Flower tips prone to blackfly.

CANNA INDICA The Indian Shot Lily,
(Spanish : Cana).

HABIT AND CULTIVATION

Category	Perennial
Family	Cannaceae
Origin	South America
Size, height x spread	1 x 0.5 metres
Situation	Full sun or some light dappled shade
Irrigation	Water freely in summer months
Temperature	To 0°C
Evergreen/deciduous	Top growth dies down in winter.
Flowering	Yellow, pink, orange, red. Summer and autumn.
Special features	-

The canna lily is a truly exotic looking plant, which will brighten up any scheme with its showy leaves and flowers. It is highly valued for bedding and pot work because of its striking and tropical-looking foliage, available in greens, bronzes, purples and some wickedly-striped colour combinations. Then, as if that were not enough, it sends up fat flower shoots, which erupt into firework-coloured lily flowers, some mottled and spotted. Water lavishly in summer for huge leaves, though it will survive on a lot less. Feed generously.

Propagation
This is a rhizomatous plant which can be split and replanted in early spring. Also try from seed, germination should be successful above 20°C.

Pruning
Cut down faded leaves and flower stalks.

Problems
Watch for slug damage to juicy emerging leaves in wet springs.

CAPPARIS SPINOSA The Caper Bush, (Spanish : Alcaparra).

HABIT AND CULTIVATION

Category	Shrub
Family	Capparidaceae
Origin	Mediterranean
Size, height x spread	0.5 x 1 metres
Situation	Full sun
Irrigation	None once established.
Temperature	To –5°C
Evergreen/deciduous	Evergreen
Flowering	Pinkish-white. Summer.
Special features	Edible flower buds.

The caper bush has a long history as a commercial crop, going back as far as the Ancient Greeks. In more modern times, in the 1800's, it was heavily cultivated along the Mediterranean coastline in Spain. Even today it is still a valuable export item and is often served up in tapa bars in Southern Spain, though not many people realise that they are actually eating pickled flower buds! A cultivated 3yr. old plant should yield around 3kg. of capers annually and will carry on in good production for 25years. The plant is a prostrate, creeping shrub found growing naturally on rocky cliffs along coastlines, inland in mountainous scree land and even in old stone walls. Thus it can be seen that it is a plant that likes hot, dry, inhospitable conditions and poor ground. A sure way to kill a caper bush is to over water and fuss over it! The flowers are a pretty pinkish-white, some 5cm across and with a large central boss of stamens.

Propagation
From very fresh seed or, if older, soak 24hrs, refrigerate for 2 months wrapped in a moist cloth in an airtight container, resoak and plant.

Pruning
Flowers are borne on new growth, so it can be severely pruned annually without loss of crop.

Problems
None.

CARISSA MACROCARPA Natal Plum, (Spanish : Carisa)

HABIT AND CULTIVATION

Category	Shrub
Family	Apocynaceae
Origin	South Africa
Size, height x spread	2 x 2 metres
Situation	Full sun
Irrigation	Moderate
Temperature	To 0˚C
Evergreen/deciduous	Evergreen
Flowering	White. Spring.
Special features	Scented flowers. Edible fruit.

The carissa is an attractive plant at all times of the year. It has dark green, very glossy, leathery leaves and white flowers, somewhat like large jasmine blooms, which stand out well against the shiny foliage and are sweetly scented. The fruits mature to a deep red and are plum like in size and taste, rich in vitamin C, and make an excellent jam. It is a thorny, dense shrub and makes a good-looking hedging plant as well as deterring unwanted visitors! It is very tolerant of adverse conditions, being quite happy in windy sites and on salt laden coastlines. It can be a little slow to establish, but once it has found its feet, it will grow away rapidly.

Propagation
From seed in spring, though somewhat slow, or semi-ripe cuttings in summer.

Pruning
Generally keeps tidy shape, but can be pruned towards the end of the year to contain its size.

Problems
None

CARPENTERIA CALIFORNICA
The Bush Anemone,
(Spanish : Anemona Californiana).

HABIT AND CULTIVATION

Category	Shrub
Family	Hydrangaceae
Origin	California, U.S.A.
Size, height x spread	2 x 1.5 metres
Situation	Full sun or some light shade.
Irrigation	Water until established, then drought tolerant.
Temperature	To –5°C
Evergreen/deciduous	Evergreen
Flowering	White. Spring and summer.
Special features	Scented flowers.

A sturdy and very attractive, dense, dome-shaped shrub, found growing naturally in the foothills of the Sierra Nevada in California, though becoming somewhat rare. It bears long, dark green, glossy leaves and erupts into fabulous bloom in late spring. The flowers are white and cup-shaped, resembling a large, single rose, with bright yellow stamens - they are very beautiful and sweetly scented. Mature plants also develop peeling bark, revealing a yellowish trunk colour underneath. A stunning specimen shrub, it will also make fantastic hedging. It will tolerate windy and salty coastal conditions, though it is not too keen on polluted city life – preferring clean air! Dislikes wet and cold winter conditions.

Propagation
From seed in autumn, but flowers will be variable, or from summer cuttings or winter layering.

Pruning
Prune yearly, when flowering has finished, to prevent sprawliness and legginess.

Problems
Watch out for aphid attacks.

CARPOBROTUS EDULIS Lion's Claw, Hottentot Fig, (Spanish : Hierba del Cuchillo, Higo del Mar).

HABIT AND CULTIVATION

Category	Succulent
Family	Aizoaceae
Origin	South Africa
Size, height x spread	0.25 metres x indefinite
Situation	Full sun, though will tolerate a little light shade at times.
Temperature	Foliage damaged below 0°C, though will re-establish.
Evergreen/deciduous	Evergreen
Flowering	Pink or pale yellow. Spring and summer
Special features	-

This is a very useful and tough ground coverer, excellent on banks and loose sandy slopes for holding soil together and avoiding erosion. Also useful as a fire inhibitor. It has juicy triangular, claw-like leaves, 1.5cm x 10cm long, on spreading, mat-forming prostrate branches, which quickly cloak the ground, rooting as they go. The large daisy flowers, some 12cm across, in either pink or pale yellow, are occasionally followed by brown fig-like fruits, which are edible, hence the name. The leaves are also reputedly eaten – a substitute for potato chips! The yellow variety seems to be slightly weaker growing. Grows in any poor soil and very tolerant of adverse conditions.

Propagation
By cuttings which will root very easily. Can also be propagated from seed.

Pruning
Cut back growth to avoid base straggliness.

Problems
None

CARYOPTERIS CLANDONENSIS
Bluebeard, (Spanish : Caryopteris, Barba Azul).

HABIT AND CULTIVATION

Category	Shrub
Family	Verbenaceae
Origin	Asia
Size, height x spread	1 x 1 metres
Situation	Full sun
Irrigation	Becoming drought tolerant.
Temperature	To –5˚C
Evergreen/deciduous	Deciduous
Flowering	Blue. Summer and autumn.
Special features	-

The bluebeard is mainly prized for its masses of delicate and lacy, feathery blue flowers produced over a long period, from summer right through to early winter cold weather. The shrub itself is finely bushy, very airy and dainty looking with upright growth and oval, grey-green leaves, which are small and serrated along the edges. It will disappear completely underground under very harsh weather conditions. This is a useful shrub that will slot into almost any scheme and provide a useful colour contrast in the garden. Often grown as a background plant and sub-shrub filler, it is, in fact, worthy of a higher placing – it's flowers will delight you.

Propagation
By fresh seed in autumn or green or semi-ripe cuttings in summer .Cuttings generally flower in the year after rooting.

Pruning
Prune back hard each year, in early spring. to promote lots of fresh new growth and flowers.

Problems
None.

CASSIA ALATA The Senna Bush,
(Spanish : Casia).

HABIT AND CULTIVATION

Category	Shrub
Family	Leguminosae
Origin	Tropical areas, exact source unknown
Size, height x spread	3 x 3 metres
Situation	Full sun
Irrigation	Drought tolerant, though appreciates an occasional summer soaking.
Temperature	To 0°C
Evergreen/deciduous	Semi-evergreen
Flowering	Yellow and black. Autumn, winter and spring.
Special features	-

The cassia genus is large, containing around 500 species, mainly native to tropical and semi-tropical zones, and ranging from shrubs through to large trees. They all have very attractive foliage and flowers, making them a popular and attractive planting. Readily cross-fertilising, there is an almost bewildering choice of hybrids. The senna bush is used in the pharmaceutical and tanning industries and has, for centuries, been recognised as a natural laxative. It has mid-green leaves, composed of alternating leaflets and lots of majestic flower spikes in yellow and black – always an attention drawer. The seed cases are long and bean like. It is happy in a poor soil, but allow it plenty of space.

Propagation
By seed in spring or late summer cuttings.

Pruning
It should be cut back severely after flowering, otherwise it can tend to get a bit lanky.

Problems
Occasionally aphids and mealy bug.

CASUARINA GLAUCA Beefwood, Swamp Cypress, Singing Cypress, (Spanish : Casuarina).

HABIT AND CULTIVATION

Category	Tree
Family	Casuarinaceae
Origin	Australia
Size, height x spread	20 x 5 metres
Situation	Full sun
Irrigation	Drought tolerant.
Temperature	To –5°C
Evergreen/deciduous	Evergreen
Flowering	Red. Spring.
Special features	-

There are some 30 species of casuarina, all noted for their extreme tolerance and adaptability to adverse conditions. It is equally happy in dry, almost desert conditions, as in swampy, marshy ground. Salty and very alkaline conditions are also acceptable. It is a quick grower and useful shade provider. A native of Australia, the Aborigines traditionally used the very hard and dense wood for hunting weapons and tools. It has long, sweeping, dark green branches with small red flowers in spring. The cones are small and grey-brown, about 1cm. long. It is an excellent front line shelter tree and its roots bind together loose earth or sandy banks. It has a tendency to sucker, so give it space. In light sandy conditions it can become invasive. Stands up well to windy conditions, its branches swaying and 'singing' in the wind.

Propagation
Easy from seed.

Pruning
None necessary. Remove an occasional untidy branch.

Problems
None.

CATALPA BIGNONIOIDES The Indian Bean Tree, (Spanish : Catalpa).

HABIT AND CULTIVATION

Category	Tree
Family	Bignoniaceae
Origin	North America
Size, height x spread	15 x 10 metres
Situation	Full sun or some light dappled shade.
Irrigation	Give young trees an occasional deep summer soak.
Temperature	Fully hardy.
Evergreen/deciduous	Deciduous
Flowering	White, sometimes tinged pink or yellow. Early summer.
Special features	Scented

The catalpa is valued for its large, lush leaves, which give dense summer shade, and for its pretty flowering. It is very tolerant of urban pollution and is perhaps best seen as a single specimen tree where its grandeur can be fully appreciated. Do not plant it in very windy, exposed positions. The pale green leaves are some 25cm long and grouped in threes. The flowers are held in thick upright clusters, some 30cm tall, and are individually bell shaped and can be roughly striated in pink or yellow and sweetly scented. These are followed by long slender seed cases, which often persist on the tree until after leaf fall.

Propagation
Seed in spring or summer softwood cuttings.

Pruning
Removal of deadwood, crossing and badly placed branches is generally all that is required.

Problems
None

CEANOTHUS ARBOREUS California Lilac, (Spanish : Lila Californiana).

HABIT AND CULTIVATION

Category	Shrub
Family	Rhamnaceae
Origin	Mexico and western states of America
Size, height x spread	5 x 4 metres
Situation	Full sun
Irrigation	Drought tolerant once established.
Temperature	To –5˚C
Evergreen/deciduous	Evergreen
Flowering	Blues. Spring.
Special features	-

There are some 50 species of ceanothus, ranging from small sub shrubs to almost trees, evergreen and deciduous. They thrive in more protected parts of England and Ireland, Mediterranean areas, Australia and, of course, their home ground, California and Mexico. In spite of their name, they are in no way related to lilacs. They prefer a protected sheltered spot in full sun with some afternoon shade. Plant in a reasonably rich soil. Shiny, glossy dark green leaves and their wonderful masses of blue flowers – now available in all shades of blue and white – make this a desirable planting.

Propagation
Seed in spring, or semi-hardwood cuttings in summer.

Pruning
Cut out any deadwood in spring and trim back shoots after flowering.

Problems
They hate root disturbance. Pot cuttings individually for planting out and anchor well in ground. Wind sway kills many plants. Root rot can be brought on by over watering.

See also **CEANOTHUS THYRSIFLORUS**, var. repens.

CEANOTHUS THYRSIFLORUS var. repens, California Lilac, Creeping Blueblossom, (Spanish : Lila Californiana Rastrera).

HABIT AND CULTIVATION

Category	Shrub
Family	Rhamnaceae
Origin	Mexico and western states of America.
Size, height x spread	1 x 2.5 metres
Situation	Full sun or with some afternoon shade.
Irrigation	Becoming drought tolerant once established.
Temperature	To -5°C
Evergreen/deciduous	Evergreen
Flowering	Many shades of blue. Spring and summer.
Special features	-

This creeping, spreading plant with oval, glossy, dark green leaves is an excellent and very pretty ground coverer. It stays low and hugs the soil, carpeting some 2 to 3m of ground. It appreciates a hot sunny spot and is tolerant of poor soil conditions and coastal climate. In extreme heat, in inland situations, provide a little afternoon shade. Racemes of blue flowers, from pale powder blue through to a deep gentian blue, are borne throughout the spring and summer, contrasting very nicely with the deep green foliage.

Propagation
From seed in spring or summer hardwood cuttings.

Pruning
A trim over after flowering keeps the plant tidy and dense.

Problems
Hates root disturbance. Pot cuttings individually for planting out and anchor well in ground. Wind sway kills many plants. Root rot can be caused by over watering.

See also **CEANOTHUS ARBOREUS**.

CEDRUS DEODARA Indian Cedar, (Spanish : Cedro Deodar).

HABIT AND CULTIVATION

Category	Tree
Family	Pinaceae
Origin	Himalayas
Size, height x spread	30 x 10 metres
Situation	Full sun to part shade
Irrigation	Drought tolerant, but appreciates occasional summer soaking.
Temperature	Hardy
Evergreen/deciduous	Evergreen
Flowering	Inconsequential. Spring.
Special features	-

The cedars have a very ancient lineage and are much respected for their scented wood. This one is a rapid grower and makes a large conical tree with very tiered branches and weeping growth at branch tips. It makes a very beautiful specimen tree where size is not a problem. Male and female cones, about 5 – 10cm, grow on separate branches. This species will grow in a wide range of conditions, from arid inland to cooler mountain areas – its size will largely be controlled by the climate and amount of water it receives. Also suitable for pots until around 2m tall.

Propagation
By seed.

Pruning
None

Problems
None

Also **CEDRUS LIBANI**, Cedar of Lebanon, (Spanish : Cedro de Libani). To around 25 x 15 metres. Grey-green needle like foliage on tiered branches, flat and spreading. Pink-grey cones, ovoid and some 15cm across. Similar conditions and cultivation to c. deodara.

CENTRANTHUS RUBER Red Valerian, Kiss-me-Quick, (Spanish : Milamores).

HABIT AND CULTIVATION

Category	Perennial
Family	Valerianaceae
Origin	Mediterranean and North Africa
Size, height x spread	1 x 0.75 metres
Situation	Full sun, partial shade.
Irrigation	Drought tolerant.
Temperature	Hardy.
Evergreen/deciduous	Semi-evergreen
Flowering	Pink-red and white. Spring through to autumn.
Special features	-

This is one of our easiest and most tolerant plants and yet surprisingly difficult to find in garden centres. It is often seen naturalised on dry banks, stony waste ground and stone walls, giving a clear indication of the conditions it likes. It is also particularly good in rock and gravel gardens, on banks and wall crevices. Take care because it can become invasive if spoilt too much, though seedlings are easily pulled up. It has blue-green glaucous foliage. Branching heads of small star-shaped flowers in dusky-pink/red or white are borne from springtime through to autumn, and are very attractive in clumps. The white, particularly, brightens up any dark, difficult corner. A good plant for a natural garden, it always seems to self sow in the right spot!

Propagation
Easy from seed in spring or autumn, but will also self-seed very readily.

Pruning
Remove spent flowers to encourage a second flush of flowers and avoid a proliferation of seedlings.

Problems
None

CERATONIA SILIQUA The Carob Tree, (Spanish : Algarrobo, Pan de San Juan)

HABIT AND CULTIVATION

Category	Tree
Family	Leguminosae
Origin	Mediterranean
Size, height x spread	12 x 8 metres
Situation	Full sun
Irrigation	Drought tolerant once established.
Temperature	To around –5˚C
Evergreen/deciduous	Evergreen
Flowering	Cream, insignificant. Spring.
Special features	Edible crop.

The carob tree is a slow growing but extremely tough tree and a great survivor. The wind moulds and twists it into wierd, gnarled forms. It has dark green, tough, leathery leaves and long, brown, bean-like pods around 25cm long. These are ready for picking in autumn time when dark brown. The inner pulp tastes sweet and juicy; and the pods are roasted and powdered for use as a chocolate substitute. It was much valued in times of famine and it is commonly known through the Mediterranean as St. John's bread. In ancient times, 1 carob bean was a measure of weight, equivalent to a one carat (derivation) diamond. This has now been standardised to 200mg. Do not plant this tree too close to the house, it needs space and its root structure can lift paving etc. Also, some people find the scent of the flowers overpowering and objectionable.

Propagation
From seed, best pre-soaked.

Pruning
Just occasional shaping.

Problems
If not cropped, the litter from the seed pods is considerable.

CERCIS SILIQUASTRUM Redbud, Judas Tree, or Love Tree, (Spanish : Arbol de Judas, Arbol de Amor).

HABIT AND CULTIVATION

Category	Tree
Family	Leguminosae
Origin	Mediterranean
Size, height x spread	10 x 4 metres
Situation	Full sun or with some afternoon shade
Irrigation	Drought tolerant once established.
Temperature	Hardy.
Evergreen/deciduous	Deciduous
Flowering	Magenta or white. Early spring.
Special features	-

This is a slender trunked tree with a rounded head, grown mainly for its spectacular flowering. Clusters of pea-like magenta or white flowers appear on the bare branches in early spring. The leaves, when they open, are attractively heart-shaped (hence love tree), often emerging bronze coloured, changing to a soft green, and then golden at leaf fall. The tree dislikes root disturbance, so buy containerised trees and do not attempt to transplant. Stake well to avoid swaying and root damage. The common name of Judas Tree refers to the legend that Judas Iscariot, having betrayed Jesus, then hung himself on one of these trees. The tree was so ashamed that it blushed with embarrassment, and this is what we see every spring!

Propagation
By seed.

Pruning
Little required. Take out any wayward or crossing branches, deadwood etc.

Problems
None.

CERINTHE MAJOR PURPURESCENS
Honeywort, (Spanish : Ceriflor).

HABIT AND CULTIVATION

Category	Annual
Family	Boragacinaceae
Origin	Mediterranean
Size, height x spread	0,75 x 0.40 metres
Situation	Full sun or partial or dappled shade.
Irrigation	Occasional summer soaking
Temperature	To 5°C
Evergreen/deciduous	-
Flowering	Indigo blue. Spring and summer
Special features	-

The honeywort seems to be a little known plant and yet one that is exceedingly easy to grow and very rewarding. A native of the Mediterranean area, it is an undemanding plant which will survive and self-seed without any help. Poor ground will suffice, though if you can give it something better, it will thank you with bigger and lusher plants. The foliage is a pale, glaucous green with creamy mottling and spots. The flowers are a really unusual indigo blue with touches of deep pink/purple and they are held in large clusters of drooping bell-shaped blooms. It is a really eye-catching plant, combining brilliantly with brighter colours. Try it grouped in borders, and also in pots. In dappled shade, it also looks wonderful in a more natural setting under trees in open woodland or meadowland.

Propagation
Very easy from early spring-sown seed. Once established in the garden, it will self-sow readily.

Pruning
None.

Problems
None.

CESTRUM 'NEWELLII' Jessamine, (Spanish : Cestrum).

HABIT AND CULTIVATION

Category	Shrub
Family	Solanaceae
Origin	Mexico
Size, height x spread	3 x 2 metres
Situation	Full sun or dappled shade.
Irrigation	Moderate, can become almost drought tolerant in a partially shaded position.
Temperature	To –5˚C. Will survive lower temperatures, but goes deciduous.
Evergreen/deciduous	Evergreen
Flowering	Burgundy red. Spring and summer.
Special features	Very poisonous

This arching evergreen shrub has slightly downy, lance shaped leaves, and the emerging new growth in spring is red tinged. The showy clusters of burgundy-red tubular flowers, which are produced over many months, are borne on the tips of the branches. Berries of the same deep red colour follow on from the flowers. It is a very attractive shrub at all times and worthy of space in the garden. It can also be pot grown but will require much more water and regular fertilising otherwise it will not be so floriferous.

Propagation
Soft tip cuttings in summer and it may produce suckering growth which can be carefully detached and replanted.

Pruning
Cut out some older wood each year in winter to promote bushier growth and plenty of flowers.

Problems
None.

See also **CESTRUM NOCTURNUM**.

CESTRUM NOCTURNUM
Night scented Jessamine,
(Spanish : Dama de Noche).

HABIT AND CULTIVATION

Category	Shrub
Family	Solanaceae
Origin	West Indies
Size, height x spread	3 x 2 metres
Situation	Full sun
Irrigation	Becoming drought tolerant, though lusher-growing with some water.
Temperature	To around 0°C
Evergreen/deciduous	Semi-evergreen
Flowering	Lime green. Summer.
Special features	Intensely perfumed. All parts very poisonous

This tropical and semi-tropical member of the cestrum family is one of the Mediterranean classics and widely grown for its amazing night time perfume which is so intense on a hot summer's evening that some people find it overpowering - others adore it! It forms an upright, fairly ordinary looking shrub with dark green leaves. The flowers are small and lime-green coloured, held in large clusters. A shrub well grown can be covered in them. During the day they have no perfume, but as soon as darkness begins to fall, the bewitching scent is wafted around on the air and can often be detected several metres away. Occasionally sets small white berries.

Propagation
Tip cuttings in summer.

Pruning
Cut out some old wood each winter to promote denser growth.

Problems
Very prone to aphid attack which can twist and distort the leaves.

See also **CESTRUM 'NEWELLI'**

CHAMAEROPS HUMILIS Dwarf Fan Palm, (Spanish : Palmito).

HABIT AND CULTIVATION

Category	Palm
Family	Palmae
Origin	Mediterranean
Size, height x spread	2.5 x 5 metres, but will grow taller in cultivation and with water.
Situation	Full sun or light dappled shade.
Irrigation	Drought tolerant, but will also accept irrigation.
Temperature	Hardy to –10°C
Evergreen/deciduous	Evergreen
Flowering	Pale yellow but insignificant. Spring.
Special features	-

This dwarf native palm is found growing wild in the Mediterranean area in poor soil and rock faces. It is perhaps the toughest of all palms and will take widely ranging growing conditions, even tolerating a sprinkling of snow. It slowly develops clumping, multiple trunks and the leaves are fine, erect and fan shaped. In a garden situation it is a useful specimen plant and looks equally well in informal groupings. It can also be grown in a large container. The strong fibrous leaves were once used in basket making. The palm hearts are often cut out and sold fresh or to the canning industry for use in salads, a practice, which sadly, kills the palm.

Propagation
Germination from seeds in approximately 6 weeks.

Pruning
Remove dead outer leaves and flower/fruiting stalks.

Problems
None.

CHOISYA TERNATA Mexican Orange Blossom, (Spanish : Naranjo de Mexico)

HABIT AND CULTIVATION

Category	Shrub
Family	Rutaceae
Origin	Mexico
Size, height x spread	2 x 2 metres
Situation	Full sun or some light dappled shade.
Irrigation	Becoming drought tolerant.
Temperature	To around –5°C
Evergreen/deciduous	Evergreen
Flowering	White. Spring with repeat flowering in autumn.
Special features	Leaves and flowers scented.

A very attractive, evergreen shrub nicely rounded and dense with bright green, shiny leaves composed of three leaflets, which are aromatic when crushed. It bears dense clusters of fragrant white flowers, mainly in spring and autumn, though flowering can carry on right through the summer months too. The sweet scent of the flowers resembles that of orange blossom, hence the common name. This is a very pretty specimen shrub and also makes a wonderful hedge. It is a very easy and maintenance-free planting, though find it a nicely sheltered spot as it is not happy in a cold wind and deserves a good position.

Propagation
In spring from seed or semi-ripe cuttings in late summer/autumn.

Pruning
Trim to keep in shape. Will transplant if cut back hard, and, as a hedging plant, it can be clipped regularly.

Problems
None.

CHORISIA SPECIOSA Floss Silk or Kapok Tree, (Spanish : Palo Borracho Rosado, Arbol de los Pajaros).

HABIT AND CULTIVATION

Category	Tree
Family	Bombacaceae
Origin	Brazil, South America.
Size, height x spread	15 x 10 metres
Situation	Full sun
Irrigation	Water moderately when in active growth and flower, but will become drought tolerant.
Temperature	To around 0°C
Evergreen/deciduous	Deciduous
Flowering	Pink and gold. Summer and autumn.
Special features	Heavily spined trunk.

The chorisia speciosa is a stunningly beautiful specimen tree. Even when leafless it draws attention with its viciously and strikingly thorned trunk. But it is grown mainly for it's fabulous flowers, which are large and orchid-like with five petals, bright pink and with a deep golden throat. After flowering, large seed cases develop which are lined with soft flossy hairs used for stuffing cushions etc., hence kapok tree. The compound leaves are hand-shaped and about 12cm long overall. Find it a warm spot and it won't disappoint.

Propagation
From seed in spring.

Pruning
Generally none necessary.

Problems
None.

Also **CHORISIA INSIGNIS**, Bottle Tree, (Spanish : Palo Borracho Amarillo, Arbol Botella). A smaller-growing and chunkier tree with even more impressive thorns on a heavily swollen trunk which stores water against times of drought. Same family as the baobab tree of Africa. Flowers yellow and white, again very beautiful, and usually earlier in flower.

CISTUS LADANIFER Rock Rose, Gum Cistus, (Spanish : Jara Pringosa, Jara de Ladano).

HABIT AND CULTIVATION

Category	Shrub
Family	Cistaceae
Origin	Mediterranean
Size, height x spread	1.5 x 1.5 metres
Situation	Full sun
Irrigation	Drought tolerant.
Temperature	To around –5°C
Evergreen/deciduous	Evergreen
Flowering	White with deep red blotches. Spring.
Special features	-

The cistus family love a hot, sunny spot in very poor soil, even a seaside cliff situation. Do not pamper them or they will die. C. ladanifer is an upright shrub with dark green, sticky leaves which emit a pleasant aroma in hot sunshine. The gum from the leaves and stems is extracted for use in the pharmaceutical industry. Shallow rooting and with matted fibrous roots, they are excellent colonisers and robust plants that help bind soil and are also useful as a fire retardant. The flowers are large, white and open cup-shaped with a deep red triangular blotch at the base of each petal. Each flower only lasts one day, but they are produced in great profusion. A great range of hybrids are available, many scented and in a good range of colours.

Propagation
Seeds in autumn or softwood cuttings in summer.

Pruning
Trim lightly after flowering to keep tidy shape, but do not prune hard.

Problems
None

CLEMATIS ARMANDI
(Spanish : Clematis).

HABIT AND CULTIVATION

Category	Perennial climber
Family	Ranunculaceae
Origin	China
Size, height x spread	8 x 15 metres
Situation	Cool root run growing into sun or light dappled shade.
Irrigation	Moderate
Temperature	To −10°C with some root protection
Evergreen/deciduous	Evergreen
Flowering	Creamy white. Early spring.
Special features	Scented flowers.

The clematis family is large and they are found in most temperate parts of the world, but many of the large-flowering type originate from China or Japan. Some of these larger flowerers will not really be happy with strong Mediterranean sunshine and all need a cool root run. They are self climbers, twisting tendrils around whatever support is available, looking particularly good on pergolas and, stronger growing varieties, through trees. The armandii has long, glossy, dark-green leaves and is vigorous when suited. The flowers are about 5cm across, open cup-shaped and almond scented

Propagation
Seed in autumn, summer softwood cuttings or winter layering.

Pruning
Prune small flowerers immediately after flowering to allow time for ripening of new growth for following season's flowers. Large flowering varieties should be pruned down hard to a pair of strong leaf buds before new growth starts in early spring.

Problems
Clematis wilt (prune hard), aphids, slugs, snails and occasional mildew.

See also **CLEMATIS CIRRHOSA, C. MONTANA** and **C. ORIENTALIS**

CLEMATIS CIRRHOSA Virgin's Bower, (Spanish : Clematis de Maria).

HABIT AND CULTIVATION

Category	Perennial climber
Family	Ranunculaceae
Origin	Mediterranean
Size, height x spread	5 x 2 metres
Situation	Cool roots, climbing into full sun or light dappled shade.
Irrigation	Drought tolerant.
Temperature	To around –5°C
Evergreen/deciduous	Classed as evergreen, but summer dormant.
Flowering	Creamy white-green. Winter.
Special features	-

A scrambling climber found growing wild through most of the Mediterranean area, it clambers up and over trees, and thickets of brambles etc. The cup shaped flowers, through winter, are pretty and are followed by distinctive feathery seedheads. Useful garden application where a wilder, more natural-looking climber is required. Propagation, and pruning as C. armandii. Small flowerers generally give less problems that their showy, larger-flowering cousins.

Also **CLEMATIS MONTANA**, an exceedingly vigorous type from China. Smothered in flat flowers, white or shades of pink, some scented, in early spring. New growth often tinged dark red. A very striking climber and less problematical than some of the large-flowered hybrids. Reaching 12 x indefinite.

Also **CLEMATIS ORIENTALIS**, from Mediterranean area. Yellow lantern shaped flowers in spring/summer, followed by typical feathery seed heads. Spread 4 x 2 metres.

CLERODENDRUM THOMSONIAE
Bleeding Heart Vine (Spanish :
Clerodendro).

HABIT AND CULTIVATION

Category	Perennial climber
Family	Verbenaceae
Origin	West Africa
Size, height x spread	4 x 2 metres
Situation	Partial to full shade
Irrigation	Moderate through summer months.
Temperature	Tender. Minimum 5°C
Evergreen/deciduous	Evergreen
Flowering	Red with white calyces. Summer.
Special features	Scented.

This very attractive shrubby climber is a little delicate and will not tolerate low temperatures or cold winds but it is delightful in a sheltered position. It has large, deep-green, oval leaves, distinctively ribbed, on a woody-stemmed, twisting framework, which requires support and tying in. The bracted flowers are particularly eye-catching, crimson-red and held in clusters, each surrounded by creamy-white calyces, the flowers being slightly scented. Use it on a sheltered patio wall, courtyard garden or small bower. It can also be grown in a large pot. Happiest in a humus-rich soil - it is definitely worth spoiling and pampering a bit! And, usefully, this is one of the few flowering vines that will tolerate full shade.

Propagation
Semi-hardwood cuttings in autumn or try spring seed sowings.

Pruning
Thin out crowded growth in early spring.

Problems
Whitefly, red spider mite and mealy bug:

CLIANTHUS PUNICEUS Parrot's Bill, (Spanish : Pico del Loro).

HABIT AND CULTIVATION

Category	Climber
Family	Leguminosae
Origin	New Zealand.
Size, height x spread	4 x 4 metres
Situation	Full sun
Irrigation	Moderate in summer.
Temperature	To around 0°C
Evergreen/deciduous	Evergreen
Flowering	Red. Spring and early summer.
Special features	-

The Maoris have cultivated this plant for hundreds of years, and treasured it for its great beauty and the extreme sweetness of the nectar. They called it kowhai ngutu-kaka, or red kaka beak. It is now almost extinct in the wild and protected. An extremely decorative shrubby climber/trailer, it grows in desert regions and loves to scramble over sandy banks or poor, rocky, alkaline soil. It has elegant ferny green foliage, which is only outdone by the stunning display of flowers in spring and early summer. These are held in drooping clusters and are brilliant red and claw-like. Although a desert plant, it appreciates regular watering and fertilising through the growing season, and will reward you with wonderfully lush foliage and plenty of those dazzling flowers.

Propagation
By seed, soaked in hot water overnight, and then sown or summer cuttings.

Pruning
Prune lightly after flowering to keep in good shape.

Problems
Snails can be a problem with the lush growth. Dislikes root disturbance, plant in situ and leave alone.

CLIVIA MINIATA Fire Lily, (Spanish : Clivia).

HABIT AND CULTIVATION

Category	Bulb
Family	Amaryllidaceae
Origin	South Africa
Size, height x spread	0.5 x 0.5 metres
Situation	Full or partial shade
Irrigation	Monthly summer soaking
Temperature	To 0°C
Evergreen/deciduous	Evergreen
Flowering	Orange or yellow. Spring and summer.
Special features	-

A native of the Natal area of South Africa, clivias are noted for their striking funnel shaped flowers, some 7.5cm long, borne in heavy clusters of 10 to 20 flowers over dark green, glossy strap-shaped basal leaves. They are currently available in a glowing orange or a pretty soft yellow. The tough, rhizomatous roots like to colonise crevices and shallow soil and it also makes an excellent pot plant. Allow it to become pot bound, and flowering will be at its best and most prolific. It also makes a good ground cover perennial, colonising thin rocky ground or between tree roots. The Zulus extracted a medicine from the leaves to alleviate childhood pains.

Propagation
From seed, though rather slow to flower, or by plant division after flowering.

Pruning
None. Simply remove spent flower heads if seeds are not required.

Problems
Generally trouble free though mealy bug can make an appearance.

COBAEA SCANDENS The-Cup-and-Saucer Plant, (Spanish : Vid de la Taza y del Platillo).

HABIT AND CULTIVATION

Category	Perennial climber
Family	Cobaeaceae
Origin	Mexico and tropical Central America
Size, height x spread	5 x 2 metres
Situation	Full sun or some partial shade.
Irrigation	Moderate summer watering
Temperature	To 5°C
Evergreen/deciduous	Evergreen
Flowering	Pale green to lilac to purple. Spring, summer, autumn.
Special features	-

The cup-and-saucer plant is one of our prettiest and most unusual climbers, very easy to grow and yet very little seen. The new foliage is purple-toned and the climber self-clings by twisting tendrils. Start it from seed in early spring and it will grow away vigorously, rapidly cloaking a pergola, trellising or similar. As long as temperatures are maintained above freezing, it will be perennial. The flowers are very elegant. The cup-shaped flowers, sitting on calyces or 'saucers' are borne on long stalks and open a very pale green. They then turn a soft lilac, maturing to a deep purple before fading. All colours are borne on the plant at the same time, and the effect is delightful. Little girls (and big ones!) love them for dolls tea parties!

Propagation
By early spring sown seeds.

Pruning
Train the new growths and keep under control. Can be pruned down low after flowering if the top growth is very matted and tangled.

Problems
None.

COLCHICUM AUTUMNALE Autumn Crocus, (Spanish : Colquico).

HABIT AND CULTIVATION

Category	Bulb
Family	Liliacaea
Origin	Europe and Asia
Size, height x spread	0.15 x 0.15 metres
Situation	Sun or partial shade
Irrigation	Will survive on seasonal rains
Temperature	Fully hardy.
Evergreen/deciduous	Disappearing underground in summer
Flowering	Lilac to purple. Autumn.
Special features	All parts highly toxic.

The large goblet flowers, up to 20cm long, of the autumn crocus always draw attention, though it is, surprisingly, little planted. It grows from a corm and produces masses of crocus-like flowers with the first autumn rains. The strap-like basal foliage emerges after the flowers and disappears as the heat of summer builds up. Flower colour ranges from a pure white in some varieties through pinky-lilacs to deep amethyst-purple. Plant the corms some 10cm below the surface of the soil and they will increase yearly. An open sunny position is liked, though they can also be used as part of bank plantings and in rock gardens. The plant is highly toxic, though the active ingredient, colchicine, is used in the treatment of certain types of cancer.

Propagation
By seed or plant division in autumn.

Pruning
None.

Problems
None

CONVOLVULUS CNEORUM Silverbush, (Spanish : Cneorum de la Enredadera)

HABIT AND CULTIVATION

Category	Shrub
Family	Convolvulaceae
Origin	Mediterranean
Size, height x spread	0.75 x 0.75 metres
Situation	Full sun or dappled shade.
Irrigation	Drought tolerant.
Temperature	Frost tender
Evergreen/deciduous	Evergreen
Flowering	White. Spring and summer.
Special features	-

The silverbush is a tough and attractive addition to any garden, always looking neat and tidy. It forms a nicely rounded, compact, small shrub with platinum-silver, small lance-shaped leaves, creating a perfect compliment to other plants. The white cup-shaped flowers are flushed pink on the outsides and are prolifically produced through spring and summer and often right through until the colder weather arrives. It is a useful plant for hot, sunny positions and will bloom most prolifically on poor soil. An ideal rockery or gravel-garden plant where it's feet can be kept well dry! It can also be grown in containers. The foliage acts as a fire retardant

Propagation
From softwood cuttings in spring and summer.

Pruning
A light trimming after flowering helps maintain it's neat shape and encourages best flowering.

Problems
None if grown hot and dry. Dislikes cold, humid conditions.

See also **CONVOLVULUS SABATIUS** syn. C. Mauritanicus.

CONVOLVULUS SABATIUS syn. **CONVOLVULUS MAURITANICUS**, Moroccan Morning Glory, (Spanish : Correhuela de Marrueco).

HABIT AND CULTIVATION

Category	Perennial
Family	Convolvulaceae
Origin	North Africa
Size, height x spread	0.3 x 1 metres
Situation	Full sun or dappled shade
Irrigation	Occasional summer soaking.
Temperature	To around –5°C
Evergreen/deciduous	Evergreen
Flowering	Blue. Spring through to autumn
Special features	-

C. sabatius is a very pretty, trailing groundcover plant, also excellent draped over walls, on banks and in hanging pots and baskets. It is also a good addition to wild scree gardens where it has space to spread. Its charming sky blue cup-shaped flowers smother the plant through all the warmer months. The plant has slender, creeping stems with soft, rounded green leaves and, although in some areas, it can become a problem it is such a pretty invader that most people welcome it! Picking off the spent flowers will encourage fresh flushes.

Propagation
From stem cuttings in spring and summer. Can also root itself into the ground when well suited.

Pruning
Only an occasional trim over to keep tidy, though can also be pruned hard if becoming over-rampant.

Problems
None apart from a dislike of cold, wet conditions.

See also **CONVOLVULUS CNEORUM**

COPROSMA REPENS Taupata,
(Spanish : Coprosma).

HABIT AND CULTIVATION

Category	Shrub
Family	Rubiaceae
Origin	New Zealand
Size, height x spread	0.5 x 2 metres
Situation	Full sun, dappled and light shade.
Irrigation	Water regularly through the summer months.
Temperature	To around 0°C
Evergreen/deciduous	Evergreen
Flowering	Pale yellow, insignificant. Spring.
Special features	-

Mainly grown for their wonderful foliage, these lush-looking, spreading shrubs are much more tolerant than you would suspect. They need warmth and water in summer, but given that they can cope with urban pollution, salty conditions and poor sandy soils without any problem and are, in fact, much used in coastal situations in New Zealand. Their rounded and highly glossy leaves are exceedingly attractive, especially in the variegated forms. Flowering is insignificant and sometimes followed by orange-red berries but it is the foliage, which always draws the eye.

Propagation
Seed in spring or semi-ripe cuttings during the summer months.

Pruning
When first planted, the plants spread and ground cover well. In later life they have a tendency to put out upright shoots – these should be pruned out unless you want a taller growing shrub. Generally a light pruning in late autumn maintains shape.

Problems
None

COREOPSIS VERTICILLATA Tick plant, (Spanish : Dahlia del Prado).

HABIT AND CULTIVATION

Category	Perennial
Family	Compositae
Origin	North America
Size, height x spread	0.75 x 0.50 metres
Situation	Full sun
Irrigation	Drought tolerant
Temperature	Fully hardy
Evergreen/deciduous	Semi-evergreen
Flowering	Yellow. Spring, summer and autumn
Special features	-

The coreopsis is a very strong growing perennial, an ideal colonising plant and useful as a cheap and bulky filler in the new garden. A native of the Great Plains of North America, it will adapt to poor stony ground and even windy coastal conditions. The leaves are lance- shaped and mid to dark green, finely divided and form a nice bushy framework. The rich- yellow flowers are carried in great abundance through the warmer months. Once the first flush of flowers is over, cut the plant back by about half and further flowers will rapidly be produced. Do not over water or over feed as this will produce soft and floppy growth, which will then need staking. Also a useful cut flower.

Propagation
By division of old clumps in winter or spring. Also by stem cuttings in spring.

Pruning
Trim over to keep in shape and promote further flowering.

Problems
None.

CORONILLA VALENTINA ssp. GLAUCA
Large Scorpion Vetch, (Spanish : Ruda Inglesa).

HABIT AND CULTIVATION

Category	Shrub
Family	Leguminosae
Origin	Mediterranean
Size, height x spread	1.5 x 1.5 metres
Situation	Full sun
Irrigation	Drought tolerant
Temperature	To around –5°C
Evergreen/deciduous	Evergreen
Flowering	Yellow. Spring.
Special features	Scented.

The scorpion vetch is a tough shrub, a native of open grassy scrubland, cliff tops etc. It makes a useful planting in the natural garden, demanding nothing more than an open sunny position and alkaline, poor, stony soil to give of its best. Although so easy going, it is also very pretty with its blue-green glaucous foliage and pea-like, yellow flowers which scent the air on a hot spring day. The common name of scorpion vetch is from the shape of the seed pods, which are curved and bear a pointed end like the sting of a scorpion's tail.

Propagation
From seed. Small self-sown seedlings will also transplant. Or from summer cuttings and autumn layering.

Pruning
Clip over the plants to keep them compact, as they have a tendency to fall apart.

Problems
None. Keep hot and dry. Will rot away if overwatered and especially dislikes overhead watering.

CORTADERIA SELLOANA Pampas
Grass, (Spanish : Cortaderia).

HABIT AND CULTIVATION

Category	Grass
Family	Gramineae
Origin	South America
Size, height x spread	3 x 2 metres
Situation	Full sun
Irrigation	Drought tolerant.
Temperature	Frost hardy.
Evergreen/deciduous	Evergreen
Flowering	Cream, dusky pink. Summer and autumn.
Special features	-

The pampas grass often receives bad press – perhaps from its ubiquitous usage in too many suburban gardens of England! However, it is a stately, magnificent grass and a wonderful accent point when correctly positioned. Certainly it looks more at home in our Mediterranean climate than in grey, wet English climes. The leaves are long and slender, curving gracefully – though beware, because they do have very sharp edges. The silvery plumes tower above the leaves, swaying in the slightest breeze. Very tolerant of poorer conditions – in fact it can become invasive if treated too kindly. Remember its homeland – the open savannah of Argentina – and imitate!

Propagation
From seed or division.

Pruning
The old practice of setting fire to the plant – somewhat scary! – is not necessary. Yes, this possibly happens in it's natural habitat, bush fires being a natural hazard, but in a cultivated setting you can simply shear the old growth down and it will quickly regenerate. Wear long, tough gloves for the job.

Problems
None

COSMOS ATROSANGUINEUS Black or Chocolate Cosmos, (Spanish : Atrosanguineus del Cosmos).

HABIT AND CULTIVATION

Category	Perennial
Family	Compositae
Origin	Mexico
Size, height x spread	1 x 0.3 metres
Situation	Full sun or light dappled shade
Irrigation	Moderate summer watering
Temperature	Almost fully hardy.
Evergreen/deciduous	Evergreen, unless particularly cold.
Flowering	Black-red. Spring to autumn.
Special features	Chocolate aroma.

This is the plant for all chocolate addicts – get your kicks from the aroma of the flowers, guaranteed non-fattening! C. atrosanguineus is a clump-forming perennial with wider pinnate leaves than the more commonly known cosmos. The wonderfully, velvety, rich maroon/black flowers, some 3cm.wide open cup-shaped with yellow stamens, emit that rich chocolatey smell on hot days right through their long flowering period. Regular deadheading keeps the flowering going longer. It is also an excellent cut flower, though the perfume may not be so noticeable indoors. Protect it from strong winds and do not over fertilise. It is intolerant of heavy clay soils and water logging.

Propagation
By seed or basal cuttings in spring.

Pruning
Only dead heading.

Problems
Watch for aphid attack on shoot tips. Mildew can appear in widely varying daytime/night-time temperatures.

Cotinus Coggygria 'Royal Purple'

COTINUS COGGYGRIA Smoke Tree, Venetian Sumach, (Spanish : Arbol de las Pelucas).

HABIT AND CULTIVATION

Category	Shrub
Family	Anacardiaceae
Origin	Southern Europe and Asia
Size, height x spread	5 x 3 metres
Situation	Full sun or some afternoon shade.
Irrigation	Occasional deep soaking in summer.
Temperature	Fully hardy.
Evergreen/deciduous	Deciduous
Flowering	Insignificant grey flowers, but see text. Spring.
Special features	Poisonous.

This is a tall, densely leafed shrub, mainly grown for its spectacular autumnal colours and flower florescences. The leaves are oval shaped and a light green, turning a glorious butter yellow and red colour in autumn, especially in colder areas. The small grey flowers, borne in masses, are insignificant but when they fade the stalks of the sterile flowers elongate and become clothed in hairs giving the effect of airy smoke puffs, hence the common name. It is unusual and utterly delightful. There are also several purple varieties, particularly 'Royal Purple' which, although not having the striking autumn tones, has very attractive rich, maroon-red leaves right through the growing season and carries pinkish puffs of 'smoke'.

Propagation
Softwood cuttings in summer. Seed in autumn.

Pruning
Prune back to about two-thirds in winter to tidy and promote new brightly-coloured growth.

Problems
None.

CROCOSMIA MASONORUM
Montbretia, (Spanish : Montbretia).

HABIT AND CULTIVATION

Category	Bulb
Family	Iridaceae
Origin	South Africa
Size, height x spread	1 x 1 metres
Situation	Full sun or with some afternoon shade.
Irrigation	Moderately through summer.
Temperature	Hardy.
Evergreen/deciduous	Foliage dies down in winter.
Flowering	Orange-red. Spring and summer.
Special features	-

Montbretias are South African natives from the Natal area, where they naturalise above 1000m. These cormed plants bear spectacular shows of flowers through spring and summer in fiery shades. Plant the corms in winter in a rich soil and they will soon mature into dense clumps of sword-shaped, pleated leaves, forming in fans. The branched flower stalk has a flattish upper part where the 6-petalled flowers are prolifically produced. The flowers are around 6cm long in orange-red coloration and funnel shaped, though there are also some yellow varieties now available. They are also excellent cut and brought indoors for arrangements.

Propagation
By division in spring, though this should not be done until they are severely overcrowded as flowering will then be delayed. Also by spring sown seed.

Pruning
Remove dead flower stalks and tidy up spent leaves.

Problems
None.

CUPRESSUS ARIZONICA Arizona Cypress, (Spanish : Cipres Arizonica).

HABIT AND CULTIVATION

Category	Tree
Family	Cupressaceae
Origin	Arizona, America
Size, height x spread	15 x 5 metres
Situation	Full sun
Irrigation	Drought tolerant
Temperature	To around –10°C
Evergreen/deciduous	Evergreen
Flowering	Insignificant. Spring.
Special features	-

The Arizona cypress is a useful planting because of its adaptability to extreme conditions. It will tolerate almost desert conditions and is perfectly at home in salt-laden windy coastal areas. Also, surprisingly, cold tolerant if kept dry. It is a pyramidal tree with glaucous, grey-green foliage and can either be used as a specimen tree or makes good solid hedging, very wind and dust resistant. It carries large chocolate brown cones about 2.5cm across and brown, ridged bark. Young plants can be carefully transplanted if necessary, but more mature specimens will not tolerate a move.

Propagation
Cuttings in winter or cold-treated seed in late autumn.

Pruning
Cut out twisted or distorted branches and can be topped out at desired height.

Problems
Cypress can be subject to canker (coryneum canker) which is a fungal disease that kills the bark and eventually the tree, but this does not seem to be such a problem in hot areas and particularly in hot, windy coastal areas where there is some speculation that the heavily salt-laden winds deter the disease. Diseased bark should be cut out and burnt.

See also **CUPRESSUS MACROCARPA** and **C. SEMPERVIRENS**.

CUPRESSUS MACROCARPA Monterey Cypress, (Spanish : Cipres Macrocarpa).

HABIT AND CULTIVATION

Category	Tree
Family	Cupressaceae
Origin	California, America
Size, height x spread	12 x 12 metres
Situation	Full sun
Irrigation	Drought tolerant.
Temperature	Hardy
Evergreen/deciduous	Evergreen
Flowering	Insignificant. Spring.
Special features	-

The stately and beautiful Monterey cypress is noted for its handsome foliage and habit of growth. When young it is compact and conical but, as it matures, it's branches spread into a large canopy. Wind can often twist and transform these into wonderful living sculptures. This is an extremely picturesque tree and one that needs, and deserves, a lot of space and a special position. It looks particularly good against an open skyline. Although hardy, it does not like a bitterly cold wind being more accustomed to the warmer, though fierce, winds of the Californian coastline. A good shelter and shade tree, it can also be clipped to form tall hedging. Dark-green, aromatic leaves and globular, glossy brown cones.

Propagation
From seed or cuttings.

Pruning
Responds well to pruning, so can be used as hedging.

Problems
Cypress canker. See entry C. arizonica.

See also **CUPRESSUS ARIZONICA** and
C. SEMPERVIRENS.

CUPRESSUS SEMPERVIRENS Italian Cypress, (Spanish : Cipres)

HABIT AND CULTIVATION

Category	Tree
Family	Cupressaceae
Origin	Southern Europe
Size, height x spread	20 x 2 metres
Situation	Full sun
Irrigation	Drought tolerant once established.
Temperature	Down to around –5˚C
Evergreen/deciduous	Evergreen
Flowering	Insignificant. Spring.
Special features	-

The Italian cypress is much seen accenting Mediterranean skylines and is a very popular 'exclamation mark' planting. It was traditionally planted in and around cemeteries' – it is said to emit microbia-killing substances – and it is still largely seen as a mourning tree in many traditional Mediterranean communities. It is a very thin, columnar tree, though with some variation between individual plants. Select thin plants when buying. It is very tolerant of hot, dry conditions - best not to overwater or overfertilise as this promotes rapid and rather lax growth which will not achieve the sought-after, thin, pencil shape. Plant, stake and water well until established, then leave it alone. Can also be used as hedging and good in small groupings.

Propagation
From cuttings.

Pruning
Can be topped out at desired height. Cut out any wayward branches.

Problems
Cypress canker. See entry C. Arizonica.

See also **CUPRESSUS ARIZONICA** and **C. MACROCARPA**.

CYCAS REVOLUTA Sago Palm, (Spanish : Cica or Palmera de la Iglesia, Palma de Sagu).

HABIT AND CULTIVATION

Category	Cycad
Family	Cycadaceae
Origin	The Island of Java
Size, height x spread	3 x 1 metres
Situation	Sun, dappled or light shade
Irrigation	If the plant receives sun, water once a week in summer.
Temperature	Down to 0°C if kept dry
Evergreen/deciduous	Evergreen
Flowering	Cream. Infrequent
Special features	Poisonous

The Sago palm belongs to the oldest plant family known to mankind. With more than 300 million years of existence, they are often called living fossils and were on the scene even before the dinosaurs! The cycas we buy today look exactly the same as their ancient ancestors. It is a very slow grower (and, therefore, costly to buy) and, perhaps because of it's great heritage and wisdom, very adaptable to changing conditions! It has a palm/fern-like appearance, though is in no way related to either, with a stout woody trunk and dark-green, recurving leaves, so hard and symmetrical that they appear to be made of plastic. Mature plants will flower intermittently and orange fruits are later produced. There are male and female plants. The Cycas is a very striking plant, worthy of a special position. Can also be grown in a large container.

Propagation
From seed – slowly - or suckers that can develop at the base of the plant.

Pruning
None.

Problems
None.

CYCLAMEN HEDERIFOLIUM syn.
CYCLAMEN NEAPOLITANUM
(Spanish : Ciclamen Silvestre).

HABIT AND CULTIVATION

Category	Bulb
Family	Primulaceae
Origin	Mediterranean
Size, height x spread	0.10 x 0.10 metres
Situation	Sun or dappled shade.
Irrigation	Seasonal rains.
Temperature	Hardy.
Evergreen/deciduous	Top growth dies down in summer.
Flowering	White, pinks, lilacs, purples. Winter.
Special features	Scented.

The hardy cyclamen (distinct from C. persicum, the florist's cyclamen) is a charming, small, tuberous plant found growing in open woodland and rocky situations throughout the Mediterranean area. Much daintier looking than C. persicum, the shiny heart shaped leaves are often marbled and mottled in silver and the softly scented flowers are carried like butterflies above the leaves. Each flower has 5 reflexed petals and a mouth, which is often of a darker shade. Colours range from a pure white through to a deep rosy purple. The tubers spring into action with the first autumn rains and flowers are produced during the winter months. The whole plant goes summer dormant. Plant the tubers in pockets of rich ground and they will multiply quite rapidly to give you large drifts, which will enchant you in their own quiet way.

Propagation
Easy from seed.

Pruning
None.

Problems
Can be prone to black root rot. Burn infected plants. Try to avoid water logging during the winter months.

CYPERUS PAPYRUS Paper Reed,
(Spanish : Papiros Egipcios).

HABIT AND CULTIVATION

Category	Grass
Family	Cyperaceae
Origin	North Africa
Size, height x spread	4 x 2 metres
Situation	Full sun or dappled shade.
Irrigation	Keep wet
Temperature	Down to around –5°C
Evergreen/deciduous	Evergreen
Flowering	Brown/green. Summer
Special features	-

A native of the Mediterranean basin, the pith from the stems of this papyrus was used by the Egyptians to make paper. A striking plant, it requires a lot of water and is perfectly positioned in, or at the side, of a pond, though it can be grown in a pot if you are prepared to give it plenty of water. The sturdy leafless stems carry the distinctive umbrellas composed of between 70 – 100 fine, drooping spikelets, creating a huge green mop head. The flowers are brownish green and carried in the umbels. Plant in moist soil or in water up to 25cm deep in a position without too much wind.

Propagation
By division of rhizomes. Or, when in flower, cut a head, trim up and insert upside down in a bucket of water. Tiny rootlets will appear from the finished flowers.

Pruning
Cut down low the brown, dying stems.

Problems
None.

Also **CYPERUS PAPYRUS 'NANUS'** a dwarf variety, to a height of 80cm.

CYTISUS BATTANDIERI Pineapple or Moroccan Broom, (Spanish : Citisus de Marrueco).

HABIT AND CULTIVATION

Category	Shrub
Family	Leguminosae
Origin	North Africa
Size, height x spread	5 x 4 metres
Situation	Full sun
Irrigation	Drought tolerant
Temperature	To around –5˚C
Evergreen/deciduous	Semi-evergreen
Flowering	Yellow. Spring and summer
Special features	Scented.

The pineapple broom is thus known because of the delightfully fruity smell of the flowers. In Morocco it grows in poor, sandy soils amongst cedar and oak trees and is another shrub that demands very little attention. It has very silvery, soft leaves composed of three leaflets and forms a rather open, lax shrub. It is often seen planted against a wall, though this is, in fact, not necessary in a Mediterranean climate. Plant in an open, sunny position in poor soil and it will be happy. Very pretty, dense racemes of yellow flowers exude their pineapple aroma over several metres.

Propagation
By seed in individual pots, as they do not like root disturbance. Also by softwood cuttings in summer.

Pruning
Best cut down low every winter to prevent straggliness.

Problems
Shoot tips prone to black fly and mealy bug can also invade.

See also **CYTISUS PRAECOX**.

CYTISUS PRAECOX Warminster Broom, (Spanish : Escobon).

HABIT AND CULTIVATION

Category	Shrub
Family	Leguminosae
Origin	Mediterranean and North Africa
Size, height x spread	1.5 x 1.5 metres
Situation	Full sun
Irrigation	Drought tolerant
Temperature	Hardy
Evergreen/deciduous	Deciduous
Flowering	Yellow. Spring
Special features	Poisonous. Musty smelling flowers.

The slightly weeping Warminster broom is a very tolerant shrub, happy in an open, exposed position on thin poor soil and is pollution tolerant and ideal for a seaside location. It is an excellent and rapid-growing, colonising shrub and a good wind break planting. It forms a densely- branched shrub with very fine, silky, grey-green leaves. In springtime it is smothered in a profusion of soft-yellow, pea-like flowers and it is eye-catching for several weeks. The musky, somewhat acrid, smell of the flowers is borne on the air for several metres around the plant, and is particularly noticeable on very hot days.

Propagation
Pre-soaked seed sown in individual pots, as it dislikes root disturbance. Or from heel cuttings in summer.

Pruning
Pinch out growing tips to encourage bushiness. After flowering can be shortened back by up to two thirds, but do not cut into old wood as it will not regenerate. Old straggly bushes should be replaced.

Problems
None.

See also **CYTISUS BATTANDIERI**.

DELONIX REGIA Royal Ponciana,
Flamboyant, (Spanish : Flamboyan).

HABIT AND CULTIVATION

Category	Tree
Family	Caesalpiniaceae
Origin	Madagascar
Size, height x spread	8 x 5 metres
Situation	Full sun
Irrigation	Water regularly during summer.
Temperature	To 5°C
Evergreen/deciduous	Deciduous
Flowering	Red. Late spring and summer.
Special features	-

The name flamboyant aptly describes this tree, as it is truly spectacular in bloom with its vivid coloration and sheer beauty. This is not one for you mountain dwellers. It needs a warm, sheltered spot, a little spoiling and may take a few years to settle into flowering but it's all worth it! The tree itself is not very large, though it forms a spreading canopy and makes a good, small, shade tree. The roots are wide spreading and somewhat aggressive, so give it space. The trunk often develops twisted and the bark is rough and grey. The leaves are very beautiful, large and fern like, some 40cm long with a dozen or so leaf pairs off the main rib, each of these composed of 12 – 20 individual rounded leaflets. Each flower is some 10cm long and they are produced in packed racemes. The scarlet red against the soft green ferny foliage is pure drama. Long bean-like seed cases stay on the tree for a complete year.

Propagation
By pre-soaked seed in spring.

Pruning
Generally none, just remove crossing or badly placed branches.

Problems
None.

Dianthus

DIANTHUS DELTOIDES Maiden Pink, (Spanish : Clavellina).

HABIT AND CULTIVATION

Category	Perennial
Family	Caryophyllaceae
Origin	Mediterranean
Size, height x spread	0.15 x 0.30 metres
Situation	Full sun or dappled shade
Irrigation	Moderate summer watering
Temperature	Fully hardy
Evergreen/deciduous	Evergreen
Flowering	White, pinks. Spring.
Special features	Scented.

The maiden pink is a cushion forming plant, ideal in cracks in paving or walls, in a rockery etc. Regular summer watering and spring fertilising will produce a fine flush of scented flowers. Removal of dead flower heads can extend the flowering well through summer and into autumn. The tiny lance shaped greyish leaves form a neat mound from which emerge the single flowers with fringing to the petals and often a dark red eye contrasting nicely with the pink or white petals. This is an undemanding plant which will spread and colonise in unexpected nooks and crannies. Most have a delightful aroma of cloves though there are specific cultivars with stronger and different perfumes.

Propagation
By summer layering or cuttings.

Pruning
None. Simply remove dead flower stems to promote growth and further flower flushes.

Problems
Watch for aphids and caterpillars. Can also be prone to rust.

DIGITALIS PURPUREA Foxglove,
(Spanish : Dedalera, Calzones de Zorra)

HABIT AND CULTIVATION

Category	Perennial
Family	Scrophulariaceae
Origin	Mediterranean
Size, height x spread	1.5 x 0.5 metres
Situation	Full sun or dappled shade
Irrigation	Drought tolerant.
Temperature	Fully hardy
Evergreen/deciduous	Semi-evergreen
Flowering	White, pink, purple, pale yellow. Spring through to autumn.
Special features	Highly poisonous, especially the leaves.

Although not often thought of as a Mediterranean climate plant, the foxglove is, in fact, a native of the area and surprisingly tolerant of heat, dryness and poor soil conditions. A short-lived perennial, they are often treated in gardens as biennials. Generally they will self seed and come up in all the best places anyway, without any help from us! When planting, they are very effective in groups in a shrub border, under tall trees and in a naturalised gravel garden. The leaves are large, oval and rough, forming rosettes close to the ground. The tall flower spikes then emerge wrapped around with tubular flowers in shades of white, pink, magenta and pale yellow, often with a spotted throat. The medicinal properties of these plants have been known since ancient times and they are still commonly used today in cardiac medicines to strengthen and regulate the heart beat.

Propagation
From seeds in autumn.

Pruning
Remove dead flower stalk.

Problems
Occasional rust.

DIPLADENIA AMABILIS syn. Mandevilla amabilis, (Spanish : Dipladenia).

HABIT AND CULTIVATION

Category	Perennial climber
Family	Apocynaceae
Origin	South America
Size, height x spread	4 x 2 metres
Situation	Partial or light, dappled shade
Irrigation	Regular summer watering
Temperature	To 0°C
Evergreen/deciduous	Evergreen
Flowering	Pink and white. Spring and summer.
Special features	-

The dipladenias are highly-valued as ornamental climbers as they produce their showy, trumpet flowers very prolifically. D. amabilis is a woody-stemmed shrubby climber, never achieving any great height but ideal on a small pergola or bower where it's pretty flowers can be admired at close quarters. It has shiny, oval, mid-green leaves and a great profusion of pink trumpet-shaped flowers. A white form is also available which has a golden yellow throat. Plant in a warm sheltered spot in good soil and water and feed regularly through the hot months.

Propagation
Semi-ripe summer cuttings.

Pruning
Thin out congested growth in early spring to encourage it to climb.

Problems
Whitefly and red spider mite.

Also **DIPLADENIA GRANDIFLORA**. A deciduous variety with large, ribbed leaves and bigger, paler-pink, trumpet flowers, preferring more sun to d. amabilis. A larger grower, to perhaps 6m. Very exotic looking. Again, give it a sheltered position. Prone to mealy bug.

DODONEA VISCOSA 'PURPUREA'
Purple-leafed Hop Bush, (Spanish : Dodonea).

HABIT AND CULTIVATION

Category	Shrub
Family	Sapindaceae
Origin	North America
Size, height x spread	5 x 4 metres
Situation	Full sun or some light shade.
Irrigation	Drought tolerant
Temperature	To around –5°C
Evergreen/deciduous	Evergreen
Flowering	Insignificant. Spring.
Special features	-

The hop bush will grow in most locations – hot and dry, irrigated or not, on thin poor soils, in very windy positions and coastal areas. It is also quite a rapid grower, a good pioneer planting and windbreak and an extremely useful hedging plant. Add to all this it's attractive colouring and it is hard to see why it isn't planted more. A plant perhaps little known, but fashion swings are about to turn in its favour! The tough, narrow, bronzy-green leaves retain their coloration best in full sun. Tiny green flowers open in clusters in spring but are fairly insignificant. What are noticeable are the pretty, pinkish seed capsules, which stay on the bush for several weeks and make a telling contrast with the bronzy foliage.

Propagation
Seed in spring, or semi-ripe summer cuttings – it strikes easily.

Pruning
Cut back after flowering, and hedging can be sheared.

Problems
Rarely, aphid attack on soft growing tips.

DOMBEYA WALLICHII Pink Snowball Tree, (Spanish : Dombeya).

HABIT AND CULTIVATION

Category	Shrub/small tree
Family	Sterculiaceae
Origin	East Africa and Madagascar
Size, height x spread	6 x 4 metres
Situation	Full sun or some dappled shade.
Irrigation	Good watering once or twice a week in summer.
Temperature	To 0°C
Evergreen/deciduous	Semi-evergreen
Flowering	Pink. Autumn and winter.
Special features	Scented.

The dombeya is one of our most enchantingly beautiful shrubs and, sadly, little known and under-planted. Large heart-shaped, felty leaves clothe the shrub, which can also be grown as a small tree. But the flowers are the jewels in the crown. Small and rosebud-like, in pink and cream, they form pendulous globes, the size of a tennis ball, and – even more – sweetly scented. Even when the flowers fade they do so elegantly, turning a faded sepia colour and remaining on the branches for many months. Plant this beauty where the flowers will hang down around you and, I promise, this will be one of your favourite plantings. Give it a warm, protected position, good fertile soil and summer watering and feeding.

Propagation
Seed in spring or semi-ripe summer cuttings.

Pruning
May be cut back after flowering.

Problems
Occasional whitefly and red spider mite

DRACAENA DRACO The Dragon Tree,
(Spanish : Drago de Canarias).

HABIT AND CULTIVATION

Category	Tree
Family	Agavaceae
Origin	Canary Isles, Cape Verde and Madeira
Size, height x spread	8 x 5 metres
Situation	Sun or shade
Irrigation	Drought tolerant.
Temperature	To around 0°C
Evergreen/deciduous	Evergreen
Flowering	Greenish-white. Summer.
Special features	-

The dragon tree is a truly prehistoric-looking plant and extremely tough and slow growing, taking approximately 10years to reach 1m high. The oldest tree still in existence is in Tenerife, known as the Millenium Dragon Tree and said to be between 1500 and 3000 years old, though estimated dating suggests around 650 years would be more accurate. After the first flowering, and thereafter approximately every 10years, the tree will branch forming the typical divided crown. Wild dragon trees are now very rarely seen. Some 500 years ago, in the Canary Isles, there was a flightless bird, around the size of a turkey, that ate the fruits and hence scattered the seed, but since the bird has become extinct, the incidence of dragon trees has also dropped dramatically. A very architectural and bold addition to any garden, it also grows happily in large containers, though will never reach its full grandeur.

Propagation
By seed, but germination difficult and slow.

Pruning
None. Simply pull off dead outer leaves.

Problems
Do not overwater or rot can set in.

Also **DRACAENA INDIVISA**, Cabbage Palm. Altogether smaller and finer growing. Leafy green fountains on thinner stems, can be multi trunked. Creamy-brown flower stalks. Fine accent plant. Also bronze form.

DURANTA REPENS Brazilian Sky Flower, (Spanish : Duranta).

HABIT AND CULTIVATION

Category	Shrub
Family	Verbenaceae
Origin	South America
Size, height x spread	3 x 2 metres
Situation	Full sun or some partial shade
Irrigation	Occasional deep soak in summer.
Temperature	To around –5°C
Evergreen/deciduous	Semi-evergreen
Flowering	Blue or white. Spring through to autumn
Special features	Berries poisonous

The duranta is a very elegant-looking, arching shrub, commonly found through the Americas and Mexico. It forms excellent informal hedging, a dense windbreak and is certainly pretty enough to form a specimen shrub. It has glossy, thin, dark green leaves cloaking it's somewhat spiny branches. The delightful, tiny, blue, white or violet-blue edged with white flowers cascade in racemes right through much of the warmer months. These are followed by very pretty strings of golden yellow berries, flowers and berries often being held on the'shrub at the same time, an eye-catching combination. The flowers are attractive to butterflies.

Propagation
By seed in spring or semi-ripe summer cuttings.

Pruning
Can be hard pruned in winter to curb vigour, but best removing selected branches so as not to spoil the shape of the bush.

Problems
Occasional whitefly.

ECHEVERIA ELEGANS Hen and Chicks, (Spanish : Echeveria).

HABIT AND CULTIVATION

Category	Succulent
Family	Crassulaceae
Origin	Mexico
Size, height x spread	0.10 x 0.50 metres
Situation	Full sun or part shade.
Irrigation	Drought tolerant
Temperature	To around 5°C
Evergreen/deciduous	Evergreen
Flowering	Pink with red or yellow tips. Spring and summer
Special features	-

The echeveria family is composed of rosette-shaped succulents in greens or blue-greys all of which reproduce by small offsets and are, therefore, sometimes commonly known as Hen and Chicks – though there are also sempervivums known by the same name.

E. elegans is one of the quickest spreading and is a very pretty, pale silvery blue-grey, occasionally edged with red if grown in cooler conditions. The broad, fleshy leaves in rosettes form spreading clumps, and the dainty bell flowers are borne on thin stems above the plant. Position in a rockery where they can be best appreciated. Also excellent in low flat pots and, for the really ambitious, try a tapestry carpet of different coloured varieties – a real talking point perhaps set into paving.

Propagation
Simply detach a 'chick' or plantlet and replant. Individual leaves will also root – detatch and allow leaf base to dry out for 24hrs. before planting.

Pruning
None

Problems
None if grown in open airy situation.

ECHIUM FASTUOSUM The Pride of Madeira, (Spanish : Echium).

HABIT AND CULTIVATION

Category	Shrubby perennial
Family	Boraginaceae
Origin	Madeira
Size, height x spread	2 x 1 metres
Situation	Full sun or some dappled shade
Irrigation	Drought tolerant, though benefits from a weekly watering in summer.
Temperature	To around 5°C
Evergreen/deciduous	Evergreen
Flowering	Blue. Spring.
Special features	-

The echium family is held in wide regard for it's stunning flower spikes, always absolute show-stoppers! The plants themselves are undemanding for us Mediterranean gardeners, liking hot dry conditions, with poor, thin soil and quite happy too in seaside gardens. Overwatering and overfeeding can cause health problems. It has long, thin, narrow, grey leaves which are slightly irritant and it develops into a nicely-mounded, low shrub. But it is the flower spikes that everyone waits for - towering to perhaps 2m and stacked out with blue, tubular flowers, rather like a large, blue foxglove. As it opens from the bottom up, the flower show is extended over quite a long period and each plant carries several of these wonders. The only problem with these plants is that, although listed as a perennial, they can be short lived, sometimes dying after flowering. A short life – but so spectacular!

Propagation
Spring seed or semi-ripe summer cuttings. Can self-sow when happy.

Pruning
None. Cut out dead flower spike.

Problems
Can be prone to whitefly and mealybug.

See also **ECHIUM WILDPRETII**.

ECHIUM WILDPRETII Tower of Jewels, (Spanish : Echium).

HABIT AND CULTIVATION

Category	Biennial
Family	Boraginaceae
Origin	Canary Isles
Size, height x spread	2.5m x 0.60 metres
Situation	Full sun
Irrigation	Weekly soaking in summer.
Temperature	To 0°C
Evergreen/deciduous	Evergreen
Flowering	Coral pink. 2nd. spring.
Special features	-

This echium is a definite biennial, but do not discard it for that reason. If you can find it, buy it, plant it, and stand back! Its common name gives it away – a tower of jewels and nothing less. It has very narrow, silvery, and soft hairy leaves that form a basal rosette. In it's second year, on maturity, it will send up – and up – one single flower spike in springtime. This is stacked with hundreds of coral-pink flowers, which slowly open up to the dense terminal spike. It is a dramatic and long-lasting sight that will bring your friends to your garden in their droves! The birds and bees also love it. Please allow the seeds to mature, thus perpetuating the plant in your garden, or pass seedlings around to friends. It is becoming a threatened species in its natural habitat and we all owe it a helping hand.

Propagation
By seed.

Pruning
None.

Problems
None.

See also **ECHIUM FASTUOSUM**.

ENSETE syn. MUSA ENSETE,
(Spanish : Musa).

HABIT AND CULTIVATION

Category	Tropical perennial
Family	Musaceae
Origin	Malaysia
Size, height x spread	10 x 5 metres
Situation	Full sun or partial shade
Irrigation	Plenty during summer months.
Temperature	To 0°C
Evergreen/deciduous	Evergreen
Flowering	Reddish-green. Spring and summer
Special features	Edible fruit

There are approximately 300 species of the ensete family, many grown purely for their large, tropical and lush foliage. A courtyard setting or similar is ideal, preferably with a high humidity, rich soil and generous summer watering - it will reward you with lots of stunning jungly foliage, sheer drama.

Around 20 varieties are commercially grown today, and it holds second place in world fruit rankings. The banana is considered to be one of the oldest cultivated fruits known in the world. There is even some debate over the original forbidden fruit in the Garden of Eden; was it an apple or banana? The Koran tells us that it was a banana. From Malaysia, Alexander the Great is credited with introducing it to the Western world. In the early 1400's Portuguese sailors brought the first banana plants to the Canary Islands, though it wasn't until 1876 that the fruits were first tasted in America to celebrate the 100th. anniversary of independence. By the 1800's the U.S. were importing 16 million bunches a year.

There are basically two varieties, the sweet banana, eaten raw, and the plantain, for cooking. Perhaps surprisingly, the plantain is much more widely grown capturing some 80% of the market. The plants reach their full height in approximately 9 months, some 8 to 10m The false 'trunk' is formed from overlapping leaf sheaths. Flowers develop into mature bananas in about 3 months and each bunch will yield around 200 bananas. After flowering the main stalk will die down to make room for new shoots, called suckers or pups and so ensure continuity of the plant.

Propagation
Plant division at anytime.

Pruning
Cut out dying main stalk after fruiting and any old, untidy leaves.

Problems
None.

ERYSIMUM LINIFOLIUM syn. CHEIRANTHUS, Spanish Wallflower, (Spanish : Alheli de Invierno).

HABIT AND CULTIVATION

Category	Perennial
Family	Cruciferae
Origin	Spain and Portugal
Size, height x spread	1 x 1 metres
Situation	Full sun
Irrigation	Drought tolerant
Temperature	To –5°C
Evergreen/deciduous	Evergreen
Flowering	Lilac. Autumn to spring
Special Features	Scented

This is a plant that is often found growing in old, abandoned gardens throughout the Mediterranean area as it self-seeds so readily and is a real survivor. It is an ideal scented addition to rock gardens, banks and general border plantings and a good gap filler. It forms a dome-shaped, small shrub with long, narrow-leafed, blue-grey foliage at the ends of the branches. It sporadically produces, throughout the year, an abundance of lilac, very sweet smelling flowers, but mainly from autumn to spring. Being such prolific flowerers, the plants themselves are short-lived, often only surviving for two or three years, but there are always plenty of self-sown seedlings coming along to replace the parent and ensure continuity of the line.

Propagation
By seed in spring or by summer cuttings which root easily.

Pruning
None.

Problems
Blackfly, whitefly and caterpillars can attack.

ERYTHRINA CRISTA-GALLI The Coral Tree, (Spanish : Crestas de Gallo, Picos de Gallo, Gallitos, Arbol del Coral).

HABIT AND CULTIVATION

Category	Shrub/small tree
Family	Leguminosae
Origin	Brazil
Size, height x spread	6 x 3 metres
Situation	Full sun
Irrigation	Drought tolerant, but appreciates occasional summer soaking
Temperature	Down to 0°C
Evergreen/deciduous	Deciduous
Flowering	Deep coral. Spring and summer.
Special features	Poisonous

Erythrina is derived from the Greek word eritros, meaning 'red'. The Coral Tree was adopted in 1942 by Argentina as their national flower. It is very beautiful and striking in flower, most often seen as a specimen tree – and can even be grown in a large container – though it can also be trained as a multi-stemmed shrub, then staying somewhat smaller. The prickly, 3-leafed foliage is carried on thorned stems and the flowers develop on the new spring growth. The rich coral-coloured flowers, each some 5cm long, bloom in loose, terminal clusters and are borne in great profusion through spring and summer. The overall effect is very stunning. Long woody seed pods. In cold areas, the branches are very prone to dieback and, under severe conditions, all topgrowth can be lost but it should shoot again from the rootstock.

Propagation
Seed in spring or summer cuttings.

Pruning
Trim after flowering. Can be hard pruned at end of winter if necessary. Cut out any branches that have died back.

Problems
None

Also
ERYTHRINA CORALLOIDES, The Flame or Naked Coral Tree. Similar to above, larger leaves and carries flowers on leafless stems in early spring.

ESCHSCHOLZIA CALIFORNICA

The Californian Poppy, (Spanish : Amapola Californiana).

HABIT AND CULTIVATION

Category	Annual
Family	Papaveraceae
Origin	California
Size, height x spread	0.30 x 0.15 metres
Situation	Full sun
Irrigation	Drought tolerant
Temperature	-
Evergreen/deciduous	-
Flowering	Cream, yellow, orange, bronze, rose, scarlet, lilac and purple. Spring and summer.
Special features	-

The Californian Poppy is the national floral emblem of the state and a more vivid one could hardly have been chosen. It is one of our brightest annuals, looking great in clumps in rock gardens, pots, cracks in paving and broadcast over natural, gravel gardens. The grey-green, fine, feathery foliage contrasts superbly with the vivid cup-shaped, poppy flowers. Grow in full sun because the flowers refuse to open in dull or shaded conditions. They love it hot and sunny and give of their best in poor, stony soil. Deadhead regularly to prolong flowering and the life of the plant. Later the plants turn into a heap of dried out straw – but not before they have thrown their seeds far and wide.

Propagation
By seed in spring, but sow in situ as they do not like being transplanted.

Pruning
None.

Problems
Watch out for snails in wet spring weather.

Eucalyptus (Gum Tree, Fever Tree)

The eucalyptus family is composed of over 600 species, ranging from truly stately trees to multi-trunked shrubs of all sizes, and the genus makes up almost 75% of Australia's endemic plant species. The name 'eucalyptus' is derived from the Greek 'eu' meaning ''well' and ''kalyptos' meaning covered, referring to the cone-shaped capping on the flower bud. The juvenile foliage often differs greatly from the mature, there is extreme variability within a given species, and hybridisation is common – all of this making exact identification difficult at times. As long ago as the 1700's botanists at Kew started to catalogue the different species and even to this day new hybrids are still being found.

Known as gum trees because of the sticky substance they exude, called 'kino', this was once used as a tanning agent in the leather manufacturing industry. Another once common name, which has somewhat fallen into disuse, is that of fever tree. Early colonists throughout the British Empire planted groves of the aromatic fever trees in tropical fever areas because most insects were deterred by the strong aroma exuded by the eucalypts. Their hungry thrusting roots also tended to dry out swampy and mosquito riddled areas making living conditions more comfortable and releasing rich fertile areas for crop planting. Nowadays, the trees are highly prized for their beauty and shade, their attractive hardwood, honey and oil. The thriving oil distillery industry, utilising the new leaves and shoot tips, is concentrated into three main products; medicinal oil for common cold preparations and aromatherapy oil where it is used as an energiser are mainly extracted from E. globulus and E. radiata; industrial oil; and perfumery oil which is mainly from E. citriodora.

The eucalypts often receive bad press, but the fault – it has to be said – is not in the plant genus, but in the human being doing the planting! Remember that some will reach 50m without trying and at a growth rate of 2m or more per year! Very little will grow under the canopy of a eucalyptus tree so, obviously, considerable thought must be given to positioning. Litter from the trees can be considerable and some have invasive roots. On the plus side, their rapid growth can be a positive advantage if screening is needed (though their branches are rather brittle so beware wind damage) and there is little weed growth within their spread. A stand of eucalypts can even feasibly be used as a firewood source, as they regenerate so quickly. They are also excellent soil binders and pioneering plants and extremely useful on newly moved, naked earth. Some are able to survive a year without any water at all in arid inland situations; others grow in swamps. Well adapted to heat and drought, there are also those which will survive as low as –20°C. They are great survivors, often reshooting after being burnt out and apparently destroyed by sweeping bush fires.

So, select, site carefully, and enjoy.

EUCALYPTUS CITRIODORA
Lemon Scented Gum,
(Spanish : Eucalipto de Limon).

HABIT AND CULTIVATION

Category	Tree
Family	Myrtaceae
Origin	Australia
Size, height x spread	30 x 10 metres
Situation	Full sun
Irrigation	Drought tolerant
Temperature	To 0˚C
Evergreen/deciduous	Evergreen
Flowering	White. Winter.
Special features	Lemon scented leaves

The lemon gum makes a tall, stately and elegant tree. It grows rapidly but its roots are generally non-invasive. The straight trunk is a very beautiful, pinkish-white which turns blood red when wet – very striking! The long, narrow, slightly roughened leaves smell strongly of lemon when crushed, and this applies even to the leaf litter. It bears small, white flowers but so high up that they are almost impossible to see. Plant as a young tree in the desired position – most eucalypts resent being transplanted - water moderately until established, then leave it alone. Stake well whilst developing. Watering of the trees encourages very rapid but weak growth which then easily breaks in strong winds.

Propagation
From seed in autumn.

Pruning
Young trees can have their branches pruned back to strengthen.

Problems
None if correctly sited.

See also **EUCALYPTUS FICIFOLIA, E. GLOBULUS, E. GUNNI** and **E. VIMINALIS**.

EUCALYPTUS FICIFOLIA The Red Flowering Gum, (Spanish : Eucalipto).

HABIT AND CULTIVATION

Category	Tree
Family	Myrtaceae
Origin	Australia
Size, height x spread	12 x 12 metres
Situation	Full sun
Irrigation	Drought tolerant
Temperature	To 0°C
Evergreen/deciduous	Evergreen
Flowering	Red/pink/orange. Intermittently, year round.
Special features	Happier in a more neutral soil.

E. ficifolia is popular, and deservedly so, for its beautiful red/pink/orange bell shaped flowers that are borne in large clusters and are extremely eye-catching. So prolific is the flowering, and later seed production, that the branches are weighed down with the sheer weight of the seed pods, even to the point of breaking at times. This is one of the prettiest eucalypts in flower and the bloom period is extensive. The leaves are dark-green, lance-shaped, quite shiny and attractive. The tree itself forms a large but compact crown and is a more moderate grower than some varieties. Again, plant young trees in ultimate position, do not attempt to move at a later date.

Propagation
Autumn sown seed.

Pruning
Generally little required, though wayward and crossing branches can be cut out during the winter months.

Problems
None

See also **EUCALYPTUS CITRIODORA, E. GLOBULUS, E. GUNNI** and **E. VIMINALIS**.

EUCALYPTUS GLOBULUS
The Tasmanian Blue Gum,
(Spanish : Eucalipto Azul).

HABIT AND CULTIVATION

Category	Tree
Family	Myrtaceae
Origin	Tasmania
Size, height x spread	50 x 12 metres
Situation	Full sun
Irrigation	Drought resistant
Temperature	To 0°C
Evergreen/deciduous	Evergreen
Flowering	Cream. Spring and summer.
Special features	Strongly eucalyptus smelling. Invasive roots.

The Tasmanian Blue Gum is the floral emblem of Tasmania and, perhaps, the most beautiful of the eucalypts. It is a column-shaped tree, an extremely fast grower and the tallest, with specimens of over 50m recorded. The smooth trunk peels its grey bark in ribbons. The silvery-blue, circular, juvenile leaf matures to a mid-green, thin, long leaf, slightly curved. Creamy, single flowers with tufty stamens are held on thin stems in clusters. This eucalypt is one of the most commonly planted for commercial purposes. The timber is used for building, the pulp for papermaking and it also has the strongest smelling oil and is, therefore, much sought after in the pharmaceutical industry.

Propagation
Autumn sown seed.

Pruning
Can be topped out if necessary, but position this one with great care – it reaches a great height!

Problems
None if sited correctly.

See also **EUCALYPTUS CITRIODORA**, **E. FICIFOLIA**, **E. GUNNI** and **E. VIMINALIS**.

EUCALYPTUS GUNNII Cider Gum,
(Spanish : Eucalipto Gris).

HABIT AND CULTIVATION

Category	Tree
Family	Myrtaceae
Origin	Tasmania
Size, height x spread	25 x 8 metres
Situation	Full sun
Irrigation	Drought tolerant
Temperature	To –5°C
Evergreen/deciduous	Evergreen
Flowering	Creamy-white. Summer.
Special features	-

E. gunnii is one of the hardiest eucalypts, even surviving as far north as Scotland where, although it's foliage may be frost damaged, it will regenerate quickly with warmer weather. It forms a conical tree, again very fast growing, and has very pretty, smooth bark in pale pinkish-grey-cream, peeling and ageing to a darker grey. The juvenile foliage is much prized, especially by flower arrangers, as it is silvery-grey and very rounded. This can last as much as four years on the tree when it then matures to a lance-shaped blue-green leaf. Yearly pollarding of the trees ensures a constant supply of juvenile foliage. Creamy- white flowers with many stamens are carried in the summer months.

Propagation
Autumn sown seed.

Pruning
Normally not required. Carry out pollarding (cutting side growths almost back to main trunk) during early spring.

Problems
None

See also **EUCALYPTUS CITRIODORA**. **E. FICIFOLIA**, **E. GLOBULUS** and **E. VIMINALIS**.

EUCALYPTUS VIMINALIS Manna Gum, (Spanish : Eucalipto).

HABIT AND CULTIVATION

Category	Tree
Family	Myrtaceae
Origin	Australia
Size, height x spread	30 x 15 metres
Situation	Full sun
Irrigation	Drought tolerant
Temperature	To 0°C
Evergreen/deciduous	Evergreen
Flowering	White. Spring/summer.
Special features	Invasive roots

One of the quickest-growing eucalypts, very vigorous and tolerant of pollution. It is also happy in a very alkaline soil. Pale, creamy-tan bark peels off in long ribbons, giving the typical, patchy effect to the trunk. The younger foliage is quite a dark green and lance shaped but, as it matures, it lightens turning to a silvery, pale-green and with a very long, narrow leaf shape. The white flowers are stacked with fluffy stamens and carried during late spring and early summer. Plant young trees in permanent position, stake well in initial stages and water until established, then leave alone.

Propagation
From seed in autumn.

Pruning
Can be topped out if necessary and cut out any crossed branches to avoid congestion.

Problems
None if correctly sited. Try to avoid a very windy position; the brittle branches can break.

See also **EUCALYPTUS CITRIODORA**, **E. FICIFOLIA**, **E. GLOBULUS** and **E. GUNNI**.

EUPHORBIA CANDELABRUM
Candelabra Cactus,
(Spanish : Euforbio).

HABIT AND CULTIVATION

Category	Succulent
Family	Euphorbiaceae
Origin	South Africa
Size, height x spread	10 x 5 metres
Situation	Full sun
Temperature	To 0°C
Evergreen/deciduous	Deciduous
Flowering	Orange-red. Spring and summer
Special features	Irritant and slightly poisonous sap

The euphorbia family is one of the most varied ranging through perennials, shrubs and succulents and e. candelabrum is perhaps one of the strangest members. It is a tree-like succulent with branching and re-branching erect candelabra-like arms which are made up of 3 to 5 angled succulent stems, deeply indented and dark green. From the edges small green lance-like leaves sprout, but these are short lived and rapidly fall. The spring and summer flowers, again produced along the edges are small and orange-red with yellow bracts. The effect is sculptural and statuesque, a giant of a plant which looks good in any large-scale succulent plantings, amongst rocks, stones and gravel. It forms a good 'punctuation point'. An extremely tough plant and tolerant of wide ranging conditions. The photo shows a bougainvillea in flower growing through the arms of the euphorbia.

Propagation
Break off an 'arm', allow to callous over for 24hrs. and plant in gravelly soil. The entire plant can be uplifted and repositioned, if necessary, at any size without ill effect.

Pruning
None, though size can be contained by simply breaking off arms.

Problems
None. Grow on dry side to prevent rotting off.

See also **EUCALIPTUS CHARACIAS**, **E. MARGINATA** and **E. PULCHERRIMA**

EUPHORBIA CHARACIAS subsp. WULFENII (Spanish : Lechetrezna).

HABIT AND CULTIVATION

Category	Succulent
Family	Euphorbiaceae
Origin	Mediterranean
Size, height x spread	1.5 x 1 metres
Situation	Part or dappled shade
Irrigation	Occasional summer watering
Temperature	Hardy.
Evergreen/deciduous	Evergreen
Flowering	Green. Spring
Special features	The sap is severely irritant to many people and poisonous.

This perennial sub-shrub has blue-green, narrow leaves, which densely coat the branches and form a nicely mounded plant. In springtime, the branches are topped by broad flower heads of an intense chartreuse green, which are actually composed of highly coloured bracts, which persist for many months. When the seeds ripen, the flower heads slowly lose their vivid coloration and the foliage yellows. The plant should then be cut down to the ground to make way for new growth. The flower heads can also be cut for use in floral arrangements, but take great care with the sap. One of the best small shrubs for general garden use, being tough and adaptable. Also looks good in paving.

Propagation
When suited can self-seed prolifically. Otherwise start from seed or basal cuttings in spring.

Pruning
Cut down old growth to ground level yearly.

Problems
Occasionally mealy bug.

See also **EUPHORBIA CANDELABRUM**, **E. MARGINATA** and **E. PULCHERRIMA**.

EUPHORBIA MARGINATA
Snow on the Mountain,
(Spanish : Nieve en las Montañas).

HABIT AND CULTIVATION

Category	Annual
Family	Euphorbiaceae
Origin	North America
Size, height x spread	0.6 x 0.3 metres
Situation	Dappled shade
Irrigation	Moderate in summer
Temperature	Half hardy, usually grown as an annual.
Evergreen/deciduous	Semi-evergreen
Flowering	Yellowish, insignificant. Summer.
Special features	Irritant sap

A delightful little annual, which, with it's white, bright colouring, makes an ideal foil for larger plants. It forms a bushy, little plant with oval, pointed, bright green leaves, which are heavily edged with white, giving rise to its common name. The broad, petal-like bracts surrounding the small, yellowish, insignificant flowers are also white. Best sown in situ, it grows fairly rapidly. Can be perennial if given winter protection, but generally used as quick gap filler, as a contrast plant in pots and baskets, in rock gardens, as an edging plant etc. As with all euphorbias, take great care with the irritant sap.

Propagation
Early spring sowings of seed and will also self seed. Young plantlets can be carefully moved.

Pruning
None, though growing tips can be pinched back for extra bushiness.

Problems
None.

See also **EUPHORBIA CANDELABRUM**, **E. CHARACIAS** and **E. PULCHERRIMA**.

EUPHORBIA PULCHERRIMA Poinsettia
(Spanish : Pascuero, Flor de Pascua).

HABIT AND CULTIVATION

Category	Shrub
Family	Euphorbiaceae
Origin	Mexico
Size, height x spread	3 x 3 metres
Situation	Full sun
Irrigation	Regular summer watering
Temperature	To 5°C
Evergreen/deciduous	Semi-evergreen
Flowering	Green and insignificant, but showy bracts. Winter.
Special features	Sap irritant

The poinsettia is one of our top-selling pot plants accounting for some 85% of sales throughout the world during the Christmas period, with nearly all being exported from America. However, in our climate, it can be grown outdoors in milder areas where it will form a large shrub, somewhat sparsely leafed. The small greenish flowers start to develop in late autumn with the large coloured bracts. It can be a somewhat difficult placing in a garden scheme; remember that, apart from the bright red bracts we all know it is also available in cream and a pale pink, which may fit better into your plantings. One for a hot position – it does not tolerate cold or wind.

Propagation
Spring cuttings.

Pruning
Prune back hard after flowering to encourage more bushy growth.

Problems
Greenfly and whitefly, stem rot. But all of these problems are worst on indoor plants, outside you should have few troubles.

See also **EUPHORBIA CANDELABRUM**, **E. CHARACIAS** and **E. MARGINATA**.

EURYOPS PECTINATUS Brighteyes, (Spanish : Ojialegre).

HABIT AND CULTIVATION

Category	Shrub
Family	Compositae
Origin	South Africa
Size, height x spread	1 x 1 metres
Situation	Full sun or some light shade during hottest hours.
Irrigation	Regular deep watering in summer.
Temperature	To around 0°C
Evergreen/deciduous	Evergreen
Flowering	Yellow. Almost continuous.
Special features	-

Brighteyes is a nicely descriptive name for this hard-working shrub with its bright yellow daisy flowers that look up at us. It is one of the easiest for our Mediterranean gardens and rewards with flowers from early autumn through to early summer, going slightly summer dormant. The leaves are silvery-green and deeply divided on a bushy mound of foliage. It is a rapid grower, immensely useful in new gardens as a filler, on banks, for mixed plantings etc. A tidy looking plant but also very colourful, it is not fussy to soil, will tolerate wind, as long as it is not too cold, and is quite happy in a seaside location. With its bright, cheery look, it combines well with many other plantings.

Propagation
Softwood cuttings in summer.

Pruning
Prune moderately after flowering to maintain bushy, mounded shape.

Problems
Occasional blackfly.

FATSIA JAPONICA syn. **ARALIA JAPONICA**, Japanese Aralia, (Spanish : Fatsia).

HABIT AND CULTIVATION

Category	Shrub
Family	Araliaceae
Origin	Japan
Size, height x spread	3 x 2 metres
Situation	Shade
Irrigation	Regular weekly summer watering, more if in sunnier spot.
Temperature	To 0°C
Evergreen/deciduous	Evergreen
Flowering	White. Autumn.
Special features	-

Well known and loved as a pot plant, the Japanese aralia can also make a wonderfully extravagant planting in our milder gardens. It likes a shady, protected spot and will then produce its shiny, green, palmate leaves in great abundance creating a very tropical, jungly effect. A very stylish look for a dull shady corner and it will happily take to a large container too. Very tolerant of industrial pollution, it is often seen unexpectedly thriving in small, dark city gardens. The upright, rounded clusters of small white flowers are borne during autumn and later followed by black berries. It can also be trained into a single-stemmed standard, resembling a small tree. There are also forms with variegation, the leaves being heavily blotched in cream.

Propagation
Seed in spring or autumn or by semi-ripe summer cuttings.

Pruning
Simply cut out any wayward shoots.

Problems
None.

FEIJOA SELLOWIANA Pineapple
guava, (Spanish : Feijoa).

HABIT AND CULTIVATION

Category	Tree
Family	Myrtaceae
Origin	Brazil
Size, height x spread	4 x 3 metres
Situation	Full sun
Irrigation	Regular summer watering
Temperature	To around –5°C
Evergreen/deciduous	Evergreen
Flowering	Pink and red. Late spring.
Special features	Edible fruit.

The pineapple guava, as well as bearing exotically-tasting fruit, is a very pretty tree, quite worthy of a siting in the decorative garden. It has silvery-green, oval shaped leaves with very pretty late spring flowers. These are thick-petalled, coral pink and white, and look almost as if formed in carved wax. The flowers as well as the fruit are edible, but, of course, eating one means loss of the other! The fruits are green, tinged red, egg-sized and the juicy pulp has a flavour exactly like a cross between a pineapple and a guava. There are self-fertile varieties available, so one tree will give you fruit. Can also be pruned and trained to form a very attractive and unusual hedging plant.

Propagation
By softwood cuttings in summer.

Pruning
After fruiting to keep in shape, but generally not much required.

Problems
Fruit fly.

FELICIA AMELOIDES Blue Marguerite, Swan River Daisy, (Spanish : Felicia, Margarita Azul).

HABIT AND CULTIVATION

Category	Sub-shrub
Family	Compositae
Origin	South Africa
Size, height x spread	0.6 x 0.6 metres
Situation	Full sun
Irrigation	Drought tolerant, though appreciates a soaking now and again.
Temperature	To around –5°C
Evergreen/deciduous	Evergreen
Flowering	Blue. Almost constantly.
Special features	-

An incredibly useful little plant, the Swan River daisy has a place in every garden. It is a quick grower so useful for gap-filling, it makes a neat edging plant, a good pot plant and, with its blue daisies, combines well with most other plantings. The leaves are small and dark green and the plant has a spreading habit. It will weave between larger plantings and can also drape over rocks or wall edgings. The sky-blue daisy flowers have bright yellow centres and are produced in great profusion for much of the year and can be picked for little posies. Tolerant of poor conditions and sea-spray, it is a great little performer.

Propagation
Easy from spring or autumn cuttings.

Pruning
Keep trimming for compact, bushy plants. Old straggly plants can be revitalised with a hard haircut.

Problems
None.

FICUS BENJAMINA Weeping Fig, (Spanish : Ficus Benjamina).

HABIT AND CULTIVATION

Category	Shrub
Family	Moraceae
Origin	India
Size, height x spread	8 x 4 metres
Situation	Dappled shade
Irrigation	Drought tolerant
Temperature	To – 5°C
Evergreen/deciduous	Evergreen
Flowering	-
Special features	-

The weeping fig can reach as much as 20m tall in it's native India, but is highly unlikely to do so here, and around 8m is a more reasonable expectation in our climate. It is a plant, which appreciates the protection of a sheltered patio or courtyard and is very susceptible to changes of location. It will drop its leaves when unhappy, though will almost always regenerate. It forms a large weeping shrub or small tree with attractive pendulous branches. The leaves are slender, oval-shaped and glossy in a rich lustrous green – though there are also available many very attractive variegated varieties. Grown as an indoor pot plant in colder climes, it is very happy in a pot and likes to be root bound. Often seen with plaited trunks etc, as developing wood is very pliable. Although drought tolerant in the ground, it appreciates an occasional soaking, and pot-grown specimens would, obviously, need more water. Often develops aerial roots to help anchorage in soil.

Propagation
Stem tip cuttings in summer.

Pruning
Very little, just to maintain shape.

Problems
Red spider mite.

See also **FICUS CARICA** and **F. ELASTICA**.

FICUS CARICA Edible Fig,
(Spanish : Higo, Higuera).

HABIT AND CULTIVATION

Category	Tree
Family	Moraceae
Origin	Mediterranean
Size, height x spread	8 x 6 metres
Situation	Full sun
Irrigation	Drought resistant
Temperature	To around 0°C
Evergreen/deciduous	Deciduous
Flowering	Insignificant. Spring.
Special features	Edible fruit.

The edible fig is a greatly valued tree in the Mediterranean area. Being indigenous, drought resistant and fruit bearing it was an integral part of every country house. It is relatively fast growing, undemanding and extremely tough, thriving in the most arid situations. Seedlings often grow up through paving or old stone walls where it would seem nothing could survive. The leaves are large and deeply lobed, providing valuable summer shade. In the winter, when the tree is bare, it's grey, gnarled, twisted-shape can best be appreciated. And, of course, the figs in green, gold or black according to taste - surely one of the most succulent of fruits and all with no care and no water! Watering and feeding induces weak sappy growth and loss of fruit quality. Position where leaf and fruit fall will not be a problem, the juice stains paving badly!

Propagation
By autumn seed or summer tip cuttings.

Pruning
Cut out any old wood, crossing branches etc.

Problems
None.

See also **FICUS BENJAMINA** and **F. ELASTICA**.

FICUS ELASTICA Indian Rubber Tree, (Spanish : Arbol del caucho de la India).

HABIT AND CULTIVATION

Category	Tree
Family	Moraceae
Origin	India
Size, height x spread	30 x 15 metres
Situation	Full sun
Irrigation	Drought tolerant
Temperature	To 0˚C
Evergreen/deciduous	Evergreen
Flowering	-
Special features	-

The Indian rubber tree is a majestic, towering tree and examples of 100 years plus can attain a massive canopy - with 30m across not unknown. This is partially achieved by it's habit of sending out aerial roots, some of which twist through the air, whilst others tortuously find their way to ground and anchor there, converting into auxiliary trunks. The leaves are broad, leathery and glossy, some 30cm long, pinkish-bronze when new and cased in a pinkish-green sheath which splits open and drops as the leaf unfurls. Variegated varieties are also available, though tend to be smaller growing. Assumed by many to be the main source of latex – this honour actually goes to Hevea Braziliensis, from which caoutchouc, the South American native word for rubber, is commercially extracted. Many plants exude latex, even the common dandelion, but not many are commercially viable.

Propagation
Summer tip cuttings

Pruning
Some branch thinning can be carried out but in gradual stages, as the tree will bleed a milky sap, the latex, which can be disfiguring and will weaken the tree.

Problems
None.

See also **FICUS BENJAMINA** and **F. CARICA**.

FREMONTODENDRON CALIFORNICUM
Flannel Bush,
(Spanish : Fremontodendro)

HABIT AND CULTIVATION

Category	Shrub
Family	Sterculiaceae
Origin	California, America.
Size, height x spread	6 x 4 metres
Situation	Full sun
Irrigation	Drought tolerant
Temperature	To – 5°C
Evergreen/deciduous	Evergreen
Flowering	Yellow. Spring and summer
Special features	Hairs on leaves highly irritant to many people

The flannel bush is a native of the dry chaparral slopes and arid, almost desert-like conditions in California. It thrives in hot sun and poor soil and quickly fills out to a sizeable shrub, good for screening, windbreak etc. The hairy, 5-lobed, dark green leaves are silvery underneath and attractive, but the hairs can cause an allergic reaction so wear gloves when handling. The lemon-yellow flowers, tinged red on the outside of the petals are 10cm across and borne prolifically, giving a fine show. Plant young plants in permanent position as they will rarely transplant successfully, stake and water moderately for the first summer, then leave it alone. A good shrub, also, for coastal conditions.

Propagation
Spring or autumn sown seed or summer softwood cuttings.

Pruning
Pinch out tips to encourage bushier growth

Problems
None

GAILLARDIA PULCHELLA Indian Blanket Flower, (Spanish : Flor Combinada).

HABIT AND CULTIVATION

Category	Perennial
Family	Compositae
Origin	North America
Size, height x spread	0.5 x 0.3 metres
Situation	Full sun
Irrigation	Weekly watering in summer
Temperature	Fully hardy
Evergreen/deciduous	Evergreen
Flowering	Red, pink or yellow. Spring and summer.
Special features	-

The Indian blanket flower is one of our toughest and hardiest garden plants, equally tolerant of hot, arid conditions as cold, and standing up well to strong and salt-laden winds. They add a real splash of colour to borders and pots with their eye-catching daisy flowers, generally two-toned, crimson red and yellow. The most distinctive feature is the deeply coloured and raised centre cone surrounded by, most often, vivid red petals with the tips being picked out in a rich golden yellow. Other colour combinations are also available. The leaves are grey-green, hairy and lance-shaped. In cooler climes, it is often a rather short-lived perennial but tends to last longer in our Mediterranean climate.

Propagation
Spring or autumn sown seed. Or cuttings taken in early spring.

Pruning
None. Deadhead to encourage further flowering.

Problems
None.

GAZANIA Treasure Flowers, (Spanish : Gazania).

HABIT AND CULTIVATION

Category	Perennials
Family	Compositae
Origin	South Africa
Size, height x spread	0.2 x 0.2 metres
Situation	Full sun
Irrigation	Weekly watering helps in summer.
Temperature	To around −5°C
Evergreen/deciduous	Evergreen
Flowering	Cream, yellow, orange, russet, pink. Winter through to summer and intermittently too.
Special features	-

The Treasure flowers are just that – a mass of glorious colours throughout much of the year and one of our hardest working garden plants. The foliage is deep green, long and often lobed with a shimmery-silver underside. There are also varieties with purely silvery-grey foliage and these tend to be more carpeting, though all spread to some degree. They are excellent ground cover and soil binders in bank situations etc. and very pretty in pots. Plant in full sun, as they need heat to open their lovely flowers. The large daisies come in a wonderful colour range from creamy buffs, soft to golden yellows, orange, copper, russet, deep reds and pink and are often dramatically marked with a darker circle near the centre of the flower. One of those happy flowers!

Propagation
From cuttings or plant division in autumn or early spring sown seed. They will also self-seed readily.

Pruning
None. Simply dead heading.

Problems
None. Give plants a good clean up at season end to avoid over wintering pests.

GENISTA HISPANICA Spanish Gorse, (Spanish : Retama).

HABIT AND CULTIVATION

Category	Shrub
Family	Leguminosae
Origin	Spain
Size, height x spread	0.75 x 1.5 metres
Situation	Full sun
Irrigation	Drought tolerant
Temperature	To around –10°C
Evergreen/deciduous	Deciduous
Flowering	Yellow. Spring and summer.
Special features	Fragrant

The Spanish gorse, as may be expected, is an extremely tough and tolerant indigenous shrub. It is very useful in natural plantings and blends in well with other shrubs, under trees, in large rockeries etc. It forms a very spiny shrub with few leaves and is low growing and spreading. This is a shrub that even goats will generally not touch! During spring and summer it bears dense clusters of golden yellow, flowers with a heavy, somewhat musty smell. It does not like being transplanted.

Propagation
From seed in spring or semi-hardwood cuttings in summer.

Pruning
Pinch out tips to encourage bushiness.

Problems
None.

Also **GENISTA TINCTORIA**, Dyer's Greenweed.' A spineless shrub with similar yellow flowers, approx. 1 x 1. Leaves and flowers contain a yellow pigment once much used for dying cloth and wool. Along with the blue from woad, an excellent green is produced. It is also used medicinally as a laxative and in the treatment of gout.

GERBERA JAMESONII Barberton Daisy, (Spanish : Margarita de Transvaal).

HABIT AND CULTIVATION

Category	Perennial
Family	Compositae
Origin	South Africa
Size, height x spread	0.6 x 0.45 metres
Situation	Full sun or light dappled shade in hottest areas
Irrigation	Regular watering in summer, but do not overdo.
Temperature	To around –5°C
Evergreen/deciduous	Evergreen
Flowering	Cream, yellow, peach, pink, red. Spring and summer.
Special features	-

A native of the Transvaal, South Africa this is one of our largest and showiest daisies. It has been much hybridised in Holland and exported as pot plants but, in a Mediterranean climate, it is a relatively easy garden plant too. Plant it where the beauty of its flowers can be fully seen and appreciated. It has large, jagged leaves, which form basal rosettes and the long flower stalks erupt from the centre in a range of stunning colours. Creamy buff, butter to golden yellows, peach, rosy pinks to scarlet and bronzy reds make the choice very difficult. Widely used in the florist's trade, it makes an excellent cut flower. Plant the crowns at ground level in rich, fibrous soil but with good drainage. Fertilise and water regularly throughout the active growing season.

Propagation
Fresh autumn sown seed germinates easily or from side shoots in summer. Large clumps can also be divided in winter.

Pruning
None. Deadhead and remove dead leaves to keep plants tidy and clean.

Problems
Stem rot – avoid over watering. Mildew if temperatures are uneven.

GINKGO BILOBA Maidenhair Tree,
(Spanish : Ginkgo).

HABIT AND CULTIVATION

Category	Tree
Family	Ginkgoaceae
Origin	Asia and Far East
Size, height x spread	40 x 10 metres
Situation	Full sun
Irrigation	Drought tolerant, but better with some summer watering
Temperature	Hardy
Evergreen/deciduous	Deciduous
Flowering	Yellow. Spring.
Special features	-

This is the only remaining member of the family and one that is not generally recognised as a conifer. It has been found in fossils over 200 million years old. In spite of its tolerance to an extreme range of conditions, it is now thought, sadly, to be extinct in the wild though fortunately many cultivated examples exist. It is a very beautiful tree and much valued for it's rich autumnal colour; the Chinese treasure it for it's edible seeds which are a delicacy there. The young tree is quite narrow but it broadens out with maturity. The bright-green fan shaped leaves, resembling the maidenhair fern, are held on arching branches and they turn an enchanting soft, butter yellow before falling. The edible fruits are orange-yellow and plum-like and follow on from small yellow flowers' – but male and female trees will be needed. Appreciates a good start in life, with deep, fertile soil though adaptable to heat/cold, drought/wet and urban pollution.

Propagation
From seed or by grafting.

Pruning
Only to maintain shape.

Problems
None

GRAPTOPETALUM PARAGUAYENSE
Mother of Pearl Plant,
(Spanish : Crassa).

HABIT AND CULTIVATION

Category	Succulent
Family	Crassulaceae
Origin	Mexico
Size, height x spread	0.15 x 1 metres
Situation	Full sun or light dappled shade
Irrigation	Drought tolerant
Temperature	To 0˚C
Evergreen/deciduous	Evergreen
Flowering	Yellow, red. Summer.
Special features	-

The Mother of Pearl plant is easy and always attractive to the eye, with its cool colouring. It is another succulent native to Mexico, so it likes hot and dry conditions. It has large juicy leaves in silver-grey, often tinged with pink or red on the edges, and that form basal rosettes spreading in clumps. The tiny, star-shaped yellow and red flowers are borne throughout the summer months. Useful in rock gardens, in crevices, and walls, and an easy pot plant, it associates well with other succulents and cacti. An easy plant for children to grow.

Propagation
Individual leaves can be carefully broken off. Left to dry and callous for 24 hours then rooted in gravelly soil. Or remove baby rosettes and replant where needed.

Pruning
None. Simply remove dead leaves and flower stalks.

Problems
None if well-drained. Excess water, especially in the winter months, can cause basal rot.

GREVILLEA ROBUSTA Silky Oak,
(Spanish : Grevilea, Roble de
Australia, Roble Sedoso).

HABIT AND CULTIVATION

Category	Tree
Family	Proteaceae
Origin	Australia
Size, height x spread	30 x 15 metres
Situation	Full sun
Irrigation	Drought tolerant
Temperature	To 0°C
Evergreen/deciduous	Evergreen
Flowering	Gold. Spring and summer.
Special features	-

The silky oak is a towering, attractive tree, robust and easy, rather conical shaped and fairly fast growing. A useful windbreak/privacy tree with its dense dark green foliage. Leaves are fern-like, some 25cm long, nicely cut and a dark silvery green. The tree will generally start flowering when 4 or 5 years old and bears upturned, bell-shaped, rich golden flowers which sit prettily on the branches giving a stunning, glowing effect to the tree. The roots are shallow and wide spreading and somewhat invasive so be careful with positioning. Young plants object to root disturbance, so take care when potting on or planting out. Stake well to avoid wind rock.

Propagation
From seed sown in spring.

Pruning
Generally none needed. Take out wayward branches and dead wood. The centre can be opened up in winter if necessary to improve air circulation and overcrowding.

Problems
None

See also **GREVILLEA ROSMARINIFOLIA**.

GREVILLEA ROSMARINIFOLIA
Rosemary Spider Flower,
(Spanish : Grevilea de Araña).

HABIT AND CULTIVATION

Category	Shrub
Family	Proteaceae
Origin	Australia
Size, height x spread	1.5 x 2.5 metres
Situation	Full sun or light dappled shade.
Irrigation	Drought tolerant once well established
Temperature	-5°C
Evergreen/deciduous	Evergreen
Flowering	Pink and cream. Almost constantly.
Special features	-

The grevilleas are one of our most useful range of plants, with a great variety ranging from trees to sub-shrubs, many with long-flowering periods and ease of growth. G. rosmarinifolia is one of the most decorative, and will tolerate a more alkaline soil than many. It has soft, needle-like leaves, resembling rosemary, but a lighter green on the undersides. The shrub forms a nicely rounded mound and bears, almost constantly, spidery, tubular flowers in a rosy-pink and cream. Plant it in normal garden soil, adding a few handfuls of peat, and water to establish. After the first year, water can be slowly reduced until it will survive with almost nothing.

Propagation
Spring sown seed or try small tip cuttings in sand.

Pruning
Only tidying an odd wayward branch.

Problems
None, but watch summer watering. On an irrigation system the plant will deteriorate.

See also **GREVILLEA ROBUSTA**.

HARDENBERGIA VIOLACEA The Happy Wanderer, Australian Wisteria, (Spanish: Hardenbergia, Wisteria de Australia).

HABIT AND CULTIVATION

Category	Perennial climber
Family	Leguminosae
Origin	Australasia
Size, height x spread	3 x 3 metres
Situation	Sun or shade
Irrigation	Best with an occasional soaking in summer
Temperature	Will tolerate short spells of 0°C or slightly under.
Evergreen/deciduous	Evergreen
Flowering	Lilac/purple. Springtime
Special features	-

This is a very delicate-looking, small climber which is, in fact, surprisingly tough. It is wind and drought tolerant and not fussy on situation or soil type. It is composed of lots of twining, woody stems that are coated in simple ovoid leaves. In springtime it erupts into flower, bearing many racemes of drooping, lilac flowers, each marked with a darker purple spot, pretty and very eye-catching. It looks like a very fine wisteria and is always much admired and shows, perhaps, to its best against a white wall. Occasionally there is a repeat, but lesser, flowering in Autumn. It bears dark brown seed cases.

Propagation
By stem cuttings in late summer/autumn. Also very easy and rapid from pre-soaked seed.

Pruning
Very little required, just an occasional tidy up best done in late autumn.

Problems
Very few; an occasional touch of mildew if temperatures vary wildly.

HEBE SPECIOSA Veronica, (Spanish : Veronica).

HABIT AND CULTIVATION

Category	Shrub
Family	Scrophulariaceae
Origin	New Zealand
Size, height x spread	1.5 x 1 metres
Situation	Semi or full shade
Irrigation	Occasional summer watering
Temperature	To –5°C
Evergreen/deciduous	Evergreen
Flowering	Purple. Summer and winter to spring.
Special features	-

Most hebes are native to New Zealand and generally recognised as excellent mound-forming evergreens in shaded or partially shaded areas and those somewhat problematical areas under trees, large shrubs etc. Often used in urban plantings, they are extremely useful plants. A wide range is available, with variations in size, leaf colour and flowers which range from white, pinks, cerise, lilacs and purple. H. speciosa is one of the best with deep green leaves and rich purple flowers that bloom in terminal clusters over a very long period. Their dense, luxurious foliage and neat shape make a useful, small, informal hedge and a good dense ground covering between larger shrubs and under trees.

Propagation
From semi-ripe cuttings in summer.

Pruning
Leggy plants can be pruned by about half in early spring. Give a general trim over after flowering to tidy plant.

Problems
Occasional mealy bug.

HEDERA CANARIENSIS 'VARIEGATA'
(Spanish : Hiedra de Canaria).

HABIT AND CULTIVATION

Category	Perennial climber
Family	Araliaceae
Origin	Canary Isles
Size, height x spread	12 x 6 metres
Situation	Partial or lightly dappled shade
Irrigation	Drought tolerant, but performs better with some summer water.
Temperature	To around –5°C
Evergreen/deciduous	Evergreen
Flowering	Yellowish-green. Summer.
Special features	-

One of our best-known self clinging climbers, hederas generally come in a wide range of leaf colours and sizes. They all cling by aerial roots and are rapid coverers of fences and walls and also make useful ground covering plants. The plain green types will happily grow in full shade, whereas variegated sorts need more light to retain their colouring. H. canariense 'variegata' is a very handsome, large-leaved ivy with particularly attractive markings and variegation, the centre of the leaf being dark green, shading to a silvery-grey and heavily bordered in cream and white. The leaves can be damaged by cold weather but will regenerate. Juvenile foliage is brighter coloured and the leaves are more lobed. Cuttings taken from mature stems with more rounded leaves will stay shrub like – a curiousity that is known as arborescent ivy.

Propagation
From cuttings or rooted stems.

Pruning
Prune during early spring to curb over-vigorous growth and remove any weather damaged stems.

Problems
In dry conditions, red spider mite can appear.

See also **HEDERA HELIX**.

HEDERA HELIX English or Common Ivy, (Spanish : Hiedra).

HABIT AND CULTIVATION

Category	Perennial climber
Family	Araliaceae
Origin	Mediterranean
Size, height x spread	15 x 8 metres
Situation	Any
Irrigation	Drought tolerant
Temperature	Fully hardy
Evergreen/deciduous	Evergreen
Flowering	Yellowish-green. Summer.
Special features	-

The common ivy will produce a dense, green cover over walls, chain-link fencing, bare ground under trees etc. – and it is particularly useful in dark, shaded areas where little else will grow. It can take a year or so to establish, but will then grow away quickly and will, almost certainly, need to have some of it's exuberance curbed. Many people worry that it can cause structural damage to buildings, but this would only be the case on old walls, already crumbling'– new mortar will not be affected. The tale probably arises from the amount of old ruins seen draped with ivy! This is the hardiest ivy available and, in fact, looks very pretty when rhimed with frost in winter – something very rarely seen in our climate. See note on arborescent ivy under H. canariensis. There are many variegated and smaller leafed cultivars available.

Propagation
From cuttings or rooted stems.

Pruning
Can be hard pruned during early spring to curb growth.

Problems
In dry conditions, red spider mite.

See also **HEDERA CANARIENSIS**.

HELIANTHEMUM Sun Rose, (Spanish : Heliantemum).

HABIT AND CULTIVATION

Category	Perennial
Family	Cistaceae
Origin	Mediterranean
Size, height x spread	0.15 x 1 metres
Situation	Full sun
Irrigation	Drought tolerant
Temperature	To –10°C
Evergreen/deciduous	Evergreen
Flowering	White, yellow, orange, pink and red. Spring, Summer and Autumn.
Special features	-

The perennial sun rose is a native of the maquis of the Mediterranean area and is often also found growing in high rocky places. They need heat and sun combined with poor, stony ground and seasonal rainfall. Imitate this in your garden and they will delight you with a constant flow of flowers – often the plants are so smothered with the bright little blooms that the foliage cannot be seen. Each flower only lasts one day so imagine how many flowers this little plant produces. Great in rock and gravel gardens, in wall crevices and as sunny groundcover. They actually resent summer watering once established. They are quite variable, but most have grey to grey-green foliage and flowers in shades of white, yellow, orange, pink and red.

Propagation
Semi-ripe cuttings in summer or autumn sown.

Pruning
Cut back lightly after flowering to maintain tight growth habit and encourage repeat flowering.

Problems
None.

HELIANTHUS ANNUUS Sunflower, (Spanish : Girasol).

HABIT AND CULTIVATION

Category	Annual
Family	Compositae
Origin	North America
Size, height x spread	3 x 0.45 metres
Situation	Full sun
Irrigation	Deep watering in summer to produce giant blooms.
Temperature	-
Evergreen/deciduous	-
Flowering	Yellow. Summer.
Special features	Edible seed crop. Birds love the seeds.

The Incas worshipped the Sunflower as a living image of their Sun God and, even today, its happy, sunny face makes people smile. Often grown by children because of its ease combined with rapid growth rate and stunning flowers, it is, of course, also an important crop plant – oil being processed from it's seeds, which are also dried and salted for consumption. The plant has rough, coarse, hairy and somewhat sticky-feeling leaves. The stout, tall stems bear the heavy flowers, which you may want to stake in a garden situation. The flower heads follow the course of the sun. Beloved by birds, they look wonderfully bright against a dark green hedge or other plain background. Many cultivars exist, both annual and perennial, often more bushy and multi-headed, but smaller, and in a range of colours through cream, all sorts of yellow, orange and russets.

Propagation
By spring seed.

Pruning
None.

Problems
None.

HELICHRYSUM BRACTEATUM
Strawflower, (Spanish : Flor Perpetua).

HABIT AND CULTIVATION

Category	Perennial
Family	Compositae
Origin	Australia
Size, height x spread	0.75 x 0.75 metres
Situation	Full sun
Irrigation	Moderate watering through summer months
Temperature	To 0°C
Evergreen/deciduous	Evergreen
Flowering	Creamy-white, yellow, pink and red. Summer.
Special features	Flowers good for drying.

The strawflower is a short-lived perennial, though in our climate it will often carry on for several years if cut down to the ground each year after flowering. The plant has an upright, branching growth habit with rather coarse basal leaves. The tough, hollow stems carry the papery, straw-like, double daisy type flowers, often two-toned, and in a good range of colours. For drying, these should be cut when just open and there is no moisture in the air and tied into bundles and hung upside down in an airy place but out of the sun, which can bleach the colours. The plant is undemanding, happy in light garden soil in a sunny position and with moderate summer watering.

Propagation
Spring sown seeds, or division of plants in late autumn.

Pruning
None. Cut out finished flower heads.

Problems
None.

See also **HELICHRYSUM PETIOLARE**.

HELICHRYSUM PETIOLARE Liquorice Plant, (Spanish : Helicriso).

HABIT AND CULTIVATION

Category	Shrub
Family	Compositae
Origin	South Africa
Size, height x spread	0.5 x 1.5 metres
Situation	Full sun or dappled shade
Irrigation	Moderate summer watering but avoid overhead.
Temperature	To around 0°C
Evergreen/deciduous	Evergreen
Flowering	Creamy-yellow. Summer.
Special features	-

The liquorice plant has delightful foliage, and it is for this that it is mainly grown – furry, silvery and rounded leaves on stems that arch gracefully and creep along the ground. It is often used as an edging or ground cover plant and looks equally good draped over large rocks. It is also a very attractive addition as background planting in baskets and pots. Trimming produces lots of fresh, new growth, which has the best coloration and is velvety soft to the touch. Flowering is insignificant. Established plants can become drought tolerant. Quite happy in light garden soil, but does not like constant overhead irrigation, keep it on the dry side and avoid water on the leaves.

Propagation
Tip cuttings taken in spring.

Pruning
Keep trimming to stop the plant going leggy and promote lots of new growth.

Problems
None.

See also **HELICHRYSUM BRACTEATUM**

HELIOTROPIUM ARBORESCENS
Hot Cherry Pie,
(Spanish : Empanada de la Cereza).

HABIT AND CULTIVATION

Category	Shrub
Family	Boraginaceae
Origin	South America
Size, height x spread	1 x 2 metres
Situation	Full sun, or light dappled shade.
Irrigation	Low water requirements.
Temperature	To 0°C
Evergreen/deciduous	Evergreen
Flowering	Lilac/purple. Spring, summer and autumn.
Special features	Poisonous. Very fragrant flowers.

The hot cherry pie is a South American shrub much prized in warmer climates for its fabulous aroma of – just as it says–– hot cherry pie. Smelling is to believe! Find it a warm, protected spot such as a sheltered corner, and the smell will amaze you on warm, sunny days. Place it where the aroma can properly be appreciated. It forms a branching, spreading shrub making good low groundcover and blending in well with other plantings. The leaves are a dark-green and finely wrinkled, whilst the flowers are lilac-purple, two-toned, held in flat clusters and in great profusion. Not fussy to soil, it dislikes a cold wind, and, once established, is almost drought tolerant.

Propagation
From semi-ripe cuttings in early autumn.

Pruning
Cut back hard in early spring to encourage bushy growth – it will soon regenerate.

Problems
None

HEMEROCALIS
Day Lily, (Spanish : Lirio de Dia).

HABIT AND CULTIVATION

Category	Perennial
Family	Liliaceae
Origin	Orient
Size, height x spread	0.5 x 0.5 metres
Situation	Sun, light or dappled shade in hottest areas.
Irrigation	Moderate summer watering
Temperature	To –10°C
Evergreen/deciduous	Foliage dies down in cold conditions.
Flowering	Cream, yellow, pink, russet. Spring and summer.
Special features	-

Hemerocalis is from the Greek meaning 'beautiful for a day" – and so it is. Each flower only lasts a day but there is no shortage of them. The elegant trumpet flowers are gracefully held on wiry stems in a vibrant range of colours through buffs, golden yellow, all shades of pink, peach and russet, some with deeper throats and a few are even scented. An ever-increasing range is coming onto the market. The grassy like leaves form the perfect backdrop. Grow in large drifts in mixed borders, in pots, and they look stunning naturalised in grassy, woodland areas. Take care when planting because the flowers will turn to always face south.

Propagation
By spring sown seed, though cultivars may not come true to type. Or divide large clumps every 3 years.

Pruning
None. Remove dead flower stalks.

Problems
Slugs and snails can be a problem with the new, juicy foliage in wet springs. Aphids and red spider mite may also attack.

HIBISCUS MUTABILIS Confederate Rose, (Spanish : Arbol de la Vida, Rosa de Jerico).

HABIT AND CULTIVATION

Category	Shrub
Family	Malvaceae
Origin	China
Size, height x spread	6 x 6 metres
Situation	Full sun
Irrigation	Moderate summer watering
Temperature	To 0°C
Evergreen/deciduous	Evergreen
Flowering	White/pink/red. Autumn.
Special features	Flowers that change colour

H. mutabilis is noted for its flowers that change colour as they mature, with all colours being held on the plant at the same time. They start off white, change to pale pink and darken down to a deep pink/red before dying. Cut flowers floating on water also have this ability, particularly pretty on a dinner table, where the flower colour changes as the evening passes. It makes a large shrub with big, hairy, heart-shaped leaves, quite impressive and a good addition to a mixed shrub planting. It appreciates a rich soil and fairly protected position with an occasional feed and watering through the growing season, though it is not as demanding as H. rosa-sinensis in this respect.

Propagation
From summer cuttings.

Pruning
Prune to curb over-vigorous growth in early spring, after cold weather has passed.

Problems
Occasionally aphids.

See also **HIBISCUS ROSA-SINENSIS** and **H. SYRIACUS**.

HIBISCUS ROSA-SINENSIS Rose of China, Shoeflower, (Spanish : Hibisco, Pacifico, Rosa de China).

HABIT AND CULTIVATION

Category	Shrub
Family	Malvaceae
Origin	China
Size, height x spread	3 x 3 metres
Situation	Full sun
Irrigation	Regular summer watering
Temperature	To 0°C
Evergreen/deciduous	Semi-evergreen
Flowering	White, cream, yellow, orange, pinks, red. Spring and summer.
Special features	-

The original coral-red flowers of the hibiscus are borne almost year round in warm climates. But there are now a large range of plants, mainly bred in Hawaii, some with double flowers and in a huge range of colours – white, cream, yellow, peach, all sorts of pinks to deep red and many are blotched or have deeper throats – the range is stunning. The glossy, dark-green leaves (though variegated are also available) clothe the branches thickly and, although sometimes the flowers only last a day, there are plenty of them through the season. They like a reasonably rich soil in a protected position, and feeding and watering regularly when in active growth. They make a wonderful hedge, an impressive specimen shrub and a very beautiful standard. The name of shoeflower derives from the common usage of a hibiscus flower to polish up shoes in the West Indies.

Propagation
Summer cuttings.

Pruning
Prune in early spring, just before active growth begins.

Problems
Aphids and hibiscus beetle.

See also **HIBISCUS MUTABILIS** and **H. SYRIACUS**

HIBISCUS SYRIACUS Rose of Sharon, (Spanish : Hibisco Siriaco).

HABIT AND CULTIVATION

Category	Shrub
Family	Malvaceae
Origin	Asia
Size, height x spread	5 x 2 metres
Situation	Full sun
Irrigation	Becoming drought tolerant
Temperature	Fully hardy
Evergreen/deciduous	Deciduous
Flowering	White, pink, lilac. Spring and summer into autumn.
Special features	-

The H. Sryriacus is the hardiest of the genus and can be trained as a small tree. The oval leaves are deep-green and shiny and somewhat lobed. It forms a densely-leafed shrub and is much more tolerant of poorer conditions than the rest of the family. Can also be used as a large, informal hedging plant, when it looks very beautiful. The flowers are single open-cup shaped, semi-double or double, and in a very pretty range of colours – white, soft pinks, raspberry red, lilac and lilac-pink and violet-blue often with a darker eye in the centre of the flower. Water moderately when first planted but, as the shrub matures, watering may be decreased and it will become drought tolerant.

Propagation
Semi-ripe summer cuttings.

Pruning
Prune back in winter or early spring to promote new, healthy growth.

Problems
Blackfly.

See also **HIBISCUS MUTABILIS** and **H. ROSA-SINENSIS**.

HOYA CARNOSA Wax Plant, (Spanish : Planta de la Cera).

HABIT AND CULTIVATION

Category	Perennial climber
Family	Asclepiadaceae
Origin	Australia
Size, height x spread	5 x 2 metres
Situation	Shade.
Irrigation	Water regularly through growing season.
Temperature	To around 5°C
Evergreen/deciduous	Evergreen
Flowering	Pink-white. Summer and autumn.
Special features	Scented.

The wax plant has incredibly beautiful, sculpted flowers that look as if they have been carved out of wax. Star-shaped and in a very delicate, shell pink with a deeper pink centre, they are also heavily perfumed. It is not one of the easiest plants to accommodate and please, but well worth the effort when those flowers open. The plant needs shade or some gentle sun otherwise the leaves will burn, and it needs warmth and protection from cold winds. They like a rich soil and regular summer watering, but not excessively. Provide support for the shiny-leafed shoots and it will reward you with clusters of the exquisite flowers. Can also be grown in a pot (allow to dry out between watering) or rambling and twining through shrubs in a shaded area.

Propagation
Semi-ripe cuttings in summer and winter layering.

Pruning
Overcrowded stems can be cut out after flowering. The flower clusters develop on the previous year's axillary spurs, so be careful not to prune them out.

Problems
Mealy bug.

HYDRANGEA MACROPHYLLA
(Spanish : Hortensia)

HABIT AND CULTIVATION

Category	Shrub
Family	Saxifragaceae
Origin	Japan
Size, height x spread	2 x 2 metres
Situation	Shade
Irrigation	Regular watering in growing season, and especially if grown in pots.
Temperature	To around –5°C
Evergreen/deciduous	Semi-evergreen
Flowering	White, pink, blue. Summer into autumn.
Special features	-

With their large heads of long-lasting flowers, hydrangeas are a favourite planting for many people. The flower colour is affected by the soil. An acid soil, up to ph 5.5, will produce blue flowers, and alkaline, anything over 5.5, will produce pink. White varieties are unaffected by the soil. Various compounds can be purchased to water into the soil and fool nature – the old, traditional approach was to bury rusty nails around the plant, thus turning the flowers blue. The dense, domed heads are known as hortensias, whilst the flatter, more open heads are lacecaps. Both have large, oval, serrated leaves that burn and collapse badly in strong sun. A shaded courtyard or patio situation is ideal, where they can also be protected from strong winds, and they are perfectly happy in a large pot.

Propagation
Softwood summer cuttings.

Pruning
Prune after flowering, though faded flower heads can be left on plants for some time. Older shoots can be pruned back to base in spring.

Problems
None.

See also **HYDRANGEA QUERCIFOLIA**.

HYDRANGEA QUERCIFOLIA

Oak Leafed Hydrangea,
(Spanish : Hortensia de Roble).

HABIT AND CULTIVATION

Category	Shrub
Family	Saxifragaceae
Origin	North America
Size, height x spread	2 x 2 metres
Situation	Partial or dappled shade.
Irrigation	Moderate summer watering
Temperature	To around –5˚C
Evergreen/deciduous	Deciduous
Flowering	Creamy white to pink. Summer and autumn.
Special features	-

The oak-leafed hydrangea is a fine addition to the shrub garden, natural plantings, under mature trees etc. and one which will settle well into our Mediterranean climate and conditions. The dark-green, deeply lobed leaves form a bushy, nicely mounded shrub, which will take some moderate sun and much less water than the H. macrophylla. The pretty creamy-white conical flower heads are borne through the summer and into autumn, often gradually fading to a very pretty delicate pink. The leaves turn a bronzy-purple before autumn leaf fall. This is a very useful and natural looking shrub for a wide range of garden applications and one needing little care and attention.

Propagation
Softwood cuttings in summer. Also propagate from autumn suckers.

Pruning
Keep pruning to a minimum. Where necessary carry out in early spring.

Problems
None.

See also **HYDRANGEA MACROPHYLLA**.

HYPERICUM CALYCINUM St. John's Wort, Rose of Sharon, (Spanish : Hiperico, Mosto del San Juan).

HABIT AND CULTIVATION

Category	Shrub
Family	Guttiferae
Origin	Balkans
Size, height x spread	0.5 x 1.5 metres
Situation	Sun or shade
Irrigation	Drought tolerant
Temperature	Fully hardy
Evergreen/deciduous	Evergreen
Flowering	Yellow. Summer and autumn.
Special features	-

This showy sub-shrub is very easy to grow and makes excellent and quick-growing ground cover, bank carpeting, or a rock garden planting. It has dark-green leaves on arching branches, with a spread of approx. 1.5m The very showy, bright yellow flowers, occasionally tinged red, with conspicuous fluffy stamens are prolifically produced through summer and autumn and give a real splash of colour to the dullest, shadiest area. Tolerant of most soils and will flower best if not treated too kindly! Over watering can induce rampant growth and the plant may then become invasive.

Propagation
Softwood cuttings in summer or by autumn sown seed.

Pruning
Best pruned back hard every year in early springtime to prevent legginess and straggly plants. Also trim off the seed cases (if not needed) which are produced in great numbers to avoid weakening the plant.

Problems
None.

IMPATIENS, NEW GUINEA HYBRIDS
Busy Lizzie, (Spanish : Impatiens).

HABIT AND CULTIVATION

Category	Perennial
Family	Balsaminaceae
Origin	New Guinea
Size, height x spread	0.5 x 0.5 metres
Situation	Sun or semi-shade
Irrigation	Frequent watering
Temperature	To 0°C
Evergreen/deciduous	Evergreen
Flowering	White, pink, salmon, cerise, orange, crimson. Spring, summer, autumn.
Special features	-

Although classed as a perennial, the busy lizzie is more commonly grown as a summer bedding plant and pot plant. The name impatiens refers to its extreme impatience to multiply and grow! The New Guinea hybrids are the result of extensive hybridisation from the species, giving us a huge range of colours in these very showy plants. Every shade between white and deep crimson, many speckled and striped in contrasting shades. The leaves are long, pointed and shiny, often in a pronounced purple-bronze colour; variegated plants are also available. The flowers are flattish, with a spur, and produced abundantly through warmer weather. Fertilise and water regularly through the growing season.

Propagation
From seed in spring or summer tip cuttings.

Pruning
Pinching out the growing tips encourages bushiness. Dead head.

Problems
When grown undercover, red spider mite, whitefly and aphids can cause problems.

IOCHROMA CYANEUM
(Spanish : Iochroma).

HABIT AND CULTIVATION

Category	Shrub
Family	Solanaceae
Origin	Columbia, South America
Size, height x spread	3 x 1.5 metres
Situation	Full sun or partial shade
Irrigation	Moderate
Temperature	To 5°C
Evergreen/deciduous	Evergreen
Flowering	Purple. Autumn, winter, spring.
Special features	-

This is a little-known shrub, but one that is easy enough given steady warmth. It does not appreciate very hot, burning sun, a cold wind or freezing temperatures and it performs better if planted in a reasonably rich soil. It looks particularly good amongst mixed shrub plantings and in natural woodland settings. Mid-green, oval leaves cloak the slender branches and the shrub has a tidy, upright form. The thin, tubular flowers, slightly flared at the ends, are borne in dense clusters and are a deep, inky purple-blue – a fairly unusual colour in the plant world. Will also grow in a large container, though will then require more summer watering.

Propagation
By softwood or semi-ripe cuttings in summer.

Pruning
Pinch out growing tips for bushier plants. Cut back, by about half, the flower stems towards the end of winter. This will induce vigorous, fresh growth.

Problems
Occasionally troubled by whitefly and red spider mite.

IPOMOEA ALBA Moonflower, (Spanish : Ipomoea)

HABIT AND CULTIVATION

Category	Perennial climber
Family	Convolvulaceae
Origin	Tropical America
Size, height x spread	8 x 3 metres
Situation	Full sun or partial shade
Irrigation	Weekly summer watering
Temperature	To 0°C
Evergreen/deciduous	Evergreen
Flowering	White. Summer
Special features	Night flowering. Scented.

The moonflower is a very rapid and beautiful climber. It is soft-stemmed, self twining and will quickly cover fences, sheds, and large old cypress trees. Position the plant where you can see it from a patio or window and it will enchant you at night. The huge, glistening white, saucer-like flowers unfurl and glow in the moonlight and have a soft, haunting perfume too. During the early hours of daylight, the flowers close up to a tight tube and often only last a day or two but they are followed by many more. The heart-shaped leaves are lushly produced and are a shiny, bright green.

Propagation
By seed in spring, which has been pre-treated in hot water, or from very fresh autumn seed and protect the young plantlets during winter. Also from semi-ripe summer cuttings, preferably from stems which bear soft nodules.

Pruning
Can be cut down hard during winter if growth becomes too tangled.

Problems
None

See also **IPOMOEA INDICA**.

IPOMOEA INDICA Morning Glory Vine, (Spanish : Ipomoea)

HABIT AND CULTIVATION

Category	Perennial climber
Family	Convolvulaceae
Origin	Tropics
Size, height x spread	Indefinite
Situation	Full sun, dappled or partial shade
Irrigation	Drought tolerant
Temperature	To –5°C
Evergreen/deciduous	Evergreen
Flowering	Blue. Almost year round
Special features	Can become invasive

The morning glory vine is an extremely vigorous climber/trailer, which, unless sighted very carefully, can quickly reach serious nuisance status! It roots as it goes and can find its way under paving and you'll find its long stems twining through everything. However, it is extremely beautiful with its deep blue trumpet-shaped flowers, which gradually fade to a dusty rose pink; particularly fresh-looking in the early morning hours. The deep green, lobed leaves are also attractive. Use it as a tough pioneer plant, and do not be kind to it! No fertiliser and a little water to establish, then it will become drought tolerant. It is perfect tumbling down a bank where nothing else is planted or covering some chain-link fencing.

Propagation
Easiest from rooted sections. Creeping stems will root in to almost anything! Also from spring seed, though setting of seed is fairly rare.

Pruning
Do not be afraid to hack this one back to base if it becomes unruly.

Problems
Only control.

See also **IPOMOEA ALBA**.

IRIS GERMANICA Bearded Iris, (Spanish : Lirio).

HABIT AND CULTIVATION

Category	Rhizomatous perennials
Family	Iridaceae
Origin	Mediterranean
Size, height x spread	Up to 1m x 0.5 metres
Situation	Full sun
Irrigation	Drought tolerant
Temperature	To –15°C
Evergreen/deciduous	Evergreen, except in very cold weather.
Flowering	All colours. Spring.
Special features	Some hybrids scented.

Iris are so named after the Greek goddess, Iris, who came down to earth on a rainbow and the range of colours available does indeed span the rainbow. They are extremely tough and tolerant plants, very well suited to our Mediterranean gardens as they like alkaline soil and plenty of heat. The sword shaped green leaves develop in clumps and, within the bearded group, there are basically three sizes; dwarfs up to about 0.20, intermediates to about 0.50 and the tall to around 1m. Planting a mixture of sizes will extend the flowering period, with the taller ones flowering later. The colour range is enormous with more constantly being introduced and the only shade unavailable, as yet, is a true red. The falls, or beard, are often very conspicuously marked in a distinct colour with lighter standard petals, some with plicata edging. Look for scented varieties. Plant, in our climate, with the rhizome just under the soil surface.

Propagation
Split large clumps after flowering and replant small fans with a section of rhizome. Or cut rhizome into sections.

Pruning
None. Remove dead leaves and flower heads.

Problems
None.

JACARANDA MIMOSIFOLIA
(Spanish : Jacaranda).

HABIT AND CULTIVATION

Category	Tree
Family	Bignoniaceae
Origin	South America
Size, height x spread	12 x 8 metres
Situation	Full sun
Irrigation	Moderate summer watering
Temperature	To 0°C
Evergreen/deciduous	Deciduous to semi-evergreen
Flowering	Spring and late summer
Special features	-

The jacaranda is one of our most hauntingly beautiful trees, one that everyone remembers in flower. It is often used as a street tree, lining main avenues in towns and cities and is also a fabulous specimen tree. The leaves are very lush and fern-like, bright green and composed of many tiny leaflets on a long rib which can reach 0.30m. But it is the flowering that is much awaited – a delicious lilac-blue haze settling on the trees – and with the falling flowers, the carpets under the trees are almost as stunning. Seen close to the blooms are tubular and held in large panicles. It can be grown in a pot as a foliage plant, pruning hard every winter. This is a reasonably fast growing tree with a nicely rounded canopy.

Propagation
Spring sown seed or summer cuttings.

Pruning
Generally none necessary. Cut out crossing branches.

Problems
None.

JASMINUM AZORICUM
(Spanish : Jazmin Moruno).

HABIT AND CULTIVATION

Category	Perennial climber
Family	Oleaceae
Origin	Azores
Size, height x spread	6 x 4 metres
Situation	Full sun or partial shade
Irrigation	Drought tolerant
Temperature	To −5°C
Evergreen/deciduous	Evergreen
Flowering	White. Summer and autumn
Special features	Scented

The azoricum is a very tough, evergreen and somewhat shrubby climber. It will often stay shrub-like for some years before putting out long leader shoots. Encourage this by never pruning the head and tying in the climbing branches. It is also an excellent ground cover jasmine. It has shiny, green leaves and quite large typical jasmine flowers, sweetly scented.

Propagation
From ripe wood cuttings in summer or by layering.

Pruning
To shape.

Problems
None

Also **JASMINUM SAMBAC**, Arabian Jasmine, (Spanish : Jazmin de Arabia).Quite similar to the Azoricum, but originating from India and a more tender plant (to 0°C).Bears large white, waxy flowers which are heavily scented and in much demand in the perfumery industry. The plant is also cultivated for jasmine tea. Care as the j. azoricum.

See also **JASMINUM MESNYI, J. NUDIFLORUM, J. OFICINALE** and **J. POLYANTHEMUM**.

JASMINUM MESNYI Primrose Jasmine, (Spanish : Jazmin de San Jose).

HABIT AND CULTIVATION

Category	Perennial climber
Family	Oleaceae
Origin	China
Size, height x spread	3 x 2 metres
Situation	Full sun
Irrigation	Weekly soaking in summer
Temperature	To around 0°C
Evergreen/deciduous	Evergreen
Flowering	Soft yellow. Spring through to summer.
Special features	Slightly scented.

The primrose jasmine is a shrubby rambler with long branches, which can be encouraged to climb, or it can be left as an arching shrub. Try, also, pruning into an unusual hedging plant, with its pretty flowers it is an attractive option. Liking a sheltered spot, it is otherwise easy and very beautiful with its soft primrose yellow scented flowers.

Propagation
By layering or ripe summer cuttings.

Pruning
Very little, to shape. Once or twice a year if used as hedging.

Problems
None.

Also **JASMINUM NUDIFLORUM**, Winter Jasmine, (Spanish : Jazmin de invierno). Another yellow-flowered jasmine, but this one is a bright, golden yellow and flowers on leafless stems in winter. It is an arching deciduous shrub, reaching about 2m high and is a good tough planting for soil retention on banks etc. Plant in sun or part shade. Care as above.

See also **JASMINUM AZORICUM**, **J. OFICINALE**, **J. POLYANTHEMUM** and **J. SAMBAC**.

Jasminum Polyanthemum

JASMINUM OFICINALE Common Jasmine, (Spanish : Jazmin Comun).

HABIT AND CULTIVATION

Category	Perennial climber
Family	Oleaceae
Origin	Asia
Size, height x spread	10 x 3 metres
Situation	Full sun or partial shade
Irrigation	Drought tolerant
Temperature	To –5˚C
Evergreen/deciduous	Semi-evergreen
Flowering	White. Summer and autumn
Special features	Scented

Jasmine is one of the classic scents of Mediterranean gardens, its evocative perfume wafting through the air on hot, summer nights. The white flowers are borne in terminal clusters mainly through summer and autumn, though usually a sprig or two can be picked at any time of the year. Its arching, squarish stems need training to climb or can be pruned to remain somewhat shrubby.

Propagation
By layering or semi-ripe summer cuttings.

Pruning
To keep in shape.

Problems
None

Also **JASMINUM POLYANTHEMUM**, Spring Jasmine, (Spanish : Jazmin de Primavera). This is a vigorous and fast-growing, twining, evergreen climber from China reaching some 6m high. In spring it is smothered in pink buds, which open out into white flowers with a fabulous exotic perfume. Prune after flowering to keep tidy and promote new ferny foliage.

See also **JASMINUM AZORICUM**, **J. MESNYI**, **J. NUDIFLORUM** and **J. SAMBAC**.

Juniperus Horizontalis

JUNIPERUS CHINENSIS
Chinese Juniper,
(Spanish : Juniperus de China).

HABIT AND CULTIVATION

Category	Tree
Family	Cupressaceae
Origin	China, Japan and Mongolia
Size, height x spread	18 x 5 metres
Situation	Full sun
Irrigation	Occasional deep soaking in summer
Temperature	To –10°C
Evergreen/deciduous	Evergreen
Flowering	Insignificant.
Special features	-

This is one of the most planted junipers and makes an upright, conical tree or it can be tipped out and retained at around 4m for tall and dense hedging. It has dark-green, glaucous foliage and peeling brown bark. It is happy in thin sandy soil and with very little water.

Propagation
Tip cuttings root easily.

Pruning
Can be sheared for hedging, otherwise none.

Problems
Humid conditions can cause fungal problems.

Also **JUNIPERUS COMMUNIS**, Common Juniper, (Spanish : Juniperus). A European native, this forms a tall conical tree to 12m with yellowish-green, needle-like foliage. The berries are used as a culinary spice and in gin production. Cultivation is as above.

Also **JUNIPERUS HORIZONTALIS**, Creeping Juniper, (Spanish : Juniperus Prostratum). A native of America, this useful ground-covering juniper can spread some 2m with a height of 0.30m and has blue-green or greyish leaves. Eye-catching variegated forms are also available. Cultivation is as above.

JUSTICIA CARNEA Brazilian Plume Flower, (Spanish : Planta de Camaron, Chuperosa).

HABIT AND CULTIVATION

Category	Shrub
Family	Acanthaceae
Origin	Brazil
Size, height x spread	1.5 x 1 metres
Situation	Dappled or partial shade
Irrigation	Moderate summer watering
Temperature	To 5°C
Evergreen/deciduous	Evergreen
Flowering	White or pinks. Summer and autumn
Special features	-

The Brazilian plume flower is a very attractive, smallish shrub and one which can very easily be slotted into a garden scheme. It has pointed, deep-green, heavily ribbed leaves, often with deep-red new growths and red undersides to the leaves. The flowers are either in white or a range of pinks, from a fairly pale, dusty pink through to a carmine shade. These are held in spikes of many tubular flowers on the terminal ends of upright branches. The peak blooming season is summer and autumn but, in mild conditions, this can extend almost right through the year. It can also be grown in pots. Beware frost - even a touch can kill this sub-tropical plant.

Propagation
Softwood cuttings in spring.

Pruning
Prune back hard in late winter to encourage branching and bushiness.

Problems
In wet springs slugs can sometimes be a problem, as can caterpillars later on. Both enjoy the lush new growth. Watch for whitefly.

KNIPHOFIA UVARIA Red Hot Poker, Torch Lily, (Spanish : Kniphofia).

HABIT AND CULTIVATION

Category	Perennial
Family	Liliaceae
Origin	South Africa
Size, height x spread	1 x 0.5 metres
Situation	Full sun
Irrigation	Becoming drought tolerant
Temperature	To –10°C
Evergreen/deciduous	Evergreen, unless particularly cold
Flowering	Orange/yellow. Summer
Special features	-

These stately perennials from the open Transvaal of South Africa give us some of the brightest and easiest summer colour for our gardens. The thin, sword-like leaves resemble dense clumps of arching grass from which rise the torch-like flowers in early summer, opening orange/red and fading to yellow. They are very statuesque and also make good and long-lasting cut flowers for indoors. The fleshy, tuberous roots like a humus-rich soil but will also settle for much poorer conditions and, if given some straw protection, will even survive snow and freezing weather. The flower stems are very strong and wind resistant making this a good coastal planting.

Propagation
Crowded clumps can be lifted and divided in early spring. They may then take a year to settle back into flowering. Also from spring sown seed.

Pruning
Clean out dead leaves and finished flower stalks.

Problems
None.

KOLKWITZIA AMABILIS Beauty Bush, (Spanish : Kolkwitzia).

HABIT AND CULTIVATION

Category	Shrub
Family	Caprifoliaceae
Origin	China
Size, height x spread	3 x 3 metres
Situation	Full sun or dappled shade
Irrigation	Occasional summer soak
Temperature	To −10°C
Evergreen/deciduous	Deciduous
Flowering	Pink. Spring.
Special features	-

The beauty bush lives up to its name and is a charming addition to general garden plantings, in mixed shrub borders and it also makes a delightful specimen shrub. It is the only species in the genus and its native habitat is rocky gulches as high as 3000m. A fast grower, it forms an attractive arching shrub, prone to suckering, with peeling bark and oval, dark-green leaves. The spring flowers are very abundantly produced and are bell-shaped, a pretty candy pink with a golden flushed throat. For best performance plant in humus rich soil and water regularly until established, thereafter it will require little. Regular mulching around the roots is also appreciated.

Propagation
From softwood cuttings in summer or carefully lift small suckers and relocate.

Pruning
Allow it to develop its arching habit, then thin out the stems each year after flowering.

Problems
None

LAGERSTROEMIA INDICA Crepe Myrtle, Pride of India, (Spanish : Reina de las Flores, Arbol de Jupiter).

HABIT AND CULTIVATION

Category	Shrub
Family	Lythraceae
Origin	Tropical Asia
Size, height x spread	6 x 4 metres
Situation	Full sun
Irrigation	Occasional deep soaking in growing season
Temperature	To 5°C
Evergreen/deciduous	Deciduous
Flowering	Pink, lilac, purple, white. Spring and summer.
Special features	Peeling bark

The crepe myrtle is grown for its very pretty flowers, which are borne during spring and summer in a range of soft pinks, lilacs and purples and have very prettily crinkled and creped petals. It makes a large upright shrub or can be trained into a small tree. The toffee coloured peeling bark is best appreciated in tree form. The mid-green, small, oval leaves colour up dramatically in autumn before falling. It is happiest in full sun in a light, even sandy soil, and will become almost drought tolerant. As a tree is looks delightful in a tub but obviously will then need more watering. Dislikes being transplanted.

Propagation
Easy from spring sown seed. Also hardwood cuttings in winter.

Pruning
Prune immediately after flowering to encourage a dense shrub.

Problems
Can suffer with mildew.

LAGUNARIA PATERSONII Pyramid tree, Primrose Tree, Norfolk Island Hibicus, (Spanish : Lagunaria).

HABIT AND CULTIVATION

Category	Tree
Family	Malvaceae
Origin	Australia
Size, height x spread	12 x 6 metres
Situation	Full sun
Irrigation	Occasional deep summer watering
Temperature	To –5°C
Evergreen/deciduous	Evergreen
Flowering	Pink. Spring and summer
Special features	Irritant hairs in seed cases

The pyramid tree is a very neat, evergreen, conical tree, often seen as a street planting. It is a member of the hibiscus family, but much tougher, and is quite happy in windy coastal situations. The olive green/greyish leaves are tough and leathery and it bears very pretty, pink, open bell-shaped flowers, fading with age to almost white. The flowers are very much like those of hibiscus, though somewhat smaller, with the typical prominent stamens. The seed cases are brown and fuzzy and hang decoratively on the tree for a very long time. Take care handling them because they have irritant hairs inside. Protecting the root run with mulch in very hot conditions promotes better flowering.

Propagation
Spring-sown seed (see note above) or semi-ripe summer cuttings.

Pruning
Generally very little, just tidying shape, removing dead and crossing wood etc.

Problems
Occasional red spider mite.

Lampranthus Spectabilis

LAMPRANTHUS Ice Plant,
(Spanish : Lampranthus).

HABIT AND CULTIVATION

Category	Succulent
Family	Aizoaceae
Origin	South Africa
Size, height x spread	0.30 metres x indefinite
Situation	Full sun
Irrigation	Drought tolerant
Temperature	To 0°C
Evergreen/deciduous	Evergreen
Flowering	White, yellow, orange, red, pinks, lilacs, purple, cerise. Spring.
Special features	-

Very few plants can match this one for sheer flower power. In springtime it is absolutely stunning, the plants are smothered in daisies – in fact, some people would say it is almost too much! But, if your tastes run to vivid, jewel like colours, this one is for you. There are very many to choose from - best to select and buy them in flower so that you get the shade you are looking for. All have tiny succulent leaves, grey-green, and many form neat rounded mounds, maybe 1m across; others are lower growing and closely hug the ground, these have an indefinite spread. All flower in spring – different colours spread the flowering season - and many have a repeat, if lesser, flowering in autumn. They are very popular and, often, huge sheets of them are used in municipal and communal plantings. Excellent as ground cover, on banks etc. and in rock gardens. After a few years they tend to become woody and are best replaced with fresh plants.

Propagation
By stem cuttings in spring, after flowering, or in autumn.

Pruning
Trim over lightly after flowering.

Problems
None if grown hot and dry.

LANTANA CAMARA The Spanish Flag, (Spanish : La Banderilla)

HABIT AND CULTIVATION

Category	Shrub
Family	Verbenaceae
Origin	Tropical America
Size, height x spread	2 x 1.5 metres
Situation	Full sun
Irrigation	Drought tolerant
Temperature	To 0°C
Evergreen/deciduous	Semi-evergreen
Flowering	White, cream, yellow, pink, orange, red. Spring, summer, autumn.
Special features	Poisonous

A very well established shrub in Spain, the red/yellow combination is known as the Spanish flag though there are very many other colour combinations available – some very pretty cream and pink mixes and others with sunset colours, often changing hue as they mature and fade. Buy in flower so you know exactly what you are getting. It is a very tough shrub, growing in poor ground and needs little care and attention. In certain parts of the world, lantana are even classed as noxious weeds. The rounded, spreading branches bear rough, deep green leaves and the flowers are tiny and tubular, held in dense domed heads. In warmer areas it can flower almost right through the year.

Propagation
From semi-ripe summer cuttings.

Pruning
Tip prune for bushiness and can be given a harder prune in late winter.

Problems
Whitefly

See also **LANTANA MONTEVIDENSIS** syn. sellowiana.

LANTANA MONTEVIDENSIS syn. sellowiana, Creeping Lantana, (Spanish : Lantana Rastrera).

HABIT AND CULTIVATION

Category	Sub-shrub
Family	Verbenaceae
Origin	Tropical America
Size, height x spread	0.75 x 3 metres
Situation	Full sun or some dappled shade
Irrigation	Drought tolerant
Temperature	To –5°C
Evergreen/deciduous	Evergreen
Flowering	White, yellow, lilac. Almost year round.
Special features	Poisonous

The creeping lantana is a very useful and pretty ground cover plant. The arching stems are mat forming and it is particularly good on difficult banks to prevent erosion, and between shrubs and trees, as long as the shade is not too dense. The tiny tubular flowers are held in dense flower heads, resembling verbena, and in warmer areas, it will flower almost right through the year. The leaves are a rather dull green, rough and serrated and can turn bronze-purple in colder conditions. It will become drought tolerant, though does rather better with a deep watering four or five times during the summer. This is one of our most undemanding plants.

Propagation
From semi-ripe summer cuttings.

Pruning
Tip prune every now and again to keep tidy and promote fresh, new growth.

Problems
Whitefly.

See also **LANTANA CAMARA**.

LAVANDULA ANGUSTIFOLIA syn.
L. OFFICINALIS, L. SPICA, L. VERA,
English Lavender (Spanish : Lavanda).

HABIT AND CULTIVATION

Category	Shrub
Family	Labiatae
Origin	Mediterranean
Size, height x spread	1 x 2 metres
Situation	Full sun
Irrigation	Drought tolerant
Temperature	To –10˚C
Evergreen/deciduous	Evergreen
Flowering	Lavender/purple. Spring and summer.
Special features	Aromatic herb

Although known as English lavender, though there is no native species there, it seems to have been introduced from the Mediterranean area in the 1600's. It became extremely popular and was greatly exploited for its aromatic qualities and thereon became known as English lavender. It forms great aromatic mounds of billowing foliage which look wonderful in natural plantings mixed with other endemic plants and also makes an excellent informal low hedge. If you live in the country, try mixing it with other herbs such as rosemary, sage, thyme, and rock roses and sun roses for a perfectly integrated look, which will need very little maintenance. It is distinguished by its grey, furry leaves and is one of the hardiest of the genus. The flowers are used in the distillation of lavender oil for the perfumery and medical trades. The blooms are edible in this species only and can be used for flavouring cakes, ice creams etc.

Propagation
Semi-ripe cuttings in summer.

Pruning
Trim over in early spring to keep compact shape and cut out dead flower stalks later.

Problems
Do not summer irrigate or shrubs will fall apart.

See also **LAVANDULA DENTATA** and **L. STOECHAS**.

LAVANDULA DENTATA Toothed
Lavender, (Spanish : Alhucema
Dentata, Alhucema Rizada).

HABIT AND CULTIVATION

Category	Shrub
Family	Labiatae
Origin	Mediterranean
Size, height x spread	1 x 1 metres
Situation	Full sun
Irrigation	Drought tolerant
Temperature	To –5°C
Evergreen/deciduous	Evergreen
Flowering	Lavender-blue. Almost year round.
Special features	Aromatic herb

The toothed lavender has fine grey-green leaves, toothed at the margins, giving a soft ferny look to the plant. It makes a nicely mounded and very leafy, aromatic shrub. The pale lavender-blue flowers are held in short, dense spikes almost right through the year, but with peak flowering through the warmer months. It is drought and lightly frost resistant, its native habitat being limestone rocks and stony, poor ground. The bees like this lavender, which is rich in nectar, and it is cultivated mainly for honey production. The essential oil in this one is not so strongly scented and it is, therefore, not used in the perfume industry. A very useful small planting grouped in natural areas. It is not edible.

Propagation
Semi-ripe summer cuttings.

Pruning
Trim over lightly in early spring to maintain tight plants.

Problems
None.

See also **LAVANDULA ANGUSTIFOLIA** and **L. STOECHAS**.

LAVANDULA STOECHAS
French Lavender,
(Spanish : Cantahueso, Cantueso).

HABIT AND CULTIVATION

Category	Shrub
Family	Labiatae
Origin	Mediterranean
Size, height x spread	0.75 x 1 metres
Situation	Full sun
Irrigation	Drought tolerant
Temperature	To –10°C
Evergreen/deciduous	Evergreen
Flowering	Purple. Almost year round.
Special features	Aromatic herb

The French lavender was traditionally used as an antiseptic wash to help clean and cure wounds. The word 'lavender' is thought to come from the Latin word 'lavare' – to wash – the Romans used it in their washing water to perfume and cleanse. 'Stoechas' is the ancient Greek name for some islands off the coast of Marseilles where the plant grows abundantly. It is recognisable by its long, grey-green, lanceolate leaves carried on a low-growing woody shrublet. It is a common maquis plant, found growing in limestone areas, amongst sparse shrubs and trees. Short, stiff, unbranched stems bear the tight flower spikes made up of small, purple flowers which are topped by a 3cm long purple, petal-like bract. The overall effect is somewhat like a tiny purple pineapple. It gives off a very intense smell during the heat of summer, a cross between a lavender and rosemary fragrance. French oil is extracted from the plants which is used in room fresheners, deodorants, insecticides etc.

Propagation
Summer cuttings.

Pruning
Tip prune to keep tidy.

Problems
None.

See also **LAVANDULA ANGUSTIFOLIA** and **L. DENTATA**.

LAVATERA ARBOREA Tree Mallow, (Spanish : Lavatera).

HABIT AND CULTIVATION

Category	Shrub
Family	Malvaceae
Origin	Mediterranean
Size, height x spread	3 x 1 metres
Situation	Full sun
Irrigation	Drought tolerant
Temperature	To –5˚C
Evergreen/deciduous	Semi-evergreen
Flowering	Pinkish purple. Spring, summer and autumn
Special features	-

The tree mallow is a large, mounding, semi-evergreen shrub, which can be trained into a mini tree. It has large, grey-green leaves, heavily lobed and grows quite rapidly and requires little care. It makes a good pioneer planting, easily adapting to poor soil and conditions - and is an ideal and rapid gap filler. The hibiscus-like flowers are pinkish purple, usually with a paler centre and heavily marked veins. Its peak blooming time is during the warmer months but, given kind conditions, it can flower almost right through the year. Each individual flower is short lived but they are produced in great abundance. A good plant for a child commencing gardening with its ease and speed of cultivation.

Propagation
Seed sown in spring germinates easily. Also by softwood spring cuttings.

Pruning
Generally none, though can be shaped into a tree.

Problems
Can be troubled with aphids.

LEONOTIS LEONURUS Lion's Ear, (Spanish : Cola de Leon).

HABIT AND CULTIVATION

Category	Shrub
Family	Labiatea
Origin	South Africa
Size, height x spread	2 x 2 metres
Situation	Full sun
Irrigation	Drought tolerant
Temperature	To –5°C
Evergreen/deciduous	Evergreen
Flowering	Orange. Late summer, autumn, winter.
Special features	-

The lion's ear is a very striking shrubby perennial that is also very tough and easy and a perfect addition to a dry garden. It can survive with very little water. It is a woody based plant which sends up erect stems with dark green, lance-shaped leaves, which are slightly aromatic. The fuzzy, tawny-orange, tubular flowers are curved, whorled and grouped around the flower stalks – an unusual and very eye-catching sight. Even when the flowers have finished the seed cases are also attractive, looking like wasps nests. Flowers and seed cases can be cut for long lasting indoor arrangements. In extremely hot conditions it can become summer dormant.

Propagation
Spring sown seed or green wood cuttings in early summer.

Pruning
When flowers and seeds are finished and the plant starts to look a little messy, cut it down to within about 15cm of ground level.

Problems
None

Leptospermum Scoparium

LEPTOSPERMUM LAEVIGATUM
Tea Tree, (Spanish : Leptospermum).

HABIT AND CULTIVATION

Category	Tree
Family	Myrtaceae
Origin	Australia
Size, height x spread	10 x 8 metres
Situation	Full sun
Irrigation	Drought tolerant
Temperature	To 0°C
Evergreen/deciduous	Evergreen
Flowering	White. Spring
Special features	-

Legend has it that Captain James Cook prepared a 'tea' from one of the Leptospermum species for his crew to help combat scurvy and the family have since been known as tea trees. Do not confuse this with Melaleuca alternifolia, which is the true source of tea tree oil. L. laevigatum is a beautiful small tree, which, as it matures develops twisting and curving branches and trunk, some even arching along the ground giving an extremely elegant, sculptural outline. The small, oblong, dull green leaves are held on the graceful pendulous branches. In springtime it flowers profusely with small, white, single rose type flowers. Grows very happily in windy coastline positions.

Propagation
Semi-ripe summer cuttings

Pruning
Generally none, let it develop its own shape.

Problems
Scale insect and sooty mould.

Also **LEPTOSPERMUM SCOPARIUM**, New Zealand Tea Tree, Manuka, (Spanish : Leptospermum). This one forms a spreading shrub, some 3 x 3, with purple-tinged leaves. The flowers are single or double, in white, pale pink and a deep rosy-pink/red. Sometimes a little hard to establish but, once settled, cultivation as above but with a little more water.

LILIUM CANDIDUM Madonna Lily, (Spanish : Azucena).

HABIT AND CULTIVATION

Category	Bulb
Family	Liliaceae
Origin	Mediterranean
Size, height x spread	2 x 0.30 metres
Situation	Full sun or partial shade
Irrigation	Occasional summer soak
Temperature	To –5°C
Evergreen/deciduous	Evergreen
Flowering	White. Spring
Special features	Scented

The Madonna lily is the oldest lily in cultivation and was traditionally much planted in Spanish gardens, being highly valued and admired not only for its beauty but also for its perfume. This is the only lily that likes shallow planting – the nose of the bulb should be planted just below soil level. With autumn rains the bulb starts to shoot with very thin, long, shiny green basal leaves. In spring the flower shoots are sent up, each bearing up to 20 individual blooms, some 15cm long. The trumpet-shaped flowers are pure white and heavily scented, a glorious sight which lasts for several weeks. The plants are summer dormant, and all top growth dies down as the temperatures rise.

Propagation
Large clumps can be lifted and carefully divided after flowering. Or, gently pull off bulb scales and plant into trays of compost until more mature. Also by spring sown seeds, though these can take some years to mature to flowering size.

Pruning
None. Remove dead flower stalks.

Problems
As with all lilies, can develop virus but the species are generally more immune. Also watch out for lily beetle.

See also **LILIUM LONGIFLORUM**.

LILIUM LONGIFLORUM Easter Lily, (Spanish : Lirio).

HABIT AND CULTIVATION

Category	Bulb
Family	Liliaceae
Origin	Asia
Size, height x spread	1.25 x 0.30 metres
Situation	Full sun or dappled shade
Irrigation	Regularly during flowering period.
Temperature	To –5˚C
Evergreen/deciduous	Evergreen
Flowering	White. Early summer.
Special features	Scented.

The Easter Lily has long been regarded as the symbol of the Virgin Mary, but it actually predates Christianity. Roman mythology tells that whilst Juno, the Queen of all the Gods, was breastfeeding her son, Hercules, some excess milk fell from the Heavens creating the Milky Way star system and, what fell to Earth, formed this white lily. Because of its more recent religious links, it is much used in decorating churches – though the prudish Victorians removed the very prominent stamens and pistils because of their overt sexuality, so as not to encourage any wicked thoughts in the congregation! Plant the bulb two to three times its own depth and every summer each flower stalk will bear up to 8 flowers, approx. 20cm. long, trumpet-shaped with reflexive petals, pure white, with golden stamens and heavily scented.

Propagation
Spring sown seed, though slow to mature to flowering size, or bulb scales, planted into trays of compost, will build up into flowering sized bulbs in approx. 3 years.

Pruning
None. Remove dead flower stalks.

Problems
Lily viral disease and lily beetle.

See also **LILIUM CANDIDUM**.

LIMONIUM LATIFOLIUM Sea Lavender,
(Spanish : Lavanda del Mar).

HABIT AND CULTIVATION

Category	Perennial
Family	Plumbaginaceae
Origin	North Africa
Size, height x spread	0.5 x 0.5 metres
Situation	Full sun
Irrigation	Occasional watering during period of peak growth and flowering
Temperature	To –10°C
Evergreen/deciduous	Semi-evergreen
Flowering	Lavender-blue or blue-white. Summer.
Special features	Flowers can be dried

The sea lavender is mainly grown for its very pretty, papery flowers, which can be cut and dried and used indoors, having a very delicate and misty appearance. It is a clump forming perennial with large, dark-green, leathery leaves. The flowers are produced during summer and cover the plant in a light haze of lilac-blue, though occasionally a bluish-white plant will also be found. These are long lasting on the plant and it makes a very attractive addition to any mixed border, with shrub plantings, on dry banks and gravel gardens. If the flowers are wanted for drying, cut them just as they open and hang in bunches upside down in an airy place out of the sun. This is a very adaptable plant that will tolerate arid inland situations as well as a seaside planting, as its common name suggests.

Propagation
Plants can be divided in very early spring, or sow seeds.

Pruning
None, simply tidy plants and cut out dead flower stalks.

Problems
None.

LINUM NARBONENSE Blue Flax, (Spanish : Lino Bravo).

HABIT AND CULTIVATION

Category	Perennial
Family	Linaceae
Origin	Mediterranean
Size, height x spread	0.5 x 0.5 metres
Situation	Full sun
Irrigation	Drought tolerant
Temperature	Fully hardy
Evergreen/deciduous	Will disappear underground in cold conditions
Flowering	Blue. Spring and summer
Special features	-

The flax family has been cultivated since at least 5000BC and the Egyptians used cloth made from the fibres of the plant to wrap their mummies. The Romans spread the cultivation of flax and it was widely used to produce a type of linen and for the extraction from the seeds of oil – linseed oil – which, even today, is widely used in the pharmaceutical industry to make a liniment for burns and rheumatic pains. It is also much used in the manufacture of printers' ink, paints and soap. L. narbonense is one of the most handsome of the family with soft green leaves forming clumps and very pretty sky-blue, funnel-shaped flowers which are profusely produced through spring and summer. Found naturally amongst rocks and dry gravelly terrain, it needs a warm position and is happy in poor ground.

Propagation
Spring-sown seed.

Pruning
Trim over after flowering.

Problems
None.

LONICERA JAPONICA Japanese Honeysuckle, (Spanish : Madreselva).

HABIT AND CULTIVATION

Category	Perennial climber
Family	Caprifoliaceae
Origin	Japan
Size, height x spread	10 x 5 metres
Situation	Sun or shade, though will generally flower less in full shade.
Irrigation	Drought tolerant
Temperature	To –10°C
Evergreen/deciduous	Semi-evergreen
Flowering	Creamy white. Spring and summer.
Special features	Scented. Berries, if produced, are poisonous

The honeysuckles have a reputation as being one of our most romantic climbers and, indeed, it is very pleasant and relaxing to sit under a bower covered by twining honeysuckle with the sweetly scented flowers wafting their perfume on a summers evening. L. japonica is the largest of the family and can become rampant so position carefully or be prepared to prune heavily. It is a perfect pioneer planting, for covering fencing, rough banks etc. and will rapidly give a mature, wild and 'romantic' look to the garden. The leaves are dark green and shiny on twisting, twining stems and the flowers are very prettily held in pairs, in a faded creamy-white-pale-yellow combination.

Propagation
Hardwood cuttings in autumn or by layering.

Pruning
Do not be afraid to take shears to this one. Prune savagely after flowering to control.

Problems
Aphids.

See also **LONICERA NITIDA**.

LONICERA NITIDA Honeysuckle, Box Honeysuckle. (Spanish : Madreselva)

HABIT AND CULTIVATION

Category	Shrub
Family	Caprifoliaceae
Origin	China
Size, height x spread	2 x 3 metres
Situation	Sun or part shade
Irrigation	Drought tolerant, though better with occasional summer watering
Temperature	To around –5°C
Evergreen/deciduous	Evergreen
Flowering	White. Spring.
Special features	Poisonous berries

L. nitida is completely distinct to the general conception of honeysuckles. This one makes a tiny-leafed, dense shrub which is ideal for hedging and can be pruned and trained, very much as box, to form mini-edging, topiary etc. The leaves are oval, small and a glossy green. The flowers are small, white, somewhat scented, but fairly insignificant – this is not one to grow for heavily scented, luxuriant flowers – and they are followed by purple-black berries, which are poisonous. This is a tough shrub that has its position in the garden – there are not so many plants that will accept such close and constant trimming for formal work.

Propagation
Semi-ripe summer cuttings, or hardwood autumn cuttings.

Pruning
Trim to shape if formal hedging is required. Do main training during winter and early spring. Tip prune anytime.

Problems
None.

See also **LONICERA JAPONICA**.

LOTUS BERTHELOTII Parrot's Beak, (Spanish : Lotus).

HABIT AND CULTIVATION

Category	Trailer
Family	Leguminosea
Origin	Canary Islands
Size, height x spread	0.25 metres x indefinite
Situation	Full sun, dappled or partial shade.
Irrigation	Occasional summer watering
Temperature	To 0°C
Evergreen/deciduous	Evergreen
Flowering	Gold or copper. Spring and autumn
Special features	-

The parrot's beak is an exceptionally useful and pretty trailer and ground coverer, looking particularly good draped over walls, cascading down banks, planted between rocks etc. and is also a good pot plant. The fine silvery-grey, soft, needle-like foliage is an asset in itself and the combination with the rich rust and copper coloured flowers is very eye-catching. There is also a variety with greener foliage and deep, golden-yellow flowers. The flowers, in the shape of a parrot's beak, smother the plant in springtime and there is a later, though generally lesser flowering, in autumn. This is an easy, undemanding plant and one that is sure to give you constant pleaure.

Propagation
From summer cuttings.

Pruning
Tip prune to prevent straggliness, and it can be cut harder in late winter if it is spreading too far.

Problems
Dislikes wet feet which can cause rot and loss of plant. Avoid winter water logging.

MAGNOLIA GRANDIFLORA
Bull Bay or Southern Magnolia,
(Spanish : Magnolio)

HABIT AND CULTIVATION

Category	Tree
Family	Magnoliaceae
Origin	North America
Size, height x spread	20 x 8 metres
Situation	Sun or shade
Irrigation	Moderate summer water
Temperature	To –10°C
Evergreen/deciduous	Evergreen
Flowering	Creamy white. Late spring to early summer.
Special features	Scented. Prefers an acidic soil but will tolerate alkaline.

The southern magnolia is one of the oldest trees that exist, pre-dating the Great Ice Age. The glacial conditions killed off the European magnolias and the genus that we now have are either from North America (evergreen) or Asia (deciduous). They were re-introduced into Europe in the 18th.C. It is a truly magnificent tree, which, in its native habitat, can reach over 30m high with a trunk diameter of 5m. In Mediterranean conditions – and here I refer to mainly alkaline soils and dry air – it will never attain such splendour and the size indicated opposite is more realistic. It has a very full, leafy head with large, shiny, green leaves, felted brown underneath. The magnificent flowers are large and cup-shaped with a strong citrus fragrance. Even the shiny red seed cones are attractive. This is a specimen tree with a capital 'S', give it space and plant carefully (the roots are delicate) into a soil enriched with peat and leaf mould. Mulch yearly to keep the root run cool. Select a grafted tree, or flowering will be slow.

Propagation
From autumn sown seed, but slow to flower, or summer cuttings.

Pruning
Simply remove crossing branches, dead wood etc.

Problems
None.

MAHONIA AQUIFOLIUM
Oregon Grape, Holly Grape,
(Spanish : Mahonia).

HABIT AND CULTIVATION

Category	Shrub
Family	Berberidaceae
Origin	North America
Size, height x spread	1 x 1.5 metres
Situation	Dappled, partial or full shade
Irrigation	Moderate summer water.
Temperature	To –10°C
Evergreen/deciduous	Evergreen
Flowering	Yellow. Spring
Special features	Scented

The Oregon grape makes a very attractive specimen shrub, a good, low, informal hedge, and windbreak plant and a medium-height ground coverer, useful amongst trees etc. The leaves are divided into shiny green leaflets, somewhat prickly and resembling holly. In cold conditions these can turn beautiful bronze and purple shades, though staying on the bush. The neat clusters of small yellow flowers, with a sweet perfume, are followed by blue-black rounded fruits, which look like small grapes. They are very attractive to birds and also make an excellent jam or jelly, if you get in before the birds! The growth rate is moderate and, once established, they are tolerant of wind, heat and drought.

Propagation
Spring sown seed or semi-ripe summer cuttings.

Pruning
Just shaping. Best pruned with secateurs to avoid spoiling leaf shape.

Problems
None.

MANDEVILLA LAXA Chilean Jasmine,
(Spanish : Mandevila, Jasmin de Chile)

HABIT AND CULTIVATION

Category	Perennial climber
Family	Apocynaceae
Origin	Argentina
Size, height x spread	6 x 2 metres
Situation	Partial or dappled shade
Irrigation	Weekly summer watering
Temperature	To 0°C
Evergreen/deciduous	Deciduous
Flowering	White. Spring and summer
Special features	Scented. Milky sap is poisonous

The Chilean jasmine is a surprisingly little grown climber, yet it is undemanding, does not overpower with its size and has beautiful and scented flowers. It is a woody stemmed climber with mid-green, ovoid leaves, heart-shaped at the bottom and large loose clusters of trumpet flowers, which resemble very large jasmine and are sweetly scented. They make very nice posy flowers. The base of the plant will go bare, so it is best to plant something at its feet. A good pergola or arch plant and it looks stunning if allowed to grow up into a large dark green cypress – the white flowers shine out like stars. It benefits from thick mulching applied around the tuberous, somewhat delicate roots.

Propagation
Very easy from spring sown seed.

Pruning
Can be cut back hard during the winter to encourage bushiness. Beware milky sap.

Problems
Occasional aphids.

MELALEUCA ARMILLARIS Paperbark,
Honeymyrtle, (Spanish : Melaleuca).

HABIT AND CULTIVATION

Category	Shrub
Family	Myrtaceae
Origin	Australia
Size, height x spread	8 x 6 metres
Situation	Full sun
Irrigation	Becoming drought tolerant
Temperature	To –5°C
Evergreen/deciduous	Evergreen
Flowering	Creamy white-yellow. Spring.
Special features	Scented.

The paperbarks are similar to the bottlebrushes (callistemon), all originating from Australasia and there is a wide range of these spectacular shrubs and trees. M. armillaris can be trained into a small tree when its grey, furrowed and peeling bark can be best appreciated. It is quick growing and can also be used as informal hedging, a windbreak and screening plant and background planting. The shrub, with its light-green, needle-like leaves explodes into a mass of creamy yellow-white bottlebrush flowers in spring, each approx. 5cm long and composed of a brush of white stamens. This is a very tough plant, adapting well to alkaline soils, hot winds and harsh sea winds. The new tip growth can be burnt by frost under extreme conditions, but it will recover.

Propagation
Spring sown seed or semi-hardwood cuttings in summer.

Pruning
Tolerates hard pruning to shape, but generally best left to their own devices.

Problems
None.

Also **MELALEUCA ALTERNIFOLIA**, Tea Tree, (Spanish : Melaleuca). The Aborigines traditionally used the leaves from this plant to help heal wounds and skin infections. Today there is a huge market for Tea Tree oil, a pale yellow extract, and some 700 tons of it are annually exported from Australia. Used in the treatment of wounds, bites and stings, skin irritations, acne etc.

MELIA AZEDERACH Persian Lilac, Bead Tree, Chinaberry, (Spanish : Melia, Lila de Persia).

HABIT AND CULTIVATION

Category	Tree
Family	Meliaceae
Origin	Asia
Size, height x spread	15 x 8 metres
Situation	Full sun
Irrigation	Drought tolerant
Temperature	To –5°C
Evergreen/deciduous	Deciduous
Flowering	Lilac. Spring.
Special features	Scented flowers. Berries poisonous.

The Persian lilac is much valued in its homeland for its fine grained timber and for the insecticidal properties of its leaves – it is closely related to the Neem tree, which is a fount of natural fertilisers and insect repellents. It is also an excellent summer shade tree, and was often traditionally planted around chicken runs etc. both for shade and to deter flies. It is a moderately fast grower and very tolerant of poor conditions. The deep-green leaves are composed of many leaflets, making a ferny looking tree. The fragrant, star-like, lilac flowers appear with the leaves in spring. The green fruit mature to a golden yellow and hang on the tree, in drooping clusters, through the winter. Although poisonous to humans and animals, they are used by the pharmaceutical industry and are relished by fruit bats in their native country – this being the only mammal that can eat them unharmed. Birds also relish them but can become partly intoxicated. The seed of the golden berries were also once dried and used for making rosaries. A widely planted street tree and deservedly popular.

Propagation
Autumn sown seed.

Pruning
Has somewhat brittle branches, which can be wind damaged. Prune to shape.

Problems
Suckers and self seeds quite readily.

MELIANTHUS MAJOR Honey Flower, Touch-me-not, (Spanish : Melianthus).

HABIT AND CULTIVATION

Category	Shrub
Family	Melianthaceae
Origin	South Africa
Size, height x spread	3 x 3 metres
Situation	Full sun, partial or dappled shade
Irrigation	Becoming drought tolerant but better with an occasional summer soaking
Temperature	To 0˚C
Evergreen/deciduous	Evergreen
Flowering	Maroon. Spring.
Special features	Poisonous

The honey bush is an undemanding and very striking open shrub mainly grown for its beautiful foliage. The luxuriant leaves start to unfurl with autumn rains and get larger and more magnificent as the wetter months of winter progress. With much summer watering, this exotic look can be retained but, if irrigation is not an option, the plant will survive the summer months semi-dormant. The blue-green leaves are composed of around a dozen heavily serrated leaflets and, during spring, a long brown-maroon flower spike is produced which is full of nectar and very attractive to bees. Altogether a stunning accent plant which will give no problems. Flowers and bruised foliage have a rather unpleasant smell, hence common name of touch-me-not.

Propagation
Spring sown seed or from suckers.

Pruning
Can be cut down late summer if plant is looking rather tired.

Problems
None.

MESEMBRYANTHEMUM CRINIFLORUM
syn. dorotheanthus bellidiformis,
Ice Plant, Livingstone Daisy,
(Spanish : Planta de hielo).

HABIT AND CULTIVATION

Category	Succulent annual
Family	Aizoaceae
Origin	South Africa
Size, height x spread	0.15 x 0.30 metres
Situation	Full sun
Irrigation	Better with occasional summer watering
Temperature	To 0°C
Evergreen/deciduous	-
Flowering	White, yellow, orange, pink, red. Spring and summer.
Special features	-

The ice plant is a dazzling little succulent that looks wonderful closely planted in masses in sunny spots in rockeries, on banks, pots, as an edging for larger containers and even as a short term lawn substitute. Best sown in situ, choose an open sunny spot, as the flowers will not open in shade or dull conditions. The plants have tiny, succulent, bright green leaves and spreading stems with vivid daisy flowers in a huge range of dazzling colours. It is also very salt-resistant and a good choice for seaside gardens. This is one of the first plants that many of us grew as children but it is worthy, still, of your attention.

Propagation
Spring seed, best sown in situ.

Pruning
None. Regular dead heading will greatly prolong the flowering season.

Problems
Watch for slugs and snails attacking vulnerable and juicy seedlings.

METROSIDEROS EXCELSA
New Zealand Christmas Tree,
(Spanish : Metrosidero).

HABIT AND CULTIVATION

Category	Tree/shrub
Family	Myrtaceae
Origin	New Zealand
Size, height x spread	10 x 4 metres
Situation	Full sun
Irrigation	Drought tolerant
Temperature	To 0°C
Evergreen/deciduous	Evergreen
Flowering	Orange/red. Summer.
Special features	-

The coastline of northern New Zealand is littered with metrosideros, some as much as 800 years old. The Maoris have long held the 'pohutukawa' in great esteem and on the very northern tip of the island is the oldest tree of all, a sacred tree, from which, it is believed that departing souls go to the afterlife. The Latin name, metrosideros excelsa, means 'ironwood of excellence', referring to its very dense reddish wood. Commercially unacceptable because of the twisting and distorting habit of its branches, it makes a very beautiful tree. Old specimens often have branches spreading and reaching the ground, where they will root and add to the life of the tree. This is one of the best plantings for exposed coastal positions and it will anchor itself with its spreading roots on sheer cliffsides where little else can survive. Shiny grey-green leaves, felted white underneath, are tough and attractive but the brilliant orange-red bottlebrush flowers smothering the branches during our summer (Christmas time in New Zealand) are show-stoppers. A variegated form is also available.

Propagation
Spring sown seed or semi-ripe summer cuttings.

Pruning
Tolerated if necessary.

Problems
None.

MINA LOBATA
(Spanish : Mina Lobata).

HABIT AND CULTIVATION

Category	Perennial climber
Family	Convolvulaceae
Origin	Mexico and Central America
Size, height x spread	5 x 2 metres
Situation	Full sun
Irrigation	Regular summer watering
Temperature	To 5°C
Evergreen/deciduous	Deciduous
Flowering	Red-orange-yellow-white. Summer and autumn.
Special features	-

A little known but very eye-catching perennial climber, which is more often grown as an annual. It would need a very protected position to stay perennial. It has large 3-lobed leaves and bears many racemes of small tubular flowers that start off a red-orange, maturing to yellow and fading to white. All colours are held on the plant at the same time and the effect is spectacular. It is a quick, vigorous climber, of a useful middle size – good on pergolas, arches, climbing up walls (given support) or brightening a dull old cypress with its flaming looks. It can also be draped over a high wall. Performs best in a fairly rich soil, with regular feeding and watering through the growing season.

Propagation
Spring sown seed.

Pruning
Train in new growths. In warm positions try cutting to ground level in winter and wait for spring growth.

Problems
Aphids.

MIRABILIS JALAPA Marvel of Peru,
4 o'clock plant, (Spanish : Don Pedro).

HABIT AND CULTIVATION

Category	Perennial
Family	Nyctaginaceae
Origin	Tropical America
Size, height x spread	1 x 0.75 metres
Situation	Full sun
Irrigation	Drought tolerant
Temperature	To 0˚C
Evergreen/deciduous	Top growth dies down in cold temperatures
Flowering	White, yellow, pink. Summer and autumn.
Special features	Scented

One of our best and easiest mid-summer to end of autumn flowerers is the 4 o'clock plant – charmingly named thus for its habit of opening its flowers in the afternoon, staying open all night and closing early morning. Not always punctual to the hour – let's call it Spanish 4 o'clock! It is a tuberous perennial forming a bushy mound of mid-green leaves. The flowers are sweetly scented and open-trumpet shaped, scattered across the plant in bright white, yellow and shocking pink. Often, through cross-pollination, striped and blotched flowers can be found on the same plant. A useful and rapid gap filler, a small informal hedging plant and pretty in pots, it likes hot, dry and poor conditions and is often seen growing in waste ground, motorway reservations etc. The top growth will die down as soon as temperatures drop and the tubers remain dormant over winter.

Propagation
Spring sown seed. Will also self seed easily.

Pruning
None.

Problems
None.

MONSTERA DELICIOSA Swiss Cheese Plant, (Spanish : Costillas de Adan).

HABIT AND CULTIVATION

Category	Perennial
Family	Araceae
Origin	Tropical America and West Indies
Size, height x spread	4 metres x indefinite
Situation	Partial or dappled shade
Irrigation	Moderate summer watering
Temperature	To 0°C
Evergreen/deciduous	Evergreen
Flowering	Cream. Summer
Special features	Edible fruit

The Swiss Cheese plant is more commonly known to Northern Europeans as an indoor pot plant but in a Mediterranean climate, it will perform splendidly outside. In its native habitat it sprawls through jungle trees, fixing itself into any crevice by means of its aerial roots. For us, it is perhaps best situated in a courtyard garden and its roots will find their way back to ground or into any soil filled nook. These roots help support the plant and, of course, nourish it – never cut them off. The dramatic glossy leaves are cut and perforated and, once the plant has established, it will produce thick, creamy-coloured spathes followed by cone-like edible fruits that are very slow to ripen. It enjoys a high degree of humidity but will adjust to most conditions, apart from severe cold.

Propagation
Stem tip summer cuttings.

Pruning
Cut out dead leaves and long stems can be shortened in early spring, if necessary.

Problems
Under open conditions, none.

MORUS ALBA White Mulberry, (Spanish : Morera Alba).

HABIT AND CULTIVATION

Category	Tree
Family	Moraceae
Origin	China
Size, height x spread	10 x 10 metres
Situation	Full sun
Irrigation	Drought tolerant
Temperature	Fully hardy
Evergreen/deciduous	Deciduous
Flowering	Greenish. Insignificant. Spring.
Special features	Edible fruit

The white mulberry tree was a very important planting in Andalucia as the preferred food crop of the silk worm and the prop of the vitally important silk industry. As far back as the 10th. century Andalucia was the main silk producing centre through Europe. When the island of La Palma was conquered in 1493 Spanish techniques of silk production were adopted by the islanders and, even today, craftsmen carry on the tradition there. The trade was very strong, with Granada being a big centre, until around the end of the 18th. century when Italy and France started taking over the market, followed later by Japan and China. The introduction of man-made dyes and cheaper production figures in the Far East largely brought about the downfall of the Spanish, and European, silk trade. In the 1980's craftsmen in La Palma reintroduced natural dyes (cochineal for yellow, eucalyptus for grey and almond shells for brown) with many contributions from endemic plants too and the industry experienced a small but important resurgence. Many small villages in Andalucia have magnificent examples of mulberry trees dating back to their time of glory. Warm daytime temperatures are essential to induce rapid and constant leaf growth to combat the ravages of the silk worm. Care as black mulberry.

See also **MORUS NEGRA** and **M. PENDULUS**

MORUS NEGRA Black Mulberry, (Spanish : Morera Negra).

HABIT AND CULTIVATION

Category	Tree
Family	Moraceae
Origin	North Africa
Size, height x spread	12 x 15 metres
Situation	Full sun
Irrigation	Drought tolerant
Temperature	Fully hardy
Evergreen/deciduous	Deciduous
Flowering	Greenish. Insignificant. Spring.
Special features	Edible fruit

The mulberry tree was, some hundreds of years ago, an important tree in Spain as the food crop for the silk worm – the silk industry then being vitally important. The favoured food of the silk worm is the white mulberry tree, whereas humans tend to prefer black mulberries. The trees are fairly quick growing and provide dense shade with their large heart-shaped leaves. The fruits (rather like large raspberries, but sweeter tasting) are ripe towards the end of springtime – humans and birds alike find them delicious! Belonging to the same family as the fig tree, the mulberry is very tolerant of drought and cold night time temperatures. The trees, being fully hardy, will also grow in Northern Europe but it does prefer warm daytime temperatures. An ideal tree for more mountainous areas of the Mediterranean basin. Self fertilising.

Propagation
Autumn sown seed or semi-ripe summer cuttings.

Pruning
Thin out overcrowded branches during winter months.

Problems
Do not plant over paved areas – falling fruit stains badly

Also **MORUS PENDULA**, Weeping Mulberry, (Spanish : Morera Colgante). A very beautiful specimen tree, high grafted with long trailing branches reaching the ground. Fruits as above.

See also **MORUS ALBA**, White Mulberry, (Spanish : Morera Blanca).

MYOPORUM LAETUM Ngaio,
(Spanish : Transparante).

HABIT AND CULTIVATION

Category	Shrub
Family	Myoporaceae
Origin	New Zealand
Size, height x spread	8 x 6 metres
Situation	Full sun or some shade.
Irrigation	Drought tolerant, though better with an occasional soaking
Temperature	To –5°C
Evergreen/deciduous	Evergreen
Flowering	White. Spring and summer
Special features	Poisonous berries

The myoporum family generally are quick, easy and tough and m. laetum is no exception. This is perhaps one of the most popular hedging plants through the Mediterranean area and, although not a stunning beauty, it is certainly extremely useful. Its plus points are speed of growth, evergreen, tolerant to drought, wind resistant, easily propagated (and therefore cheap to buy) and that it can be sheared very severely. Surely, for a hedging plant, one can't ask for much more and this explains its popularity. Its long dark green shiny leaves are attractive enough and it bears small white bell-shaped flowers, often followed by purple-black berries. It can reach tree proportions of 8m or more but is more generally seen pruned.

Propagation
Semi-ripe cuttings in summer.

Pruning
For hedging, it will need to be pruned at least twice a year to keep it under control. Large unwieldy plants can be very severely pruned, back to the trunk, and they will regenerate very quickly and with amazing vigour.

Problems
None.

MYRTUS COMMUNIS Myrtle, (Spanish : Mirto).

HABIT AND CULTIVATION

Category	Shrub
Family	Myrtaceae
Origin	Mediterranean
Size, height x spread	3 x 3 metres
Situation	Full sun or some shade
Irrigation	Becoming drought tolerant
Temperature	To –8°C
Evergreen/deciduous	Evergreen
Flowering	White. Spring
Special features	Scented flowers and foliage.

The common myrtle is known to have been around for some 2000 years and has been much used in the Mediterranean area for formal hedging and topiary work, much as box is in colder climates. It is a very neat and attractive shrub, with an abundance of mid green leaves, which are aromatic when crushed. It is a prolific spring flowerer with small white cup shaped flowers with a central boss of prominent stamens, the flowers also being sweetly scented. The blue-black berries are edible. It is drought and heat tolerant and very easy to grow given good drainage and little water. A very traditional planting which, sadly, has lost some of its popularity more due to fashion change than any practical reason.

Propagation
Spring sown seed or semi-ripe summer cuttings.

Pruning
Tip prune constantly to keep good tight shape but will also accept harder pruning in early spring.

Problems
Occasional mildew.

NANDINA DOMESTICA Heavenly Bamboo, Sacred Bamboo, (Spanish : Nandina).

HABIT AND CULTIVATION

Category	Shrub
Family	Berberidaceae
Origin	China and Japan
Size, height x spread	3 x 1 metres
Situation	Full sun or some shade
Irrigation	Drought tolerant but better with some watering
Temperature	To – 10°C
Evergreen/deciduous	Deciduous
Flowering	Pinkish white. Spring
Special features	-

Although this shrub is not a true bamboo, it does resemble one with its elegant cane-like stems and long, sheathed leaves. The advantage with this look alike is that it is not invasive and although it will reach some 3m tall, it only has a spread of about 1m. and is very contained. The new foliage is a handsome reddish colour and in autumn it turns orange, bronze and purple-red before leaf fall, admittedly better in cooler areas. The pretty pinkish-white flowers are held in clusters at the ends of the branches with red berries later (females only). Can also be grown to great effect in a pot.

Propagation
Semi ripe summer cuttings.

Pruning
Thin out the older branches every couple of years. Clean plant generally after growing season to remove litter.

Problems
Can be prone to chlorosis in alkaline soils. Dose with iron chelate.

NEPETA x faassenii, Catmint, (Spanish : Menta de Gatos).

HABIT AND CULTIVATION

Category	Perennial
Family	Labiatae
Origin	-
Size, height x spread	0.5 x 1 metres
Situation	Full sun or some shade
Irrigation	Occasional summer soaking
Temperature	To –10°C
Evergreen/deciduous	Top growth dies down in cold conditions
Flowering	Lavender-blue. Spring and summer
Special features	Aromatic. Adored by cats!

Catmint is a bushy mounding perennial with greyish-green leaves that are aromatic when crushed. Beware frantic, frenzied felines who will roll in the plant and crush it! The nepeta comes from the Italian town of Nepete, where the plant was cultivated for medicinal purposes, being a sedative and good for stomach disorders. The leaves are also mildly hallucinogenic. The upright flower spikes carry hundreds of small lavender blue flowers, which combined with the grey green foliage create a soft misty look invaluable between stronger colour plantings. Any reasonable soil will suit this easy and pretty herb, which is useful for edging, between paving and mixed plantings.

Propagation
Softwood cuttings in spring and summer or by plant division in early spring.

Pruning
Shear after flowering to promote a further flush of flowers. Old straggly plants can be regenerated by cutting down to 15cm in winter.

Problems
None

NERIUM OLEANDER Oleander, (Spanish : Adelfa).

HABIT AND CULTIVATION

Category	Shrub
Family	Apocynaceae
Origin	Mediterranean
Size, height x spread	5 x 4 metres
Situation	Happiest in full sun but will tolerate partial or even full shade.
Irrigation	Drought tolerant
Temperature	To –5°C
Evergreen/deciduous	Evergreen
Flowering	White, apricot, pinks, red. Spring, summer and autumn
Special features	Highly poisonous

The oleander is one of the mainstays of Mediterranean gardening and is deservedly so popular. It is an immensely useful and long flowering shrub with numerous uses. It makes a very effective screening and windbreak planting, a long flowering hedging plant, a very pretty specimen shrub and an enchanting small, slightly weeping tree. Add to this its large colour range, with flowers in singles and doubles, and the fact that it is evergreen and extremely tolerant and it is easy to see why it is so used and yet never becomes overused! Found growing naturally in rocky ravines where some water is available until early summer, try to emulate this in your garden. Stop watering as we enter summer and your plants will be happy. But this is a shrub that will grow in arid situations as well as in brackish, salty water. Flowering will be reduced in shady spots. Perhaps its only drawback is that all parts of the plant are extremely poisonous, though also very bitter tasting – so much so that even goats leave it alone. But take care, even when burning prunings, as inhaled smoke can cause severe problems.

Propagation
Stem cuttings will root easily in water.

Pruning
Prune individual branches to promote branching. Do not shear as this greatly disfigures the plant.

Problems
Scale insect which can set up fungal infections

NICOTIANA ALATA syn. affinis, Tobacco Plant, (Spanish : Planta del Tabaco).

HABIT AND CULTIVATION

Category	Perennial
Family	Solanaceae
Origin	South America
Size, height x spread	1 x 0.30 metres
Situation	Full sun or dappled shade
Irrigation	Regular summer watering
Temperature	To 0°C or grow as annual
Evergreen/deciduous	Evergreen
Flowering	White. Spring and summer
Special features	Scented

The tobacco plant is an ornamental species of the family long cultivated for tobacco. A short lived perennial it is often grown as an annual especially in cooler climates. Its main attractions are its delightfully scented flowers, particularly noticeable on hot sultry summer evenings. Although many new strains and new colours are constantly coming onto the market, it is the original N. alata that is, for me, still the best. Its beautiful pure white funnel shaped flowers mainly open at dusk and they have a wonderful haunting perfume that the newer varieties have not yet approached. The leaves are oval and mid-green forming basal rosettes and are somewhat sticky and unpleasant to the touch.

Propagation
Spring sown seed.

Pruning
None. Dead head.

Problems
Watch for slugs and snails on newly emerging leaves and caterpillars.

OENOTHERA SPECIOSA

Evening Primrose, (Spanish: Enotera, Onegra, Primavera de Tarde).

HABIT AND CULTIVATION

Category	Perennial
Family	Onagraceae
Origin	North America
Size, height x spread	0.50 x 0.50 metres
Situation	Full sun or partial shade
Irrigation	Drought tolerant
Temperature	To –10°C
Evergreen/deciduous	Top growth dies back in cold conditions
Flowering	Whiteand pink. Spring and summer
Special features	Scented

The evening primrose is drought tolerant and likes stony, thin or sandy soils. Under these poor conditions it will give of its best and be smothered in open cup-shaped white flowers, ageing to pink, all through spring and summer. The scented flowers open in the evening and are short lived but produced in great abundance. They are pollinated by night flying insects and waft a soft haunting evening fragrance. The plants are clump forming with narrow dark green leaves and they spread by rhizomes. Take care, when happy these beautiful plants can become somewhat invasive, but an ideal planting for a hot sunny bank. Oil is extracted from the seeds and much used in the pharmaceutical and natural medicine industries.

Propagation
From seed or plant division in spring. Also softwood cuttings in late spring.

Pruning
Trim over exuberant growth.

Problems
Dislikes overhead summer irrigation and can rot.

Also **OENOTHERA MISSOURIENSIS**, 0.10 X 0.50 metres. Spreading perennial with large lemon yellow flowers.

Olea Europaea (Olive Tree)

According to legend, Zeus asked all his Gods to offer to him the most useful gift. Competition was fierce and the two front runners were Athena and Poseidon. Poseidon created the horse which could be used in battle; Athena created the olive tree to nourish the people and help protect them from illness – a gift to humanity. Zeus chose 'the tree of peace' and awarded to Athena the protection of the city, since known as Athens. Thereon the olive symbolically represented a divine blessing and the whole tradition of the olive wreath of peace and the crowning of our Olympiads stems from this legend.

There is archaeological evidence that olive trees existed as long ago as 8,000B.C. and the trees first seem to have been cultivated in Crete and Syria. From there they were introduced to Greece, Italy and Spain. The trade in olive oil was an essential part of the building of the Roman Empire and as demand for the rich oil increased, so olive trees were planted all around the Mediterranean and well into Africa. They are not native to the Americas and are thought to have reached there with early Spanish settlers. They were introduced into California during the 1800's, where they were widely planted and then later introduced also into South Africa and Australia.

The production of olives, and their oil, is the mainstay of employment and economy in many rural agricultural areas. Today there are approximately 800 million olive trees throughout the world and some 2,500 million litres of olive oil are annually produced. Of this figure, 80% is produced within the E.U., who also consume 70% of the world's olive oil. Whilst 90%

of the crop is used for oil, Spain is also the world's largest producer of table olives with some 25% of the market. Over 5,000,000 hectares of land in the E.U. are down to olive groves, and one third of all E.U. farmers are olive growers.

The most popular cultivars in Spain for oil are 'hojiblanca' and for olives 'manzanilla' and 'gordal'. Pollination is by wind and huge numbers of flowers are produced to this purpose, often causing great problems to allergy sufferers. The crops are picked in late autumn/winter, generally by hand or with a mechanical shaker. The trees tend to be alternate bearing, with a good cropping year usually being followed by a poorer.

The world market is still steadily expanding as the health benefits of this oil are increasingly appreciated. It is very high in monounsaturated fat (oleic acid) and in polyunsaturated fat (linoleic acid), both now recognised as an important factor in reducing heart disease. 'The Mediterranean Diet', of which the cornerstone is olive oil, is becoming increasingly cited as an aid in the prevention of many chronic diseases. Together with grapes, figs, almonds and dates this is one of our most traditional crops and yet still one of the most valued.

OLEA EUROPAEA
Olive, (Spanish : Olivo).

HABIT AND CULTIVATION

Category	Tree
Family	Oleaceae
Origin	Mediterranean
Size, height x spread	8 x 6 metres
Situation	Full sun
Irrigation	Drought resistant
Temperature	To –5°C
Evergreen/deciduous	Evergreen
Flowering	White/yellow. Spring
Special features	Edible crop. High pollen emission

The olive tree is one of the enduring emblems of the Mediterranean landscape and an essential part of the economy of many countries. Traditional life in the area is still largely centred on the tree and its crop, which as well as being pressed for various grades of oil, are also picked and cured for eating. One of the most planted is the variety 'manzanillo' which is lower growing and with a more spreading canopy than most making it ideal for cropping. Many of the trees seen on the terraced Mediterranean hillsides are very old and form twisted and gnarled shapes with maturity. The trunks are grey and the long thin leaves tough and silver backed. Flowering is in spring and generally prolific and can cause problems to allergy sufferers. Cropping starts around the end of the year, depending on variety, and continues through to February or March.

Propagation
Trees are generally grafted, though 'wild' trees spring up from fruits dropped by birds.

Pruning
Carry out after cropping to shape tree and top out. Remove basal suckers.

Problems
Scale insects and black soot. Plant in open sunny spot with good air circulation to avoid.

OLEARIA ARBORESCENS Daisy Bush, (Spanish : Olearia).

HABIT AND CULTIVATION

Category	Shrub
Family	Compositae
Origin	Australia and New Zealand
Size, height x spread	5 x 3 metres
Situation	Full sun
Irrigation	Moderate summer watering
Temperature	To –5°C
Evergreen/deciduous	Evergreen
Flowering	White. Summer
Special features	-

The daisy bushes are some of the easiest and most attractive shrubs for our Mediterranean climate gardens. In full flow, the bush is an impressive sight, being smothered in daisy flowers. O. arborescens forms a large many-branched shrub with oval serrated leaves and dense panicles of white daisy flowers throughout late spring and summer. They form excellent windbreak and shelter plantings, and even thrive in very exposed salt-laden coastal conditions. Unfussy to soil type, they will settle well into quite alkaline conditions or poor thin soils but do need some summer watering. Do not cultivate around the roots, they are shallow rooting and dislike disturbance. Adding a thick annual mulching helps.

Propagation
Semi-ripe summer cuttings

Pruning
Trim over after flowering to promote further flower flushes and keep bushes tidy. Prune by about half annually, in late winter to prevent bushes from becoming straggly. Take out any dead wood at same time.

Problems
None

OPUNTIA FICUS-INDICA Prickly Pear,
Barbary Fig, (Spanish : Chumbera).

HABIT AND CULTIVATION

Category	Succulent
Family	Cactaceae
Origin	Mexico
Size, height x spread	5 x 5 metres
Situation	Full sun
Irrigation	Drought resistant
Temperature	To 0°C
Evergreen/deciduous	Evergreen
Flowering	Yellow. Spring and summer
Special features	Edible fruits. Vicious thorns and irritating hairs.

The prickly pear is one of the most traditional plantings on smallholdings in the Mediterranean area and was often employed as a stout, stock-proof fencing. The plant branches into oblong thick green pads and can reach almost tree-like proportions. Yellow flowers, some 10cm long, are carried along the edges of the pads during spring and summer and these turn into edible pear-shaped fleshy golden-red fruits. Do not attempt to touch any part of the plant or fruit without some stout gloves. The pads are covered in vicious thorns and the fruits, seemingly innocent and inviting, bear a coating of very fine irritant hairs. The fruits, once peeled, are very juicy and quite tasty. Plant well away from pathways etc. and areas where young children play.

Propagation
Leaves can be broken off and planted. Fallen leaves will root into the ground without any help.

Pruning
None

Problems
None

OSTEOSPERMUM FRUTICOSUM Cape Daisy, (Spanish : Osteospermum).

HABIT AND CULTIVATION

Category	Perennial
Family	Compositae
Origin	South Africa
Size, height x spread	0.50 x 1 metres
Situation	Full sun
Irrigation	Drought tolerant once established
Temperature	To –5˚C
Evergreen/deciduous	Evergreen
Flowering	White, yellow, pink, purple. Winter and spring
Special features	-

The Cape daisy is a quick and pretty filler for our gardens, equally useful in mixed plantings, front row to shrubs, in rockeries and for dry banks. It spreads on long leafed stems to form dense groundcover and can easily reach a metre or more across. The daisy flowers are quite large and range through a bright, sparkling white, buttermilk yellow, soft pinks to a deep rich purple. All the colours have their own special appeal and easily blend into planting schemes. It only asks for a warm sunny position, well-drained soil and an occasional mulching to keep the root run cooler. Look for one called 'whirlygig' which has spooned petals and is unusually eye-catching.

Propagation
Self seeds readily. Cuttings of non-flowering shoots in mid-summer.

Pruning
A light pruning after flowering confines its spreading habit. Old straggly plants can be hard pruned to rejuvenate.

Problems
None.

PAPAVER SOMNIFERUM Opium Poppy,
(Spanish : Adormidera).

HABIT AND CULTIVATION

Category	Annual
Family	Papaveraceae
Origin	Middle East
Size, height x spread	0.75 x 0.30 metres
Situation	Full sun
Irrigation	Moderate summer watering
Temperature	-
Evergreen/deciduous	-
Flowering	White, pinks, lilacs, purple, red. Spring and summer.
Special features	Highly poisonous

The opium poppy has achieved fame and notoriety for its extractions rather than for its beauty. But it is also a very elegant yet easy garden plant with grey-green glaucous foliage, serrated at the leaf edges. The large and delicate looking flowers are produced during spring and summer in white and red and a range of soft pinks/lilacs. These can be single or double and many are blotched in the eye. The word opium is derived from the Greek opion, meaning poppy juice. All parts of the plant, apart from the mature seeds, are highly poisonous. The latex exuded is used by the pharmaceutical industry to obtain morphine, thebaine, codeine, narcotine, papaverine and narceine. These drugs have not yet been superceded by any synthetic product. The growing of opium poppies in any bulk is strictly prohibited, but a few plants in the garden are acceptable, and most garden varieties do not have the narcotic strength of the species.

Propagation
Spring sown seed, though will also self seed readily.

Pruning
None, simply deadhead.

Problems
None.

PARKINSONIA ACULEATA Jerusalem Thorn, Mexican Palo Verde, (Spanish : Palo Verde).

HABIT AND CULTIVATION

Category	Tree
Family	Leguminosae
Origin	Mexico and California
Size, height x spread	6 x 6 metres
Situation	Full sun
Irrigation	Drought tolerant
Temperature	To 0°C
Evergreen/deciduous	Evergreen
Flowering	Yellow. Spring
Special features	Scented. Very vicious thorns

The Jerusalem thorn is an exceedingly tough planting, asking only for the hottest, driest spot. It is a useful colonising tree, growing fairly quickly in very arid conditions. It grows into an extremely light, airy tree with very fine, feathery leaves with a central midrib and long linear leaves with tiny leaflets, creating a weeping effect. The fragrant, 5-petalled yellow flowers are produced in spring in arching racemes. This is a useful planting where some height and bulk is required without producing dense shade and cutting down the light. It is somewhat disliked for its vicious thorns, which can pierce a shoe but, thoughtfully placed, it is pleasing and daintily delicate looking.

Propagation
Soak seeds in water for 24 hours before sowing. Germinates easiest in springtime.

Pruning
Tolerates pruning but generally this spoils its naturally graceful habit. Cut out crossing branches.

Problems
None.

PARTHENOCISSUS TRICUSPIDATA
Boston Ivy, (Spanish : Parra Virgen).

HABIT AND CULTIVATION

Category	Perennial climber
Family	Vitaceae
Origin	China and Japan
Size, height x spread	20 metres x indefinite
Situation	Full sun, dappled or partial shade
Irrigation	Drought tolerant, but better with an occasional watering
Temperature	To –15°C
Evergreen/deciduous	Deciduous
Flowering	Greenish, insignificant. Late spring
Special features	Self clinger

Parthenocissus is from the Greek parthenos, meaning virgen, and kissos, meaning creeper. It is a very beautiful foliage climber and can cover vast areas of walling with its charming snaking branches, and can also look delightful climbing up into an old tree, cypress etc. The 3-lobed leaves, some 20cm, across, unfurl in spring in a deliciously fresh green shade, maturing to a shiny deep green and, in autumn, turning the most wonderful fiery shades before leaf fall. Admittedly this firework show is at its most splendid in cooler climes than our own but it is still stunning here too. The plant climbs by means of tiny sucker like pads, clinging tightly to any surface and closely following the contours of house walls etc. Trim around windows and it will carpet your house.

Propagation
Hardwood cuttings in late spring, or by layering.

Pruning
Cut back, at any time of the year, if becoming invasive.

Problems
None.

PASSIFLORA CAERULEA Hardy Blue Passionflower, (Spanish : Passiflora, Flor de la Pasion).

HABIT AND CULTIVATION

Category	Perennial climber
Family	Passifloraceae
Origin	Brazil and Argentina
Size, height x spread	10 metres x indefinite
Situation	Full sun
Irrigation	Drought tolerant
Temperature	To -5°C
Evergreen/deciduous	Semi-evergreen
Flowering	White and blue. Spring and summer
Special features	Edible fruit

There are approximately 400 species of passionflowers known to us, most originating from the jungles of South America, all with the typical intriguing flower and some with edible fruits. Varying greatly in size of growth and flower colour, there is one for every position. Some of the more delicate are perfect in pots, others can be imagined cutting swathes through their jungle homeland! P. caerulea is the hardiest and, indeed, in our climate can become somewhat invasive. However, if a fast and rampant climber is what you need then this enters on the list of possibilities. It climbs by twining tendrils, the flowers are white, often flushed in pale pink, and with the central corona picked out in a combination of blue and green. The egg sized golden fruits are produced throughout much of the year in great abundance and are edible, though not particularly tasty.

Propagation
Spring sown seed, or semi-ripe summer cuttings.

Pruning
Thin out crowded growth during winter or early spring.

Problems
None.

Also **PASSIFLORA MANICATA**, Flame Passion Flower, (Spanish : Passiflora, Flor de la Pasion). To about 6m with flame red flowers with purple and white coronas. Edible fruit.

See also **PASSIFLORA EDULIS**.

PASSIFLORA EDULIS Edible Passion Flower, Purple Granadilla, (Spanish : Passiflora, Flor de la Pasion).

HABIT AND CULTIVATION

Category	Perennial climber
Family	Passifloraceae
Origin	Brazil and Paraguay
Size, height x spread	8 metres x indefinite
Situation	Full sun
Irrigation	Occasional summer soaking
Temperature	To 0°C
Evergreen/deciduous	Semi-evergreen
Flowering	White and blue. Spring and summer
Special features	Edible fruits

The edible passion flower is, surprisingly, little grown and yet is easy, quick, beautiful and bears fabulous fruit. It is at its happiest in reasonably good soil, with its feet in shade and growing up into full sun, though it will fairly happily perform with less than ideal conditions. It is slightly coarser growing than P. caerulea with angular stems and larger leaves though similarly clings with tendrils. The flowers are white, often flushed with purple-blue and the inner corona is purple-blue. The fruits start green, ping-pong ball shape and size, turning a deep aubergine colour. As they start to wrinkle, they are ready for eating. Cut open and that delicious aroma sets the mouth watering! The pulp can just be scooped out and eaten, or used in fruit salads, ice creams, sorbets etc. and it is also commercially used in fruit drinks and liqueurs. This is an ideal plant to grow through ugly chain-link fencing, thus keeping the fruit within easy reach.

Propagation
Spring sown seed or sem-ripe summer cuttings.

Pruning
Thin out tangled growth during early spring.

Problems
None.

See also **PASSIFLORA CAERULEA** and **P. MANICATA**.

PAULOWNIA TOMENTOSA Foxglove Tree, Empress or Princess Tree, (Spanish : Paulownia).

HABIT AND CULTIVATION

Category	Tree
Family	Scrophulariaceae
Origin	China
Size, height x spread	15 x 10 metres
Situation	Full sun
Irrigation	Occasional summer soaking
Temperature	To –10°C
Evergreen/deciduous	Deciduous
Flowering	Lilac. Spring
Special features	Scented.

The foxglove tree is grown for its very impressive foliage and beautiful flowers. It grows fairly rapidly and the flowers emerge before the foliage in large upright panicles of very elegant lilac trumpets, heavily scented, and resembling foxgloves. The large lobed leaves later unfurl. Young trees can be stooled every year to get huge, dramatic leaves and the plant will then attain perhaps some 3m in a season. This cutting down to ground level will mean no flowers, but the leaves are so wonderful that, depending upon the siting, this can sometimes be desirable. The timber is also used in Asian countries to make furniture. Plant in rich soil, they are very cold hardy, reasonably drought tolerant and shallow rooting. This can be a difficult plant to buy; if all else fails, try from seed – it is easy and quick.

Propagation
Spring or autumn sown seed. Winter hardwood cuttings.

Pruning
Generally little required, shaping, removing crossing branches etc. For pollarding, cut down to approx. 15cm. early in springtime.

Problems
Although hardy, late frosts can sometimes burn new growth but it will regenerate. Being large-leafed and somewhat brittle branched try and plant out of the wind to avoid excessive damage.

Pelargonium (Geranium)

This is such a popular planting in the Mediterranean basin that few people, perhaps, realise that the genus originates from the Cape area of South Africa, though distribution spreads up through Malawi, Zimbabwe, Kenya, Tanzania, Ethiopia and as far as the Middle East. Commonly, and misleadingly, called geraniums, they belong to the family Geraniaceae. There is much confusion over the nomenclature of this group and it is often presented, for the layman, in an over-detailed form by botanists. So, to cut it down to its absolute simplest, let's look at 4 main groups:

Zonal – plants with fairly rounded leaves, often with a darker central zone or ring. A huge range of flower colours, through white, pinks, reds, salmon and lilac, and available in singles and doubles. These are the ones that most people would call geraniums!

Ivy-leafed – trailing plants wich have similar leaves and flowers to the zonals. These are useful in hanging baskets and pots, trailing down banks, walls etc. Commonly called trailing geraniums.

Regal – these are shrubby, woody perennials with stiff, pleated leaves. The large flowers are often blotched or two-coloured. Usually known as pelargoniums.

Scented-leafed and species – not so showy as the above, these plants usually have smaller leaves, many with silky hairs, and flowers in pale colours. The scented-leafed varieties are grown for their aromatic foliage, the flowers usually being fairly insignificant. Often known as species or hardy geraniums and scented geraniums.

Because of their huge adaptibility and range of brilliantly coloured flowers, there are probably few gardeners who have never grown pelargoniums. The genus is composed of more than 250 species, the majority of which are native to South Africa. The name stems from the Greek 'pelargos' meaning 'stork' from the shape of the seed heads. One of the common names of this family is cranesbill, though nowadays this name has somewhat fallen into disuse. Some of the family members are commercially important as sources of geranium oil, particularly p. graveolens, p. odoratissimum and p. capitatum, which is used in the food and perfume industries and in the production of insecticides. Many of our most common insects dislike the aroma emitted by pelargoniums and they are a very successful companion plant.

During the 17th. century plant hunters in South Africa were sending back to Northern Europe a huge range of plants, at first those for medicinal purposes but then later more decorative types too. The wealthy started a 'fashion boom' breeding and hybridising pelargoniums and other plants in their hothouses, reaching a peak during the Victorian era. During the 19th. century there was great competition between those that could afford it to employ teams of gardeners to create new and ever more spectacular displays of plants in a myriad of colours. The First World War, shortage of labour, and the necessity to produce food, largely brought an end to this and it wasn't until the 1950's that the fashion in pelargoiums saw an upsurge again. Nowadays the plant is generally used for colourful bedding and potwork though, of course, in our climate it is perennial and lends itself to much more imaginative usage, adapting well to a range of conditions.

PELARGONIUM x domesticum, Regal Pelargonium, (Spanish : Pelargonio).

HABIT AND CULTIVATION

Category	Perennial
Family	Geranaceae
Origin	South Africa
Size, height x spread	1 x 0.5 metres
Situation	Full sun
Irrigation	Becoming drought tolerant, but better with an occasional summer soaking
Temperature	To 0°C
Evergreen/deciduous	Evergreen
Flowering	White, pinks, lilacs, purple, red. Spring and autumn
Special features	-

The regal pelargoniums are generally considered more as a garden planting - they can also be used in pots though they do not flower as prolifically as p. x zonale. They are woody and more shrub-like with a distinct flowering season, mainly spring with a lesser flowering in autumn. They have stiff pleated leaves and exotic clusters of flowers in a large range of colours, often blotched or two-toned. They can turn straggly with age and are better replaced.

Propagation
Softwood cuttings, spring to autumn

Pruning
Cut back after flowering to promote bushiness.

Problems
Is also affected by the geranium moth but not so badly as it is woodier stemmed. Also mealy bug.

Also **SCENTED LEAFED - PELARGONIUM CRISPUM** (lemon scented), **P. x fragrans** (pine scented), **P. GRAVEOLENS** (rose scented) and **P. TOMENTOSUM** (peppermint scented). All like hot, dry, sunny conditions and will aromatically groundcover – perfect for edging pathways. Seem to be unaffected by geranium moth and, in fact, can be used as companion plants for other pelargoniums to deter the moth.

PELARGONIUM x zonale, Geranium, (Spanish : Geraneo).

HABIT AND CULTIVATION

Category	Perennial
Family	Geranaceae
Origin	South Africa
Size, height x spread	Up to 40 x 30 metres
Situation	Full sun
Irrigation	Moderate summer watering
Temperature	To 0°C
Evergreen/deciduous	Evergreen
Flowering	White, pinks, lilacs, salmon, red. Almost constantly
Special features	-

The zonal geranium is one of our most colourful and popular plants, hard to beat for its sheer flower power. It is immensely useful in pots and baskets, on balconies, roof terraces, patios etc. It is one of the most enduring images of the Mediterranean area, potfuls of brilliant geraniums stacked on village house balconies. It is usually grown as an annual in colder climates, but here it is perennial and, indeed, can achieve bush-like proportions in the open garden. In the ground, emulate conditions in South Africa – give them plenty of sun, poor soil and only an occasional summer watering. They dislike being fussed over and over-watering and fertilising can kill them. Obviously, the situation in pots is different – here they will need regular, though not excessive, watering and feeding.

Propagation
Softwood cuttings from spring through to autumn.

Pruning
Deadhead regularly to tidy plants and promote further flowers. Tip prune for bushiness.

Problems
A fairly new and devastating introduction is the geranium moth. Control with specific systemic insecticides or, organically, with Neem oil.

Also **PELARGONIUM IVY LEAFED**, Trailing Geranium, (Spanish : Gitanillas). Trailing form of the above. Same care. New hybrids and cultivated garden varieties are constantly being produced in both.

Pennisetum Orientale

PENNISETUM SETACEUM African Fountain Grass, (Spanish : Penisetum).

HABIT AND CULTIVATION

Category	Grass
Family	Gramineae
Origin	Africa
Size, height x spread	1 x 0.50 metres
Situation	Full sun or dappled shade
Irrigation	Occasional summer watering
Temperature	To –5°C
Evergreen/deciduous	Semi-evergreen
Flowering	Copper red. Autumn and winter
Special features	-

The African fountain grass is a clump forming decorative grass that is very attractive as a feature planting or inter-planted between shrubs. It has very rough and narrow mid-green leaf blades. In late summer the dense conical heads of flowers begin to appear and last well through the winter. The coppery red colouring and long bristles look very attractive with a late autumn afternoon sun shining through them. Try them also in front of a row of dark green cypress trees, the contrast is telling. A well behaved grass which stays nicely clumped.

Propagation
From spring sown seed or plant division.

Pruning
Cut back dead foliage and flower stalks during dormant months.

Problems
None.

Also **PENNISETUM ORIENTALE**, Japanese Fountain Grass, (Spanish : Penisetum Orientale). As above but with very striking purple-bronze foliage and long lasting coffee coloured flower spikes. A very unusual and attention calling colour combination.

PEROVSKIA ATRIPLICIFOLIA Russian Sage, (Spanish : Perovskia).

HABIT AND CULTIVATION

Category	Shrub
Family	Labiatae
Origin	Pakistan
Size, height x spread	1.25 x 0.5 metres
Situation	Full sun
Irrigation	Drought tolerant
Temperature	To –10°C
Evergreen/deciduous	Deciduous
Flowering	Lavender-blue. Summer and autumn
Special features	Aromatic foliage

The Jerusalem sage is the sort of plant that will fit into any garden and will become one of your favourites. It likes hot, dry, sunny situations and quite poor soil. It has wonderful colouring, which contrasts splendidly with other more vibrant plantings and can add a touch of coolness and yet is a very pretty plant within its own right. The coarsely toothed leaves and stems are a subtle silver-grey and aromatic and contrast delightfully with the hazy lavender-blue flower spikes of summer and autumn. It forms an open shrublet with a somewhat snaking form and is equally happy in windy and salty coastal conditions as in cooler mountainous areas.

Propagation
Softwood cuttings in spring. Also by plant division in autumn.

Pruning
Deadhead to promote further flower flushes. Cut old growth on plants back to the base as the new spring growth starts.

Problems
None

PHASEOLUS CARACALLA Snail Plant,
(Spanish : Viña de Caracol).

HABIT AND CULTIVATION

Category	Perennial climber
Family	Leguminosae
Origin	South America
Size, height x spread	5 x 2 metres
Situation	Full sun
Irrigation	Occasional summer watering
Temperature	To 0°C
Evergreen/deciduous	Semi-evergreen
Flowering	White, yellow and purple. Summer
Special features	Scented

The snail plant is an utterly delightful climber – try it, you'll love it. It has soft green foliage composed of three leaflets on twining woody stems and is a fairly rapid perennial climber. The flowers are perfect replicas of snails' shells and open creamy white, maturing to a lilac purple and fading to a delicious honey yellow. All colours are held on the plant at the same time and the effect is enchanting – and enhanced even more by the sweet perfume that will carry several metres on a hot day. It bears long bean-like seed pods after flowering, and belongs to the same family as runner and haricot beans. The name phaseolus comes from the Greek word phaselos meaning 'little boat', supposedly because of the appearance of the pod. It likes a fairly rich soil and some watering during the hotter months but is otherwise easy and obliging. Always causes comment - and admiration - in the garden.

Propagation
Spring sown seed.

Pruning
Thin out crowded stems or cut back hard the tangled growth in early spring.

Problems
None.

PHILADELPHUS CORONARIUS Mock Orange, (Spanish : Celindo).

HABIT AND CULTIVATION

Category	Shrub
Family	Hydrangeaceae
Origin	Europe
Size, height x spread	3 x 2
Situation	Full sun or partial shade
Irrigation	Occasional summer watering
Temperature	To –10°C
Evergreen/deciduous	Deciduous
Flowering	Creamy white. Spring.
Special features	Scented

The mock orange is one of the most popular flower-bearing shrubs in our gardens, mainly because of its pretty, fresh looks and delightful orange blossom perfume. Performing best in a fertile and well-drained soil, they are very versatile. In very hot inland areas they are best with some afternoon shade and will become almost drought tolerant though look better with a soaking every couple of weeks through the hotter months. They bear mid-green oval leaves on an upright shrub, somewhat prone to suckering. The flowers are open cup-shaped, held in terminal clusters. There are some species that are variegated and others with frilly double flowers, but for perfume the single is generally the best. The flowers are also good cut for indoor arrangements.

Propagation
Softwood cuttings in summer.

Pruning
After flowering, cut out some of the older shoots to make space for new young flowering growth.

Problems
Aphids.

PHLOMIS FRUTICOSA Jerusalem Sage, (Spanish : Candilera).

HABIT AND CULTIVATION

Category	Shrub
Family	Labiatae
Origin	Southern Europe
Size, height x spread	1 x 0.75 metres
Situation	Full sun
Irrigation	Drought tolerant
Temperature	To –5°C
Evergreen/deciduous	Evergreen
Flowering	Yellow. Late spring and summer.
Special features	-

The Jerusalem sage associates well with other drought tolerant Mediterranean natives such as lavender, rosemary, brooms and gorse, rock and sun roses. It is frost, drought, alkaline and salt tolerant, making it an extremely versatile and useful planting. It looks very good in natural gardens amongst shrubs and will cling to rough banks and dry and rocky hillsides. Coastal gardeners find this one a winner too. It also associates well with mixed border plantings. From amongst the sage-like, slightly woolly, wrinkled green leaves, stout flower stems shoot up with strangely attractive, whorled and hooded flowers – a deep golden-yellow colour. These are produced in great abundance throughout the summer months. This is an undemanding, yet quietly showy plant.

Propagation
Autumn sown seed or softwood cuttings in summer.

Pruning
Prune back by about half after flowering and tidy away dead leaves etc.

Problems
Mealy bug.

PHLOX SUBULATA Moss Phlox, Creeping Phlox, (Spanish : Estrellita).

HABIT AND CULTIVATION

Category	Perennial
Family	Polemoniaceae
Origin	North America
Size, height x spread	0.10 x 0.50 metres
Situation	Full sun or lightly dappled shade
Irrigation	Moderate summer watering
Temperature	To –10°C
Evergreen/deciduous	Evergreen
Flowering	White, pink, lilac. Spring and summer
Special features	-

The name 'phlox' means flame, and it aptly describes these very colourful little ground coverers, which smother themselves in blossom during spring and summer. They are ideal for rock gardens, where they will form large mats of foliage. The soft green mounds of foliage are composed of very fine, needle-like leaves, which erupt into a profusion of flat star-shaped flowers with notched petals with a colour range from white, pale pinks, rosy pinks to lilacs. In particularly arid inland areas, they are better with a little light shade. They are also very pretty in spring pots and the plants can later be moved to the garden.

Propagation
Cuttings from non-flowering shoots in spring and early summer. Large plants can also be divided in very early spring.

Pruning
Trim over after flowering.

Problems
In confined areas can be prone to powdery mildew.

PHOENIX CANARIENSIS Phoenix Palm, Canary Island Palm, (Spanish : Palmera de Canarias).

HABIT AND CULTIVATION

Category	Tree
Family	Palmae
Origin	Canary Isles
Size, height x spread	18 x10 metres
Situation	Full sun
Irrigation	Drought resistant
Temperature	To 0°C or lower if kept dry.
Evergreen/deciduous	Evergreen
Flowering	Brownish yellow. Summer
Special features	-

The phoenix palm is the most common palm planting in the Mediterranean climate belt and one of the most widespread palms in the world. It generally has a solitary trunk, up to 1m in diameter and long mid-green feathery leaves on a stout stem with a central valley. The lower leaflets develop into very sharp spines - take extreme care when handling. Very showy clusters of orange fruits, each some 5cm. long and 10cm wide, which are not edible. There is often confusion between the Canary Island and date palms. Basically, the Canary Island has a stouter trunk, which almost always grows upright; the date palm has a finer trunk and is often curved – as romantically portrayed in postcards etc! The date palm also has greyer leaves and less of them, it does not make such a luxuriant head of foliage as the Canary Island – and, of course, it has larger and edible fruits. Plant the phoenix palm allowing plenty space for the head to develop. To encourage a more rapid growth rate water during summer months only though, once established, irrigation is not needed.

Propagation
Summer sown seeds, they need over 25C to germinate. Large trees can be transplanted but should have their crowns tied up and be propped until re-established.

Pruning
Lower dying leaves need to be cut off.

Problems
Palm beetle

See also **PHOENIX DACTYLIFERA**.

PHOENIX DACTYLIFERA Date Palm, (Spanish : Palmera Datilera).

HABIT AND CULTIVATION

Category	Tree
Family	Palmae
Origin	Mediterranean
Size, height x spread	24 x 8 metres
Situation	Full sun
Irrigation	Drought resistant
Temperature	To 5°C
Evergreen/deciduous	Evergreen
Flowering	Yellow-brown. Spring and summer
Special features	Edible fruit. Both sexes of tree needed.

The date palm has been cultivated for at least 5000 years - the dates, once dried, keeping for very long periods without deterioration and therefore a very useful crop. It is smaller than P. canariensis with a thinner, and often curved, trunk – perhaps 0.30 diameter. The crown is scantier and the leaves are stiffer and have a distinctive grey tinge to them. Both sexes are needed to fruit, but the male produces such an abundance of pollen that 1 male is sufficient for up to 100 females – quite a harem! A mature female tree can produce around 45kg. of dates. But the tree has been adapted for many other uses too. The trunk is used for furniture, the leaves for brushes, the leaflets for weaving into baskets and hats, the stones of the dates for animal fodder and a type of coffee, from the sap is extracted a syrup for palm honey and a sweet, milky liqueur and the sweet and tender heart is used in salads – a sad practice that kills the tree! Cultivation as P. canariensis.

Propagation
From seed at over 25°C. Also from basal suckers. Large palms can be transplanted but should have the crowns tied up and be propped until re-established.

Pruning
Cut down outside dying leaves.

Problems
Palm beetle.

See also **PHOENIX CANARIENSIS**.

PHORMIUM TENAX New Zealand Flax,
(Spanish : Phormium).

HABIT AND CULTIVATION

Category	Perennial
Family	Agavaceae
Origin	New Zealand
Size, height x spread	3 x 2 metres
Situation	Full sun
Irrigation	Drought tolerant
Temperature	To –5˚C
Evergreen/deciduous	Evergreen
Flowering	Dull red. Spring and summer
Special features	-

The New Zealand flax, thus named for the fibres obtained from its leaves, is large and extremely tough and makes a handsome and bold architectural planting. It has giant, sword-like leaves radiating in fans, which spread in clumps. The towering flower stalks are a zig-zag shape with dull red tubular flowers in clusters, again very striking. It works well in mixed plantings, amongst large rocks and in gravel areas and looks particularly good against a clear blue sky or a simple background, white wall etc. There are several varieties available apart from the plain green; an attractive green and cream variegated, a very striking and useful bronze-purple colour and a dazzling bronze, salmon pink and yellow combination. Although drought tolerant, it grows more extravagantly with an occasional watering and is unfussy to soil. This is a good coastal planting too.

Propagation
Spring sown seed or by plant division.

Pruning
Pull off dead outer leaves.

Problems
Can be prone to rot, do not overwater.

PHYLLOSTACHYS BAMBUSOIDES
Hedge or Timber Bamboo,
(Spanish : Bambu).

HABIT AND CULTIVATION

Category	Perennial Bamboo
Family	Bambusoideae
Origin	China
Size, height x spread	6 metres x indefinite
Situation	Full sun, partial or dappled shade
Irrigation	Regular summer watering
Temperature	To −15°C
Evergreen/deciduous	Evergreen
Flowering	Flowering very rare, can happen once in 100 years, and the plant will then die.
Special features	Can be invasive

The bamboos generally are wonderfully structural plants, adding definite impact to a garden yet without being in any way heavy and overpowering. The sun/shade patterns created by the vertical stems with horizontal banding can be stunning. The plants actually become very drought tolerant, but they always look better with water – the problem then is that they can become very invasive. The 'canes', known as 'culms', grow from a branching underground rhizome that produces long offshoots before sending up more culms. Try and plant them in a contained situation, in a pot or well-constructed planter that the roots cannot break through. P. bambusoides makes a wonderful hedge, as illustrated, if contained both sides with metal. In China it can reach 10m high with 15cm diameter culms, but those dimensions will not be achieved here. Highly cultivated in Japan for bamboo poles, with the aid of a fertilisation and pruning programme.

Propagation
By plant division. Cut through thick root system with sharp spade or machete.

Pruning
Cut out old canes and any over-vigorous growth.

Problems
Only invasiveness

PINUS PINEA Stone Pine, Umbrella Pine, (Spanish : Pino Piñonero).

HABIT AND CULTIVATION

Category	Tree
Family	Pinaceae
Origin	Mediterranean
Size, height x spread	20 x 20 metres
Situation	Full sun
Irrigation	Drought tolerant
Temperature	To -10°C
Evergreen/deciduous	Evergreen
Flowering	Insignificant. Spring
Special features	Edible pine nuts. High pollen emission

The distinctive domed shape of the umbrella pine on a short stout trunk gives it its common name. In its youth it is a quick grower, slowing down as it reaches adulthood. The new needle like leaves are a bluish green and change to a dark green as they mature. It likes sandy soil with, preferably, some moisture around its roots though will grow in more arid mountainous conditions too. It is an excellent pioneer tree that will grow in difficult ground. This is the pine that is also commercially grown for its valuable crop of edible pine nuts, which are held in large, shiny brown cones. A problem for allergy sufferers with its high levels of pollen.

Propagation
From spring sown seed.

Pruning
As the tree develops, prune out any branches developing low down to form the typical umbrella shape. Cut out any dead wood during early spring.

Problems
As with many Mediterranean pines, it is susceptible to Thaumetopoea pityocampa, the processionary caterpillar.

PISTACIA LENTISCUS Mastic Tree, Lentisc, (Spanish : Lentisco)

HABIT AND CULTIVATION

Category	Shrub
Family	Anacardiaceae
Origin	Mediterranean
Size, height x spread	4 x 3 metres
Situation	Full sun
Irrigation	Drought resistant
Temperature	To –5°C
Evergreen/deciduous	Evergreen
Flowering	Insignificant. Spring
Special features	-

The lentisc is one of the classic plants of the Mediterranean maquis and is very widespread and indifferent to heat, drought, wind (both dry and salty) and will take a reasonable degree of cold too. It is a tough survivor, not the most beautiful shrub perhaps, but with its uses. The very leathery leaves turn prettily red with cooler weather and it bears small red then black berries that are edible. It belongs to the same family as the mango. Plants can be trimmed to make a neat and trouble free hedge and it blends in well in natural gardens. Incisions are made in the trunk to extract the mastic, which is used in the manufacture of high quality varnishes.

Propagation
From seed, first soaked 24hrs or from semi-ripe summer cuttings.

Pruning
Can be sheared for hedging and shaping.

Problems
None if grown dry. Root rot can develop in waterlogged soils.

Also **PISTACIA VERA**, Pistachio, (Spanish : Pistachio). A native of Greece and Syria, deciduous and growing to some 8m tall. Cultivated in Greece and California for its edible crop, pistachio nuts. One male tree to five females for pollination.

PITTOSPORUM TENUIFOLIUM Kohuhu, (Spanish : Pitosporo).

HABIT AND CULTIVATION

Category	Shrub/tree
Family	Pittosporaceae
Origin	New Zealand
Size, height x spread	10 x 5 metres
Situation	Full sun or partial shade
Irrigation	Occasional summer watering
Temperature	To –5°C
Evergreen/deciduous	Evergreen
Flowering	Purple. Spring
Special features	Scented

The kohuhu is valued in our gardens as a very attractive foliage shrub or small tree, though the scented flowers too add to its desirability. The developing young growth is a deep purple verging on black colour with mature leaves slowly changing to a calming grey-green, small, rounded and wavy-edged. The spring flowers are purple, tubular and honey scented. It naturally forms a nicely rounded shrub, or lower branches can be pruned to form a small tree, very densely leafed, which makes a good thick background planting or is ornamental enough to be front stage too. A humus rich soil with regular mulching is appreciated with occasional watering through the hotter months.

Propagation
Seed sown in autumn or spring. Also from semi-ripe summer cuttings.

Pruning
Tolerates shaping and lower branches should be removed during the winter months to form a small tree.

Problems
Position out of a cold wind.

PLATANUS ORIENTALIS Oriental Plane, (Spanish : Platano de Sombra).

HABIT AND CULTIVATION

Category	Tree
Family	Platanaceae
Origin	Mediterranean to Himalayas
Size, height x spread	25 x 15 metres
Situation	Full sun
Irrigation	Drought tolerant
Temperature	To –10°C
Evergreen/deciduous	Deciduous
Flowering	Green. Spring
Special features	Peeling and patchy bark. High pollen emission

The oriental plane is a giant of a tree and greatly admired for its shade giving qualities and beauty. It is widely used in Mediterranean climes and is often seen planted along city streets, walkways and in parks. They are extremely tolerant of urban pollution, dry heat, drought, poor and compacted soil and are fully hardy and quick growers. Their trunks are extremely beautiful, pale silvery grey with peeling bark revealing creamy, sometimes pink tinged, patches. The leaves are light green, shiny and palmate with five deep lobes and some 20cm across. Clusters of greenish flowers, which emit vast quantities of fine pollen – beware allergy sufferers - are followed by spherical brown seed cases. Suckers readily – these are best pulled off.

Propagation
Autumn sown seed.

Pruning
Can be hard pruned. Municipal plantings are often pollarded (pruning back to main trunk) and they very quickly regenerate.

Problems
None.

PLUMBAGO CAPENSIS Cape Leadwort, (Spanish : Celestina, Jazmin del Cielo).

HABIT AND CULTIVATION

Category	Shrub
Family	Plumbaginceae
Origin	South Africa
Size, height x spread	5 x 3 metres
Situation	Full sun
Irrigation	Best with regular watering during summer
Temperature	To 0°C
Evergreen/deciduous	Semi-evergreen
Flowering	Blue, white. Spring. Summer and autumn
Special features	-

Plumbago derives from the Latin plumbum for lead, this plant reputedly being used by the ancient Romans against lead poisoning. Traditionally its sap was also used to alleviate toothache and gum inflammation. Nowadays it is more appreciated for its very pretty flower colour, an enchanting sky-blue - though a pure white form is also available. It has small, oblong pale green leaves, the entire plant being slightly sticky, and the phlox-like flowers, held in panicles, are borne through the warmer months. It likes a warm, protected situation and will happily scramble through large bougainvilleas etc. often creating a delightful colour contrast. It is probably at its best rambling, but it can confined and may also be used as a large and informal hedging plant.

Propagation
Semi-ripe summer cuttings and from suckers.

Pruning
Early spring pruning will control its growth.

Problems
Prone to whitefly.

PLUMERIA ACUTIFOLIA Frangipani, (Spanish : Plumaria).

HABIT AND CULTIVATION

Category	Shrub/tree
Family	Apocynaceae
Origin	Mexico
Size, height x spread	4 x 4 metres
Situation	Full sun
Irrigation	Moderate summer watering
Temperature	To 10°C
Evergreen/deciduous	Deciduous
Flowering	White with yellow. Summer and autumn
Special features	Scented flowers. Poisonous sap

The frangipani is grown for its stunningly beautiful flowers. The plant has thick, grey, fleshy, swollen-looking branches and forms a sparsely branched small tree or shrub. The leaves are lance-shaped, dark-green and can reach 30cm long. Each flower unfurls 5 thick waxy petals, a dense creamy-white with a yolk-yellow central eye and with a haunting perfume. There are also varieties with pink and copper flowers and some that combine pink/copper/yellow, though generally they have less perfume. This is a plant that needs warmth, protection and good soil. They can be a little tricky to place because, during the winter when the branches are bare, they are not the most attractive looking of plants. Will take quite happily to pot cultivation. The sap is poisonous.

Propagation
Stem tip cuttings in spring. Allow to callous for 24hrs., then plant.

Pruning
Branch tips can be cut back in spring to induce further branching.

Problems
Red spider mite.

POLYGALA MYRTIFOLIA Milkwort,
(Spanish : Polygala).

HABIT AND CULTIVAT ION

Category	Shrub
Family	Polygalaceae
Origin	South Africa
Size, height x spread	4 x 4 metres
Situation	Full sun, partial or dappled shade
Irrigation	Moderate summer watering
Temperature	To 5°C
Evergreen/deciduous	Evergreen
Flowering	Purple. Autumn, winter and spring
Special features	-

The polygala is principally grown for its attractive purple pea-like flowers with white veins produced over much of the year. The leaves are somewhat glaucous and it forms an erect, well-cloaked shrub, though it has a tendency to be somewhat bare at the base. Disguise this with smaller plantings in front, or it can be trained as a semi-standard, which it lends itself to very easily and thus forms an attractive feature planting. Grow it in a reasonably good soil enriched with humus and, in very hot areas, it will appreciate partial or dappled shade. It also makes an attractive pot plant, but will then require more watering and feeding.

Propagation
Spring sown seed or semi-ripe summer cuttings.

Pruning
Cut back lanky growth after flowering and can be tip pruned during growing season to promote bushier growth.

Problems
Prone to whitefly.

POLYGONUM AUBERTII syn. fallopia aubertii, Russian Vine, Mile-a-Minute plant, Silver Lace Vine, (Spanish : Milla un Minuto, El Vuelo del Novio).

HABIT AND CULTIVATION

Category	Perennial climber
Family	Polygonaceae
Origin	Asia
Size, height x spread	12 metres x indefinite
Situation	Full sun, partial or dappled shade
Irrigation	Occasional summer watering
Temperature	To −10°C
Evergreen/deciduous	Deciduous
Flowering	Creamy white. Summer and autumn
Special features	Can become invasive

This rampant climber has one of my favourite common names in Spanish – el vuelo del novio, the flight of the bridegroom, which exactly explains the speed of growth of this plant, as does its other common name, the mile-a-minute plant! For me it is a rather messy and very difficult to control plant, but if you must have it then plant it where it can smother without problem. It is self-twining with heart-shaped leaves and masses of frothy creamy white flowers, which can turn a pale pink as they mature. Often these are then followed by pinkish-white berries.

Propagation
Semi-hardwood cuttings in summer.

Pruning
Prune hard during the winter months. It can even be cut to the ground if it has become a tangled mess.

Problems
Only in control.

POPULUS ALBA White Poplar, Silver Poplar, Abele. (Spanish : Alamo).

HABIT AND CULTIVATION

Category	Tree
Family	Saliaceae
Origin	Central Europe
Size, height x spread	20 x 12 metres
Situation	Full sun
Irrigation	Drought tolerant though better with some water
Temperature	To −10°C
Evergreen/deciduous	Deciduous
Flowering	Insignificant. Spring.
Special features	Invasive root system

The white poplar is so called for its silky grey bark and the frosty white under-surface to the leaves. It rapidly forms a large conical tree, and being resistant to cold and salt-laden winds therefore makes a good shelter tree. More drought-tolerant than most in the family, it nevertheless does better with a deep soaking now and again. The lobed leaves have waved edges and are a striking dark green on the upper surface and heavily lined with white down underneath – the dancing effect in the wind is very eye-catching. In autumn, the leaves turn a delightful soft yellow before falling. It has two disadvantages. One is that it suckers readily, especially from cut trees and the other is that the roots are deep, wide-spreading and invasive. Do not plant it near to buildings, water tanks etc. Note : The Spanish 'alameda"– a word still much used for tree-lined city walkways - refers to a poplar grove.

Propagation
Hardwood cuttings in winter.

Pruning
Very little, simply removing dead or crossing wood.

Problems
Can be prone to canker and fungal diseases. Invasive roots.

PORTULACA GRANDIFLORA Moss Rose, Sun Plant, (Spanish : Portulaca).

HABIT AND CULTIVATION

Category	Annual succulent
Family	Portulacaceae
Origin	South America
Size, height x spread	0.20 x 0.20
Situation	Full sun
Irrigation	Drought tolerant but best with occasional summer watering.
Temperature	To 5°C
Evergreen/deciduous	-
Flowering	White, yellow, pink, orange, red. Spring and summer
Special features	-

The little moss roses are a delightful summertime plant. They relish hot, sunny and sheltered spots and in return will give you a glorious display of colour through all the hottest months. They look particularly at home in rock gardens, creeping and spreading, and also in gravel gardens where they will spread their colourful carpets. Try them too in summer pots, though with extra water and fertilising to keep them performing well. They have tiny bright green succulent leaves on spreading stems and open bowl-shaped flowers, 2.5cm across, with a central boss of stamens. The colours are jewel bright, pure white, fiery yellows, oranges and reds and a truly shocking pink! The flowers close in dull conditions so choose the sunniest spot, any soil will suffice.

Propagation
From spring sown seed. Will also self seed readily.

Pruning
Deadheading prolongs flowering.

Problems
Aphids.

PUNICA GRANATUM Pomegranate,
(Spanish : Granado).

HABIT AND CULTIVATION

Category	Shrub
Family	Punicaceae
Origin	S. Asia
Size, height x spread	5 x 4 metres
Situation	Full sun
Irrigation	Drought tolerant but better with occasional summer soaking
Temperature	To – 5°C
Evergreen/deciduous	Deciduous
Flowering	Orange/red. Spring
Special features	Edible fruit

Ancient folklore tells us that a man who eats a pomegranate whilst in love with a woman will become immortal! Certainly this fruit has many mythical stories attached to it and it is one of the fruits with the longest history of cultivation. The Latin name is from 'pomuni granatum' which means 'seeded apple' – the given name during the Middle Ages. Although now naturalised through the Mediterranean area and the Middle East, it is a native of Asia and 'Punica' was the ancient name for the city of Carthage, where it was much grown. It is a very attractive shrub, with shiny new red growth with bright scarlet flowers giving way to the juicy, if somewhat seedy, fruit. Drinks, jams and jellies are made from this. The leaves turn a soft yellow before falling. Very tolerant of a wide range of conditions, it can also be trimmed to a hedge and needs high summer temperatures to crop well.

Propagation
Semi-ripe summer cuttings or from suckers.

Pruning
Can be shaped during the dormant months.

Problems
None.

PYRACANTHA ANGUSTIFOLIA
Firethorn, (Spanish : Piracanta).

HABIT AND CULTIVATION

Category	Shrub
Family	Rosaceae
Origin	China
Size, height x spread	3 x 3 metres
Situation	Full sun, dappled or partial shade.
Irrigation	Drought tolerant but better with occasional summer watering
Temperature	To –5°C
Evergreen /deciduous	Evergreen
Flowering	White. Spring
Special features	Very decorative berries

The firethorn is an arching evergreen shrub, very pretty in flower, but probably mainly grown for its long-lasting and colourful berries. It is very dense growing and spiny and acts as a good animal barrier - though not goat proof! - it is often used as informal hedging. The leaves are long and narrow, dark-green above and a silvery felty white below. In springtime the small, 5-petalled white flowers are profusely produced and later followed by very impressive clusters of orange-red berries. It looks particularly good sprawling over large rocks and can also be trained to grow up against a wall. Happy in poor, stony soil and, although they will become drought tolerant, they berry better with an occasional soaking through the hotter months.

Propagation
Semi-ripe summer cuttings

Pruning
Hedging can be left to its own devices. Wall trained plants should have the long shoots shortened back after flowering.

Problems
Fireblight and scab

QUERCUS ILEX Holm Oak, Holly Oak, (Spanish : Encina).

HABIT AND CULTIVATION

Category	Tree
Family	Fagaceae
Origin	Mediterranean
Size, height x spread	25 x 20 metres
Situation	Full sun
Irrigation	Drought tolerant
Temperature	To –5°C
Evergreen/deciduous	Evergreen
Flowering	Insignificant. Spring
Special features	Edible nuts. Invasive roots

The Holm Oak once featured widely in the Mediterranean landscape but, sadly, is now very much depleted. Really only suitable for large gardens, it is a very slow grower but makes an imposing tree with time. The roots go down very deep and are wide-spreading so do not plant near any structures and, although needing abundant winter rainfall, they do not like summer irrigation. The young leaves are holly like, maturing to a glossy dark-green and white felted underneath and the edible acorns are also much appreciated by pigs! It has been much felled in the past for its close-grained, durable and beautiful timber. They will grow on thin rocky soil, and are happy in a coastal frontline situation.

Propagation
From autumn sown acorns.

Pruning
Simply removing dead or crossing wood.

Problems
Can suffer from fungal disease in maturity.

Also **QUERCUS SUBER**, Cork Oak, (Spanish : Alcornoque). To 15m tall with a wide-spreading evergreen crown. Greatly valued for its crop of cork, the dense, soft bark, which is systematically stripped every 7 years.

RESEDA ODORATA Mignonette, (Spanish : Odorata de Reseda).

HABIT AND CULTIVATION

Category	Annual
Family	Resedaceae
Origin	Egypt and Libya
Size, height x spread	0.50 x 0.30 metres
Situation	Full sun, partial or dappled shade
Irrigation	Moderate summer watering
Temperature	To 5°C
Evergreen/deciduous	-
Flowering	White. Summer and autumn
Special features	Scented

Although mignonette is generally classified as an annual, it will usually stay perennial in our climate and will, in any case, self seed to perpetuate itself. It quite rapidly forms an erect and well-branched plant with fresh green oval leaves and the flowers, although unspectacular to look at, have the most wonderful perfume. The name 'reseda' comes from the Latin meaning 'healer/restorer' in reference to its'aphrodisiac' scent and its restorative powers! The conical heads of small star-shaped white blossoms are filled with dark orange stamens and are much loved by bees. Tuck it into odd corners, in protected and sheltered spots where the warmth of the sun can send its scent wafting up to you – any reasonable soil will suit. It is also good in pots and can be cut for indoor posies. This is an unassuming little plant that has lost some of its popularity nowadays and is perhaps generally under-used.

Propagation
Spring sown seed.

Pruning
Dead head to promote further flowering.

Problems
Mildew in widely varying temperatures.

RETAMA MONOSPERMA syn. genista monosperma, Bridal Veil Broom, (Spanish : Retama).

HABIT AND CULTIVATION

Category	Shrub
Family	Leguminoseae
Origin	Mediterranean
Size, height x spread	4 x 3 metres
Situation	Full sun
Irrigation	Drought tolerant
Temperature	To –5°C
Evergreen/deciduous	Deciduous
Flowering	White. Spring
Special features	Scented

This native broom is ideally suited to large and natural type gardens, associating well with other endemic plants, on rocky, poor or sandy ground imitating its natural habitat. The almost leafless whip-like branches form a light and airy arching shrub, of an overall grey-green colour. It is a quick grower, given the poor conditions it grows in, and very pretty in full flower. The strongly scented, white, pea-like flowers smother the slender branches in spring, giving rise to its common name of 'bridal veil broom'. Do not water or fertilise this one – it will not thrive - and will sulk with too much kind treatment. It also dislikes being transplanted, so plant it, give a little water to establish, then leave it alone.

Propagation
Semi-ripe summer cuttings or by autumn sown seed.

Pruning
None necessary but will tolerate shaping if desired.

Problems
None if grown in hard conditions.

RICINUS COMMUNIS Castor Oil Plant, (Spanish : Ricino, Aceite del Echador).

HABIT AND CULTIVATION

Category	Shrub
Family	Euphorbiaceae
Origin	India and Tropical Africa
Size, height x spread	2 x 2 metres
Situation	Full sun
Irrigation	Drought tolerant, though lusher with summer water
Temperature	To –5°C
Evergreen/deciduous	Semi-evergreen
Flowering	Red. Summer
Special features	Seeds highly poisonous

The Castor Oil plant is famous for the laxative powers of its oil, but it is also a very handsome plant with large, exotic, red-tinged leaves, red fluffy flower heads and prickly seed cases. It can look wonderful against a vivid blue sky or brilliant white wall. It is very easy to grow, tolerating poor soil and usually self-seeds in all sorts of inhospitable places. It has been cultivated world wide since very ancient times for the seed oil which the Ancient Egyptians and Orientals used for beautifying their skin and hair. The seeds are highly poisonous, ingestion of even two or three can be fatal, and, unfortunately the seeds are very attractive to children being shiny and prettily marked. The name 'ricinus' is from the Greek meaning a 'tick' (as in the blood sucker) because the seeds look like this insect. During the processing of the oil the toxic ricins are removed leaving the oil safe for usage in medicinal compounds, for skin diseases such as ringworm and it is also commonly used in paint and soap products.

Propagation
Spring sown seed.

Pruning
Assiduous dead-heading stops seeds developing.

Problems
None.

ROMNEYA COULTERI California Tree Poppy, Matilija Poppy, (Spanish : Amapola Arbustiva de California).

HABIT AND CULTIVATION

Category	Shrub
Family	Papaveraceae
Origin	Mexico and California
Size, height x spread	2.5 x 1 metres
Situation	Full sun
Irrigation	Becoming drought tolerant but water initially
Temperature	To –5°C
Evergreen/deciduous	Semi-evergreen
Flowering	White. Spring and summer
Special features	Scented

The California Tree Poppy is a very beautiful woody shrub that in its homeland is so prolific as to be almost out of hand. However, in Europe it can be difficult to establish, though once happy it will grow away at a fast rate. It likes a fairly deep soil, a warm sheltered position and some initial watering but will become more tolerant to all of these with age. It does not like root disturbance, so plant very carefully and do not attempt to grow anything else within its root spread. The deeply-divided, silvery-blue leaves contrast beautifully with the pure white crinkled and satinised petals of the open cup flowers with their central boss of golden stamens. The flowers are sweetly scented, and moderate irrigation during flowering will prolong their life.

Propagation
Spring sown seed or from basal shoots.

Pruning
An annual early spring pruning promotes stronger growth.

Problems
Only in establishment.

ROSA BANKSIAE Lady Banks Rose, Banksian Rose, (Spanish : Rosa Banksia).

HABIT AND CULTIVATION

Category	Perennial climber
Family	Rosaceae
Origin	China
Size, height x spread	10 x 10 metres
Situation	Full sun, partial or dappled shade
Irrigation	Drought tolerant
Temperature	To –5°C
Evergreen/deciduous	Semi-evergreen
Flowering	White or yellow. Spring
Special features	Scented

This delightful climbing rose is little known and planted, though it is a pure charmer! The white version was first discovered in China in 1807 and introduced to the Royal Botanical Gardens at Kew. It was thus named for Lady Banks, the wife of Sir Joseph and then director of Kew. The double yellow was a slightly later introduction via the Calcutta Botanical Gardens. Nowadays we have white or yellow, single or double, with the white perhaps winning on the perfume stakes, being deliciously scented of violets but the soft yellow flowers will melt the coolest heart! It bears fountain-like, fine, thornless shoots with tiny fresh green leaves and clusters of the tiny rosebud like flowers. Relishing a warm protected spot, it looks enchanting tumbling over a wall or out of a dark cypress but can also be grown up a pergola, used as groundcover or even in a pot where its size will be restricted.

Propagation
Semi-ripe summer cuttings.

Pruning
Shorten back long shoots during winter to control growth.

Problems
Occasional mildew.

See also **ROSA RUGOSA**.

ROSA RUGOSA Japanese Rose, Sea Tomato, (Spanish : Rosa Rugosa).

HABIT AND CULTIVATION

Category	Shrub
Family	Rosaceae
Origin	China, Japan and Korea
Size, height x spread	2 x 2 metres
Situation	Full sun, partial or dappled shade
Irrigation	Moderate summer watering
Temperature	To –15°C
Evergreen/deciduous	Deciduous
Flowering	White and violet. Spring and summer
Special features	Scented. Edible hips

R. Rugosa does not seem to be very readily available in Spain though it is an excellent planting choice for our climate being very easy to grow and free from disease. This is one of the toughest of roses, with a long history, and it will do well even in poor sandy soil. It forms an excellent and very pretty hedge full of colour for much of the year. The leaves are a fresh green, heavily wrinkled (rugose) and borne on a very spiny and dense framework. The spring and summer flowers are about 10cm across, either white or a rose-purple colour, single and open cup-shaped with a centre boss of golden stamens. They are deliciously clove-scented and later followed by big, fat hips. These are one of the few species roses that are repeat flowering and it is the parent of many modern introductions.

Propagation
Summer hardwood cuttings.

Pruning
Prune lightly during early winter to shape, especially on hedging plants.

Problems
None.

See also **ROSA BANKSIAE**.

ROSMARINUS OFICINALIS Rosemary, (Spanish : Romero).

HABIT AND CULTIVATION

Category	Shrub
Family	Labiatae
Origin	Mediterranean
Size, height x spread	1 x 0.5 metres
Situation	Full sun
Irrigation	Drought resistant
Temperature	To –5°C
Evergreen/deciduous	Evergreen
Flowering	Blue, white, lilac. Autumn, winter and spring
Special features	Aromatic herb

Rosmarinus takes its name from the Latin names 'ros-marinus' or 'ros maris' meaning 'dew of the sea' because of its propensity for growing in coastal sites, though it is now much more widespread in its natural habitat and can be found growing happily in inland limestone mountainous areas too. In youth it makes an erect, compact shrub with dense green needle-like leaves, though becoming woodier and leggier with old age. The pretty flowers are long lasting, generally in blue but also in white and lilac. Plant it in poor soil and do not fertilise or irrigate, once established. The whole plant is very aromatic and has been used since ancient Greek and Roman times medicinally and in the culinary and perfumery trades.

Propagation
Spring or summer cuttings or by winter layering.

Pruning
Can be pruned to shape but never cut back into old wood.

Problems
None.

Also **ROSMARINUS PROSTRATUS**, Creeping Rosemary, (Spanish : Romero Rastrero). As above but with delightfully snaking branches, which form an excellent tough, but pretty groundcover. To about 25cm high and with an indefinite spread.

RUDBECKIA FULGIDA Coneflower, (Spanish : Rudbeckia).

HABIT AND CULTIVATION

Category	Perennial
Family	Compositae
Origin	North America
Size, height x spread	1 x 0.5 metres
Situation	Sun or shade
Irrigation	Moderate summer watering
Temperature	To –15°C
Evergreen/deciduous	Top growth dies down in cold weather
Flowering	Yellow. Summer and autumn
Special features	-

The coneflower is one of our most spectacular perennials, a mass of flower through summer and autumn. The large golden yellow daisy flowers have a prominent raised black centre, hence their common name. The leaves are thin and lance shaped, somewhat rough, and the flower stalks are strong and erect making this an excellent cut flower too. Plant in normal garden soil in mixed borders to add a splash of colour or amongst shrub plantings. It looks very colourful at the base of a wall or row of cypress trees. Once established and happy with its position, it can become rather rampant – cutting back on watering will contain this tendency.

Propagation
Spring sown seed or by plant division in early spring or late autumn.

Pruning
Deadheading prolongs the flowering season, and the entire plant can be trimmed over after flowering.

Problems
Occasional mildew.

RUSSELIA EQUISETIFORMIS
Coral Plant, (Spanish : Russelia).

HABIT AND CULTIVATION

Category	Shrub
Family	Scrophulariaceae
Origin	Mexico
Size, height x spread	1 x 1 metres
Situation	Full sun, partial or dappled shade
Irrigation	Drought tolerant but better with occasional summer watering
Temperature	To 5°C
Evergreen/deciduous	Evergreen
Flowering	Red. Almost year round
Special features	-

This colourful native of Mexico forms a very slender sub-shrub with many thin reed-like branches lined with tiny green leaves, forming a green fountain which looks very pretty spilling over a wall or tumbling down a bank, at step edges etc. It also makes a useful addition to pots and hanging baskets, its fresh green cascading foliage providing a nice backdrop to other plantings. The showy clusters of scarlet thin tubular flowers cover the plant for much of the year. Plant it in a rich humus soil and mulch annually but otherwise it is not fussy and will take full sun or some shade, better with an occasional watering through the hotter months, but will survive without, and it is happy in a coastal situation. It does not like cold winds and is frost tender, the growths blackening with frost damage.

Propagation
Spring cuttings or plant division.

Pruning
Can be cut back when not in flower to tidy and retain size.

Problems
None.

SALVIA LEUCANTHA Mexican Bush Sage, (Spanish : Salvia).

HABIT AND CULTIVATION

Category	Shrub
Family	Labiatae
Origin	Mexico
Size, height x spread	1 x 1 metres
Situation	Full sun
Irrigation	Drought tolerant
Temperature	To 0°C
Evergreen/deciduous	Evergreen
Flowering	White and purple. Summer and autumn
Special features	Tactile foliage

The Mexican Bush Sage is a very tough member of the large sage family and is very suitable for dry gardens. It has typical sage-like leaves, a dull green on the upper surface, downy white underneath, and wrinkled. In summer and autumn long arching flower branches are produced lined with spikes of woolly white flowers surrounded by a violet calyx. These droop and cascade in a very pretty manner. The entire spike is velvety soft to the touch, the sort of tactile plant that you stroke every time on passing! This is an easy plant, without any great demands, happy in a sunny spot in poor soil. It is drought tolerant and will stand up well to strong and salt-laden winds. Not edible.

Propagation
Softwood cuttings in summer or by plant division in early spring.

Pruning
Cut back plant after flowering to promote fresh new growth.

Problems
None.

Also **SALVIA PATENS**, Gentian Sage, (Spanish : Salvia). Another Mexican native, 60cm x 45cm, full sun or partial shade. Mid-green leaves and whorled gentian blue flowers on upright spikes. Needs a little more water.

See also **SALVIA OFFICINALIS**.

SALVIA OFFICINALIS
Sage, (Spanish : Salvia).

HABIT AND CULTIVATION

Category	Shrub
Family	Labiatae
Origin	Mediterranean
Size. height x spread	0.60 x 1
Situation	Full sun
Irrigation	Occasional summer watering
Temperature	To −10°C
Evergreen/deciduous	Semi-evergreen
Flowering	Purple-blue. Summer
Special features	Aromatic herb

Salvia is from the Latin 'salvere' meaning 'to be in good health' and sage has long been recognised as an important medicinal herb alongside its more modern day usage as a homeopathic medicine, and in the pharmaceutical, perfumery, liqueur and food industries. It is a commercially viable crop in many parts of the world, and reputed to give longevity and wisdom to users! All parts of the plant are strongly aromatic and it has great decorative use in our gardens too. It forms a bushy mound of a shrub with dull grey-green, oblong leaves and whorls of bluish-purple flowers in racemes during summer, loved by bees. There are also 2-tone and 3-tone variegated forms and a purple variety, all of which are very decorative. Try also the deliciously scented pineapple sage.

Propagation
Spring sown seed or softwood summer cuttings.

Pruning
Trim over after flowering but never cut into old wood.

Problems
Mealy bug.

See also **SALVIA LEUCANTHA** and **S. PATENS**.

SANTOLINA CHAMAECYPARISSUS
Cotton Lavender,
(Spanish : Abrotano Hembra).

HABIT AND CULTIVATION

Category	Shrub
Family	Compositae
Origin	Mediterranean
Size, height x spread	0.75 x 1 metres
Situation	Full sun or dappled shade
Irrigation	Occasional summer watering
Temperature	To –5°C
Evergreen/deciduous	Evergreen
Flowering	Yellow. Summer
Special features	Aromatic herb

The cotton lavender is a useful little plant in our gardens and pots, with its silver filigreed and indented foliage providing a telling contrast and foil to many other plantings. In fact the tight button yellow flowers produced through summer are sheared off by some people as they prefer to grow it simply for its foliage. It makes good dense groundcover, a useful bank planting between larger shrubs and perennials and can also be used as a low divider/hedging plant. This is a plant for a sunny position, though in very hot and arid inland situations some dappled shade is acceptable. Plant in normal well drained garden soil that is not too rich.

Propagation
Semi-ripe summer cuttings.

Pruning
Dead head. Old straggly plants can be cut back hard to encourage new basal shoots. Trim over annually after flowering.

Problems
Will not tolerate waterlogged soil and can be short lived if grown in damp and humid conditions.

SCABIOSA CAUCASICA Pincushion Flower, (Spanish : Escabiosa).

HABIT AND CULTIVATION

Category	Perennial
Family	Dipsacaceae
Origin	Caucasus
Size, height x spread	0.50 x 0.50 metres
Situation	Full sun
Irrigation	Occasional summer watering
Temperature	To – 10°C
Evergreen/deciduous	Evergreen
Flowering	White, cream, pink, lavender, violet. Summer and autumn
Special features	Scented

The pin cushion plant is another easy and pretty perennial for our hot summer gardens. So called because of its flower form and shape – domed and with multiple tiny flowers in the centre with protruding filaments giving a pin-cushion effect. The light-green, lance-shaped leaves are mainly basal with a few on the wiry flower stems. The tall-stemmed flowers are long lasting and honey-scented and make good cut flowers for indoor arrangements. Thriving in well-drained and alkaline soils, they mix in well with dense, heavier plantings with their more airy, dainty looks. There are now many hybrids available in a good range of colours, but the original lilac blue is very pretty and has delicate looks.

Propagation
Summer cuttings from young basal shoots, autumn sown seeds or by plant division in early spring.

Pruning
Dead head to promote a longer flowering season.

Problems
None.

SCAEVOLA AEMULA Fan Flower, Blue Shamrock, (Spanish : Escaevola).

HABIT AND CULTIVATION

Category	Perennial
Family	Goodeniaceae
Origin	Australia
Size, height x spread	0.30 x 1 metres
Situation	Full sun, partial or dappled shade
Irrigation	Moderate summer watering
Temperature	To 5°C
Evergreen/deciduous	Evergreen
Flowering	Blue and white. Spring, summer and autumn
Special features	-

The fan flower is a very pretty little plant, often used in pots and hanging baskets, but also entirely suitable for garden use in rockeries, or as colourful short term groundcover. The genus is quite large, mainly being endemic to semi-tropical areas and all have the distinctive 5-petalled flower in a fan shape. This one has mid-green paddle-shaped leaves on a network of spreading stems with very striking sapphire blue flowers with a white throat. In pots they will need regular watering and feeding to keep them in good flower production, but planted into the ground they can make do on considerably less. Start them off in a humus rich soil and give moderate amounts of water and fertiliser. In mild areas, they will stay evergreen and can flower for much of the year.

Propagation
Stem cuttings in spring and summer.

Pruning
Can be cut back to encourage bushiness.

Problems
None.

SCHEFFLERA ACTINOPHYLLA
Queensland Umbrella Tree,
(Spanish : Arbol Paraguas).

HABIT AND CULTIVATION

Category	Tree
Family	Araliaceae
Origin	Taiwan
Size, height x spread	12 x 8 metres
Situation	Partial or dappled shade
Irrigation	Regular summer watering
Temperature	To 5°C
Evergreen/deciduous	Evergreen
Flowering	Red. Spring
Special features	-

The Queensland Umbrella Tree gives a magnificently lush and tropical look to protected Mediterranean gardens, ideal in patio or courtyard settings where it can be protected from the wind and given some shade and mild temperatures. When suited it can reach tree-like proportions, but much smaller in adverse conditions. Also suitable for pots but, again, this will restrict its size. The leaves are glossy, like sections of an umbrella, and divided into some dozen or so leaflets that can span 0.50m across. In warmer areas it will flower in springtime. Plant it in good rich soil and give a yearly application of organic manure. Although perhaps happiest with regular watering and humidity, it will make do on considerably less. Can easily be transplanted.

Propagation
Semi-ripe summer cuttings or from fresh seed.

Pruning
Tolerates heavy pruning during cooler months to control size.

Problems
Red spider mite can be troublesome in confined conditions.

SCHINUS MOLLE False Pepper Tree, Peruvian Pepper Tree, (Spanish : Falsa Pimienta).

HABIT AND CULTIVATION

Category	Tree
Family	Anacardiaceae
Origin	South America
Size, height x spread	12 x 8 metres
Situation	Full sun
Irrigation	Drought tolerant
Temperature	To 0°C
Evergreen/deciduous	Evergreen
Flowering	Creamy yellow. Spring
Special features	Edible berries

The false pepper tree is a popular planting and deservedly so. It makes a very elegant weeping tree with long, pendulous, feathery foliage that can sweep down to the ground. The small, creamy white flowers are followed by strings of deep pink berries resembling peppercorns (though several trees may be needed for good fruiting) and these are, in fact, edible and can be used as a pepper substitute. As the trunk matures, the bark takes on a very gnarled and corrugated look. It is a very quick grower and makes an excellent windbreak and shelter tree with its wide canopy of foliage without ever becoming oppressive. The downside of the tree is that its roots can be invasive, lifting paving etc. and the litter from the tree is quite considerable but planted judiciously it certainly is a very attractive planting.

Propagation
Spring sown seed or summer cuttings.

Pruning
Generally not necessary. Cut out any deadwood.

Problems
None

SEDUM SPECTABILE Ice Plant, (Spanish : Uva de Gato).

HABIT AND CULTIVATION

Category	Perennial succulent
Family	Crassulaceae
Origin	Asia
Size, height x spread	0.50 x 0.50 metres
Situation	Full sun
Irrigation	Drought tolerant
Temperature	To – 15°C
Evergreen/deciduous	Top growth dies back in cold conditions
Flowering	Pink-red. Summer and autumn
Special features	Flowers attract butterflies

The ice plant is an easy and decorative succulent that is well suited to rock gardens. Drought and cold tolerant and happy in poor soil with minimum care – this is one you can plant and forget and in late summer and autumn it will surprise you with its attractive flowers that are a magnet for butterflies. It has juicy, soft green leaves, oval shaped and the small star-shaped flowers appear in flat clusters on fleshy stems in various shades of dusky pink to pink red. They are very long lasting, attractive to both bees and butterflies and will dry out on the plant, turning a darker shade, or can be cut and dried conventionally.

Propagation
From cuttings of non-flowering shoots or by plant division in early spring as it starts to shoot.

Pruning
Cut down flower stalks when finished. Top growth will disappear underground in cold weather.

Problems
Can rot in wet conditions

Sempervivum Arachnoideum

SEMPERVIVUM TECTORUM Common Houseleek, Hens and Chickens, (Spanish : Siempreviva).

HABIT AND CULTIVATION

Category	Succulent
Family	Crassulaceae
Origin	Europe
Size, height x spread	0.15 x 0.25 metres
Situation	Full sun
Irrigation	Drought tolerant
Temperature	To –15˚C
Evergreen/deciduous	Evergreen
Flowering	Reddish-purple. Summer
Special features	-

The sempervivum, the 'live-for-ever' plant, and 'tectorum' meaning 'of the roofs', has a long and complex mythical past. The name houseleek is from the Anglo Saxon 'leac' meaning plant. But the Irish description of the plant takes some beating – 'the wee cabbage sat on the roof'! They were traditionally grown on roofs to ward off evil spirits and lightning – neither proven! Medicinally they were used, much as aloe vera is today, for the relief of stings, bites, burns and even to clear warts and freckles. The fleshy rosettes are mat forming, often red-flushed and the star shaped flowers appear on erect stems during summer. The 'hen' rosette produces many 'chicks' and can take several years to reach flowering size. Once this has been achieved, the 'hen' will die, leaving space for the 'chicks' to develop. Grow in pots and troughs, in rock gardens and scree beds where there is good drainage.

Propagation
Break off a 'chick' and replant where desired or by breaking off a leaf, allow to callous over for 24hrs. and plant.

Pruning
Deadhead.

Problems
Can rot in wet soil.

Also **SEMPERVIVUM ARACHNOIDEUM**, Cobweb Houseleek, (Spanish : Siempreviva). As above but fleshy red-tinged green leaves are webbed with fine white hairs.

SISYRINCHIUM STRIATUM Satin Flower,
(Spanish : Sisyrinchium).

HABIT AND CULTIVATION

Category	Perennial
Family	Iridaceae
Origin	South America
Size, height x spread	0.50 x 0.30 metres
Situation	Full sun
Irrigation	Occasional summer watering
Temperature	To –15°C
Evergreen/deciduous	Semi-evergreen
Flowering	Creamy yellow. Summer
Special features	-

From the same family as the iris, the satin flower is much finer and daintier looking and is an excellent plant for poor, dry ground, between rocks, in gravel etc. They look especially good in naturalised gardens where their narrow grassy and grey-green leaves will go largely unnoticed until they burst into flower. They bear many slender spikes of small, creamy-yellow flowers which are delicately striped in purple. These are produced in great profusion, all through summer, and the plant can often be short lived because of the sheer effort of generating so many flowers. However, they easily self seed, especially in gravel, so you will never be without offspring. Take care not to uproot mistaking them for grass! Do not over water or feed, these little plants like it tough.

Propagation
Spring or autumn sown seed or by plant division in early spring.

Pruning
Can be deadheaded, but generally better left to self-seed.

Problems
None.

SOLANDRA MAXIMA Chalice Vine, Cup of Gold, (Spanish : Copa de Oro).

HABIT AND CULTIVATION

Category	Perennial Climber
Family	Solanaceae
Origin	Mexico
Size, height x spread	15 x 8 metres
Situation	Full sun
Irrigation	Moderate summer watering
Temperature	To –5°C
Evergreen/deciduous	Semi-evergreen
Flowering	Pale golden yellow. Spring and summer
Special features	Scented

This tropical-looking native of Mexico is a huge and rampant climber. Its branches are wide spreading and woody and, although classed as a climber, it is not very flexible and is perhaps better stretching along a bank or tied in to chain link fencing or some other form of very sturdy support. The large, glossy leaves, often purple tinged when juvenile, are certainly impressive and the fragrant flowers add to the drama. Their common name of cup of gold describes them exactly and they can be 25cm across. The five petals of each flower carries a central fine purple stripe. Happiest in a fertile soil and full sun, they will tolerate wind and salt spray and are reasonably drought tolerant. Do not overwater as this will produce much leaf growth and few flowers - they will show you when dry by drooping at the tips.

Propagation
Semi-ripe summer cuttings.

Pruning
Thin out crowded stems after flowering, and all stems can be shortened back to encourage more blooms.

Problems
None.

SOLANUM JASMINOIDES Potato Vine, (Spanish : Solano).

HABIT AND CULTIVATION

Category	Perennial Climber
Family	Solanaceae
Origin	South America
Size, height x spread	6 x 3 metres
Situation	Full sun, partial or dappled shade
Irrigation	Drought tolerant
Temperature	To –5°C
Evergreen/deciduous	Semi-evergreen
Flowering	Pale blue or white. Almost year round.
Special features	-

The potato vine is a very ordinary name for a very pretty and reliable plant though, as it belongs to the same family as the potato and tomato, the name is logical. It is a rapid and easy climber that will give few problems being tolerant of wind, sea spray, drought and dry air, sun or shade and reasonably cold hardy. Its dark green lobed leaves provide a nice backdrop for the star shaped flowers which, in the white form, are often mistaken for jasmine, hence s. jasminoides. Buy the plant in flower because there are many variations between the white and blue, some being quite wishy-washy. It will quickly grow along fencing, up a pergola or wall, with support, and can also scramble over rocks etc.

Propagation
Semi-ripe summer cuttings or spring sown seed.

Pruning
Cut out over congested growth during early spring.

Problems
None.

See also **SOLANUM WENDLANDII**.

SOLANUM WENDLANDII Divorce Vine, (Spanish : Solano).

HABIT AND CULTIVATION

Category	Perennial Climber
Family	Solanaceae
Origin	South America
Size, height x spread	6 x 3 metres
Situation	Full sun
Irrigation	Occasional summer watering
Temperature	To 5°C
Evergreen/deciduous	Semi-evergreen
Flowering	Lilac blue. Summer and autumn
Special features	-

S. wendlandii is rarely seen in gardens or garden centres but search it out because it is a very trouble-free and easy climber belonging to the large solanum family. It has robust grey-green stems, somewhat prickly, with large lobed mid-green leaves rather sparsely produced. The flowers are borne in abundant clusters and are a charming lilac-blue, opening cup-shaped, and lasting for several months. This climber probably looks best trained up a pergola or bower where you can laze back and look up at the enchantingly coloured flowers though it also appreciates the extra warmth and protection of a wall, where it can be trained in to suitable supports.

Propagation
Semi-ripe summer cuttings.

Pruning
Shorten back leader stems during the winter months to encourage bushier growth and more flowers.

Problems
None.

See also **SOLANUM JASMINOIDES**.

SOLLYA HETEROPHYLLA Bluebell
Creeper, (Spanish : Solia).

HABIT AND CULTIVATION

Category	Perennial Climber
Family	Pittosporaceae
Origin	Australia
Size, height x spread	4 x 2 metres
Situation	Full sun, partial or dappled shade
Irrigation	Occasional summer watering
Temperature	To 0°C
Evergreen/deciduous	Evergreen
Flowering	Blue. Late spring and summer
Special features	-

The bluebell creeper is a delicate and pretty little twining climber that is best planted at close quarters to be able to fully appreciate its subtlety – perhaps up a patio pillar or on a pergola or trellising, or it can tumble over a garden wall quite successfully. As it never reaches any great size, it can be grown in a pot on a terrace. It bears narrow, oval leaves that are shiny and mid-green and nodding clusters of around 8 bell-shaped, sky-blue flowers. The base of the plant can get a little bare and woody but this can be disguised with some lower plantings. It is happiest in a humus rich soil and appreciates a yearly mulching. Fertilise at regular intervals, especially if pot grown.

Propagation
Spring sown seed or softwood summer cuttings.

Pruning
Very little required, just a general tidy up during the cooler months.

Problems
None.

SPARTIUM JUNCEUM Spanish Broom, (Spanish : Retama de Olor).

HABIT AND CULTIVATION

Category	Shrub
Family	Leguminosae
Origin	Mediterranean
Size, height x spread	3 x 3 metres
Situation	Full sun
Irrigation	Drought tolerant
Temperature	To –5°C
Evergreen/deciduous	Deciduous
Flowering	Yellow. Spring
Special features	Scented

The Spanish broom is a rather sparse and leggy shrub with thin almost leafless stems, upright in its youth and later developing into an arching bush. In springtime it is smothered with long spikes of showy golden-yellow pea type blooms which are quite strongly aromatic. It does best in poor, thin and stony ground with little water and no fertiliser and is therefore well suited to a natural garden setting. It is also tolerant of pollution and seaside situations and can be used as a front line fire retardant plant. Initially it will grow quite quickly to around 2m and, although it can be fairly short-lived, it is a very useful colonising plant or gap filler until slower and more select plantings get established. Forms a good, loose and informal hedger or divider.

Propagation
Autumn sown seed.

Pruning
Prune in early spring to maintain a compact form and encourage bushiness.

Problems
Can become invasive when well suited.

SPATHODEA CAMPANULATA Flame Tree, African Tulip Tree, Flame of the Forest, (Spanish : Arbol de la Llama).

HABIT AND CULTIVATION

Category	Tree
Family	Bignoniaceae
Origin	Tropical Africa
Size, height x spread	15 x 10 metres
Situation	Full sun
Irrigation	Occasional summer watering
Temperature	To 5°C if kept dryish
Evergreen/deciduous	Semi-evergreen
Flowering	Orange-red. Spring, summer, autumn
Special features	-

The common names reflect the magnificence of this tree when in full flower. Two centuries ago, it was discovered by European explorers in Central Africa who were captivated by the wonderful scarlet flowers – like flames in the forest. Obviously, a native of Tropical Africa, this one needs warmth and shelter but can make a stunning shade tree with its large spreading canopy. The velvety flower buds are grouped together in clusters, rather like a tightly gloved fist, and as they open, bit by bit, the fingers fill out developing their fiery colouring. Each individual flower is shaped like a bell (hence campanulata). It can take some years to settle into flowering, and it will always perform best after a hot summer and mild winter, but the wait will certainly be worthwhile. Plant in rich soil.

Propagation
Spring sown seed (though rather slow to flower) or semi-ripe summer cuttings.

Pruning
Cut out any dieback.

Problems
None.

SPIRAEA DOUGLASII Garland Flower, Bridal Wreath, (Spanish : Spiraea).

HABIT AND CULTIVATION

Category	Shrub
Family	Rosacea
Origin	North America
Size, height x spread	2 x 2 metres
Situation	Partial or dappled shade
Irrigation	Occasional summer watering
Temperature	To –15°C
Evergreen/deciduous	Deciduous
Flowering	Pink. Late spring
Special features	Suckering

The spiraea family are mainly grown for their profusion of spring flowers and s. douglasii is no exception. It forms a vigorous upright shrub with oblong, mid-green leaves and grey-white undersides. It suckers freely, so is best planted where this will not be a problem. Use it as spreading mid-sized ground cover, perhaps on a bank. The late spring flowering of dense, deep-pink panicles made up of 5-petalled flowers is spectacular and even prettier if underplanted with spring flowering bulbs such as muscari, narcissi, anemone etc. An annual dressing with manure in early springtime will also help the flowering. Mulch to conserve moisture at the roots.

Propagation
By plant division during the winter months or by detaching suckers and replanting where required in early spring.

Pruning
Cut young growths back annually in late autumn and cut out completely some of the very old branches for rejuvenation.

Problems
None.

STACHYS BYZANTINA syn. s. lanata, Lambs Ears, Lambs Tongues, (Spanish : Oidos de Cordero).

HABIT AND CULTIVATION

Category	Perennial
Family	Labiatae
Origin	Near East
Size, height x spread	0.50 x 0.50 metres
Situation	Full sun
Irrigation	Drought tolerant
Temperature	To –15°C
Evergreen/deciduous	Top growth dies down in cold conditions
Flowering	Mauve. Spring and summer
Special features	Tactile leaves

The thick, white, tongue-shaped leaves of this little perennial give it its common names. The sunnier the conditions, the whiter and furrier the leaves. No one can resist stroking them, so soft and silky are they, so position perhaps along the side of a pathway. They make excellent low ground cover, forming spreading mats between shrubs, front border position or where ever it is hot and sunny. The leaves will be spoilt by heavy rainfall and will collapse if frosted but new growth will soon push through as soon as the conditions are more favourable. The spikes of mauve-pink flowers can be pinched out in bud to encourage lusher leaves. Happiest in very poor ground and looks well planted in clumps in gravel.

Propagation
Plant division in early spring.

Pruning
Dead head.

Problems
Can rot in very wet conditions.

Stipa Tenuissima 'Pony Tails'

STIPA TENACISSIMA Esparto Grass, (Spanish : Esparto Comun).

HABIT AND CULTIVATION

Category	Grass
Family	Gramineae
Origin	Mediterranean
Size, height x spread	2 x 1 metres
Situation	Full sun
Irrigation	Drought tolerant
Temperature	To –10°C
Evergreen/deciduous	Evergreen
Flowering	Cream. Spring and early summer
Special features	Commercial use

Esparto grass is a robust perennial found through Spain, Portugal and North Africa. It is tall and clump forming and the dense flower plumes can reach 30cm long. It is native to arid and rocky ground and mountainsides and can make an elegant specimen plant in dry gardens. It is still commercially cropped for its fibres that are now mainly used in papermaking. The Spanish grade is generally regarded as better quality than the 'Tripoli' from North Africa. First used in Great Britain in 1850, it is still widely sought after throughout Europe. The, sadly, dying trade of weaving the tough leaves into mats, soles for shoes, and ropes is now little seen. There has been a very small resurgence, mainly through the demands of tourism, but it is hardly cost effective.

Propagation
Spring sown seed or by plant division.

Pruning
Dead head when flower plumes are finished.

Problems
None.

Also **STIPA TENUISSIMA** 'Pony Tails' a delightfully fluffy grass, forming arching fountains to approx. 1m

STRELITZIA REGINAE Bird of Paradise, (Spanish : Ave del Paraiso).

HABIT AND CULTIVATION

Category	Perennial
Family	Musaceae
Origin	South Africa
Size, height x spread	1 x 1 metres
Situation	Good light but not necessarily sun
Irrigation	Regular summer watering
Temperature	To 0°C
Evergreen/deciduous	Evergreen
Flowering	Orange and blue. Spring and autumn
Special features	-

The unusual beak-like flower of the bird of paradise is fairly well known and it is the official flower of the city of Los Angeles, U.S.A. It makes an excellent pot plant, or in narrow beds where its roots can be restricted as it is under these conditions that it flowers most prolifically. It likes a rich soil, with regular watering and feeding – it admittedly will survive on much less but, if you want it to look good, pamper it a bit. The blue-green boat shaped leaves are decorative in their own right and the flowers are very long lasting.

Propagation
By division when the plants are really overcrowded. Can take a while to settle into flowering again.

Pruning
Dead head.

Problems
None.

Also **STRELITZIA NICOLAI**, (Spanish : Ave del Paraiso Gigante). A member and look alike of the banana family, in windy positions this is a better bet than the soft leafed banana. The large, exotic leaves will still shred but not as much. Reaches palm like proportions, 8 x 5, and has typical bird of paradise flowers, large-sized, and in navy blue and cream.

STREPTOSOLEN JAMESONII
Marmalade Bush,
(Spanish : Estreptosolen).

HABIT AND CULTIVATION

Category	Shrub
Family	Solanacea
Origin	South America
Size, height x spread	1.50 x 1.50 metres
Situation	Full sun, partial or dappled shade
Irrigation	Occasional summer watering
Temperature	To 0°C
Evergreen/deciduous	Evergreen
Flowering	Yellow or orange. Almost year round
Special features	-

The marmalade bush is a very hard working and pretty little shrub. It has a fairly lax and open habit with oval, finely wrinkled leaves and small but very eye-catching open flared trumpet shaped flowers in either a rich yolk yellow or marmalade orange. These are held in terminal clusters. It always gives the impression of being a happy little shrub, with no pest problems and tolerant of widely ranging conditions – and to show it, it flowers almost year round. A normal garden soil is adequate, moderate amounts of water through the hotter months, and it will tolerate wind and sea spray. It never quite takes centre stage but adds a lot to mixed shrub plantings.

Propagation
Semi-ripe summer cuttings.

Pruning
Pinch out tips regularly when young to obtain a good bushy shape. In early spring cut back flowered shoots to avoid congestion and train in new growths.

Problems
None.

TAMARIX PARVIFLORA Tamarisk,
(Spanish : Tamarisco).

HABIT AND CULTIVATION

Category	Shrub/small tree
Family	Tamaricaceae
Origin	Mediterranean
Size, height x spread	4 x 4 metres
Situation	Full sun
Irrigation	Drought tolerant
Temperature	To –5˚C
Evergreen/deciduous	Deciduous
Flowering	Pink. Spring
Special features	-

The tamarisks are very tough shrubs or small trees native to deserts and wind-battered, salty coastlines. Generally planted for their extreme tolerance to poor conditions, they make excellent windbreaks, pioneer plantings and screening hedges. Their foliage is light and ferny so large groups can be incorporated without ever becoming oppressive. Their slender weeping branches cloaked with pale pink tiny starry flowers turn the entire shrub in springtime into a frothy delight. Really hot summers provoke the best flowering. The lower whippy branches can be pruned off to create an impressive small tree. Poor rocky ground suffices, though the foliage will be more luxuriant on better ground and with just an occasional watering.

Propagation
Semi-ripe summer cuttings or hardwood winter cuttings strike easily and can be planted straight into ground.

Pruning
Prune after flowering to shape and thin out congested branches. Hard pruning promotes lots of vigorous new growth.

Problems
Can become invasive.

TAXUS BACCATA Yew, (Spanish : Tejo).

HABIT AND CULTIVATION

Category	Shrub/tree
Family	Taxaceae
Origin	Europe and Asia
Size, height x spread	15 x 10 metres
Situation	Full sun. partial, dappled or full shade
Irrigation	Occasional summer soaking
Temperature	To –15°C
Evergreen/deciduous	Evergreen
Flowering	Greenish, insignificant. Spring
Special features	Highly poisonous. High pollen emission

The yew is a coniferous and extremely slow growing shrub or tree with an ancient lineage. In Scotland is what is believed to be the oldest tree, somewhere between 3000 and 5000 years old. The timber is close-grained, non-resinous, flexible and tough – qualities that were esteemed for making longbows, hence the name taxus which is derived from the Greek 'taxon' meaning bow. The poison was also used on arrowheads. The dark green leaves are needle like and yellowish underneath and there are male and female trees. The males bear vast quantities of pollen, and the female flowers later develop into red fleshy fruits. Yew was once quite widespread throughout Europe but it is now quite rare in the wild. A concoction from the seeds was once used against snake bites and rabies, and to abort but the extreme toxicity of the treatment often had worse effects than the initial problem and medicinally it fell into disuse until some recent, and promising, research as a cancer treatment. It is very tolerant of heat or cold, dry or wet conditions and can be pruned and transplanted without problem, though it is happiest in an alkaline soil and with some humidity. It is a very useful hedging and topiary plant.

Propagation
Spring sown seed or spring cuttings.

Pruning
Can be hard pruned or shaped as required, but remember it will take a long time to recover!

Problems
Scale insect.

TECOMARIA CAPENSIS
Cape Honeysuckle,
(Spanish : Madreselva del Cabo).

HABIT AND CULTIVATION

Category	Shrubby climber
Family	Bignoniaceae
Origin	South Africa
Size, height x spread	6 x 4 metres
Situation	Full sun
Irrigation	Drought tolerant
Temperature	To –5°C
Evergreen/deciduous	Evergreen
Flowering	Orange. Autumn and winter
Special features	-

The Cape honeysuckle is a stalwart of our Mediterranean gardens. Its long rambling branches can weave through shrubs or it can be trained and tied in as a climber against a wall or left to tumble down a bank. It likes an open sunny position with good airflow and is ideal in coastal gardens. Its dark-green, glossy leaves are a perfect backdrop to the tubular fiery orange blooms held in short spikes. This is a very versatile and easy plant. Looks good associated with plumbago capensis, the blue and orange contrasting well and both liking similar conditions. Takes well to transplanting if first cut back hard.

Propagation
Spring sown seed or semi-ripe summer cuttings. Also by winter layering.

Pruning
Thin out congested growth in early spring. Over crowded growth increases risk of mildew.

Problems
Mildew is common with vastly differing daytime/night-time temperatures, bad air flow, damp autumn and springtime conditions and overcrowded growth.

TEUCRIUM FRUTICANS Bush or Tree Germander, (Spanish : Olivilla).

HABIT AND CULTIVATION

Category	Shrub
Family	Labiatae
Origin	Mediterranean
Size, height x spread	2 x 2 metres
Situation	Full sun
Irrigation	Drought tolerant
Temperature	To –5˚C
Evergreen/deciduous	Evergreen
Flowering	Blue. First half of year
Special features	Aromatic foliage

The bush germander is a native of the area, an extremely tough and tolerant, yet pretty, shrubby plant. It is named after the first King of Troy, Teucer, who reputedly held the plant in great esteem for its medicinal powers, mainly in healing wounds. It has small, aromatic grey leaves with white undersides and pretty blue tubular lipped flowers with prominent stamens for a good six months of the year. The entire effect is pale and silvery. It is variable and flower colour can range from white through palest blues to a mid-blue. Plant it in a hot, sunny spot on poor soil and it will give of its best and be totally trouble-free. It contrasts well weaving through darker leaved shrubs and can also be trimmed as a hedging plant.

Propagation
From semi-ripe summer cuttings.

Pruning
Cut out dead wood, trim over dead flowerheads. Can also be trimmed to keep confined.

Problems
None.

THEVETIA PERUVIANA Yellow Oleander, (Spanish : Adelfa Amarilla, Cascabel, Guarache, Arbol de la Suerte).

HABIT AND CULTIVATION

Category	Shrub
Family	Apocynaceae
Origin	South America
Size, height x spread	10 x 6 metres
Situation	Full sun
Irrigation	Moderate summer watering
Temperature	To 10°C
Evergreen/deciduous	Evergreen
Flowering	Yellow or peach. Almost year round.
Special features	Scented flowers. All parts of plant poisonous

The yellow oleander is thus called because of its resemblance to the oleander, though, in fact, this is somewhat superficial. It actually belongs to the same family as the frangipani, and is highly toxic in all parts, like the oleander. It has thin green leaves, but much softer and a brighter and glossier green than the oleander, and overall it makes a much more lax growing shrub. The yellow or peach coloured trumpet shaped flowers are fairly well held throughout the year but with their main flowering season in springtime. It likes a light and well-drained soil and is generally seen as a large shrub though it can also be pruned and trained to form an attractive tree.

Propagation
Spring sown seed or semi-ripe summer cuttings.

Pruning
Can be tip pruned during the winter months to encourage a bushy habit. Remove the lower growths and train one main leader stem to form tree.

Problems
Aphids.

THUNBERGIA GRANDIFLORA

Bengal Clock Vine, Blue Sky Vine,
(Spanish : Thunbergia).

HABIT AND CULTIVATION

Category	Perennial climber
Family	Acanthaceae
Origin	India
Size, height x spread	8 x 6 metres
Situation	Full sun
Irrigation	Occasional summer soaking
Temperature	To 0°C
Evergreen/deciduous	Semi-evergreen
Flowering	Lilac-blue. Summer and autumn
Special features	-

The Bengal clock vine has been described as 'the most beautiful vine in the world' and I have to admit, it would be hard to disagree. Everyone loves its amazingly beautiful flowers. It is a huge climber with large and lush, toothed leaves that lavishly snake over supports. The large drooping corymbs of flowers start to develop as soon as the weather warms up and are produced right through the warmer months. Each individual flower is a wonderful lilac-blue with a lighter striped centre and carried in great abundance. The vine in full flower is truly breathtaking. Grow it up and over some strong structure, or tumbling down a wall. It is a colour that just longs to be mixed – try it with orange campsis grandiflora, white ipomoea alba, pink bignonia ricosoleana – all stunning combinations, but you'll need a lot of space.

Propagation
Semi-hardwood summer cuttings.

Pruning
Can be cut hard back to ground in winter if very tangled. Or thin out excessive growth.

Problems
None.

Also **THUNBERGIA RIGIDA**. A shrub to around 2 x 2 metres, new growth purple coloured and flowers as above, smaller and darker. A much shyer flowerer.

Thymus Citrodorus

THYMUS VULGARIS Common Thyme, (Spanish : Tomillo).

HABIT AND CULTIVATION

Category	Subshrub
Family	Labiatae
Origin	Mediterranean
Size, height x spread	0.30 x 1 metres
Situation	Full sun
Irrigation	Drought tolerant
Temperature	To –5°C
Evergreen/deciduous	Evergreen
Flowering	Pink-lilac. Summer
Special features	Aromatic herb

Common thyme is one of our best recognised and loved herbs, no kitchen garden would be complete without it and it is an essential part of the traditional 'bouquet garnis'. Historically it has long been used for its antiseptic properties and the ancient Egyptians used the oil for embalming. Today it is widely used in the pharmaceutical, cosmetic and food industries. It is an essential constituent of the liqueur Benedictine. Its tiny but strongly aromatic leaves form an open wiry shrublet, which can tend to sprawl with old age. It likes a hot and sunny position on poor soil and is immensely useful in rock gardens, wall or paving crevices etc. A favourite plant of bees.

Propagation
Semi-ripe summer cuttings or winter layering.

Pruning
Trim over after flowering to keep bushy.

Problems
Mealy bug.

Also **THYMUS** x citriodorus, Lemon-Scented Thyme, (Spanish : Tomillo de Limon). A more compact grower than the above with tiny golden-yellow leaves which are deliciously and freshly lemon-scented. Very useful in the kichen.

TIPUANA TIPU Pride of Bolivia, Tipu Tree, (Spanish : Tipu).

HABIT AND CULTIVATION

Category	Tree
Family	Leguminosae
Origin	South America
Size, height x spread	10 x 8 metres
Situation	Full sun
Irrigation	Occasional summer soaking
Temperature	To 0°C
Evergreen/deciduous	Semi-evergreen
Flowering	Yellow. Spring
Special features	-

The Tipu tree is the only member of its species and forms a fabulous shade tree with its far-reaching and spreading branches forming a vast canopy. A reasonably quick grower, it is often seen as a street planting and is very attractive with its bright green foliage and form. The ferny leaves, some 25cm long, are composed of around 20 oval leaflets in a very fresh green colour – the whole effect is cooling and lush. In spring profuse racemes of bright golden-yellow pea-like flowers are produced which are later followed by brown winged seed pods, which hang well through autumn and winter. Generally evergreen, except in cooler areas, it appreciates a good fertile soil with an annual mulch to maintain a cool root run, but is otherwise very easy and tolerant.

Propagation
From spring sown seed. Can also self seed.

Pruning
Generally none necessary – allow it to form its own shape.

Problems
None.

TRACHELOSPERMUM JASMINOIDES
Star Jasmine,
(Spanish : Trachelospermum).

HABIT AND CULTIVATION

Category	Perennial climber
Family	Apocynaceae
Origin	China
Size, height x spread	6 x 4 metres
Situation	Full sun, partial, dappled or light shade
Irrigation	Moderate summer watering
Temperature	To –10°C
Evergreen/deciduous	Evergreen
Flowering	White. Spring and summer
Special features	Scented flowers

The star jasmine is a very pretty climber, somewhat slow to establish, but then growing away strongly. It has very attractive, fresh-looking evergreen foliage year round and the hanging clusters of white, jasmine-like flowers are borne throughout spring and summer in great profusion. Their perfume is delightful and travels for several metres. It can make a wonderful pergola plant, or be trained up through trellising or fencing and will also tumble down a bank and provide good dense groundcover. It is very heat tolerant and will become almost drought tolerant once established. Summer watering initially encourages quicker growth, but can then be phased out. Will grow in light shade, though the perfume from the flowers is better appreciated in sun.

Propagation
Semi-ripe summer cuttings. Layer into humus rich soil and it will root itself.

Pruning
Thin out congested growth in late autumn. Tip back long growths.

Problems
None.

TRADESCANTIA SILLAMONTANA

White Velvet, White Gossamer, (Spanish : El Sillamontana de Tradescantia, Gossamer Blanco).

HABIT AND CULTIVATION

Category	Perennial
Family	Commelinaceae
Origin	Mexico
Size, height x spread	0.30 x 0.50 metres
Situation	Full sun
Irrigation	Drought tolerant
Temperature	To 0°C
Evergreen/deciduous	Top growth dies down with cold weather
Flowering	Lilac-purple. Summer
Special features	Tactile foliage

This is a little known plant that is perfectly adapted to our climate and makes an easy and very pretty addition to rock gardens, gravel or scree, in crevices in paving etc. The silver woolly stems and leaves are wonderfully tactile and blend in perfectly with brighter plantings. The purple-coloured flowers produced through late spring and summer are a very pretty contrast to the foliage. It revels in a hot sunny position and its worst enemy is wet weather. Too much rain will make the leaves collapse, as will cold weather, and it will disappear underground until better weather returns. Plant it in a light and well-drained soil. Keep it dry and warm and it will give you no problems.

Propagation
Break off and root stem cuttings in sandy soil.

Pruning
None necessary. If foliage collapses with bad weather, trim back to ground level and it will reshoot from the base.

Problems
None if grown dry.

TROPAEOLUM MAJUS Nasturtium, Indian Cress, (Spanish : Capuchina).

HABIT AND CULTIVATION

Category	Annual
Family	Tropaeolaceae
Origin	South America
Size, height x spread	0.50 x 1 metres
Situation	Full sun or lightly dappled shade
Irrigation	Occasional summer watering
Temperature	-
Evergreen/deciduous	-
Flowering	Yellow, orange, red. Spring, summer, autumn.
Special features	Edible leaves and flowers

The nasturtium is one of the cheapest, easiest and most colourful plants for our gardens. Many children are introduced to the world of growing plants with a few nasturtium seeds. And which child hasn't 'cultivated' caterpillars on nasturtium leaves? But all of this should not detract from the immense value of these plants which will provide masses of colour tumbling down banks, growing over semi-wasteland, ground covering and even in pots and tubs. It is very fast growing and will quickly 'eat up' the ground with its rounded leaves and spurred flowers in brilliant fiery shades. The leaves and flowers are edible, both having a hot peppery taste and the flowers, particularly, make a pretty addition to salads. Nowadays the colour range is great, through creams to deep russet reds, some blotched and in single or double form.

Propagation
From spring sown seed.

Pruning
Only cut back when becoming too invasive.

Problems
Aphids, especially blackfly. Caterpillars from cabbage white butterfly can demolish a plant very quickly.

VERBASCUM BOMBYCIFERUM
Woolly Mullein, Giant Silver Mullein,
(Spanish : Bombyciferum de
Verbasco, Verano de Artico).

HABIT AND CULTIVATION

Category	Biennial
Family	Scrophulariaceae
Origin	Turkey
Size, height x spread	2 x 0.75 metres
Situation	Full sun
Irrigation	Drought tolerant
Temperature	To –15°C
Evergreen/deciduous	Evergreen
Flowering	Lemon yellow. Summer
Special features	Poisonous

V. bombyciferum is one of the woolliest and whitest of the family, contrasting splendidly with dark conifers, cypress etc. and forming a stunning exclamation point! It is a biennial, so growth is made during one season, with flowering in the following summer and then the plant will generally die, though in our climate it can be longer lived. In any case, it self seeds readily so you should never be without offspring. The large oval leaves and stems are completely covered in white 'wool' and the tall flower spikes, to some 2m, bear tightly packed cool lemon flowers. Again, happy in a warm sunny spot and poor soil suffices. The verbascum family generally object to fertiliser, preferring a harder life style. Try it too with a vividly coloured bougainvillea as a backdrop, sheer showmanship!

Propagation
Spring sown seed. Also self seeds readily.

Pruning
Remove dead flower stalk after seeding.

Problems
None.

See also **VERBASCUM NIGRUM**.

VERBASCUM NIGRUM, Black Mullein, Hag Taper,(Spanish : Nigrum de Verbasco, Mullein Oscuro).

HABIT AND CULTIVATION

Category	Perennial
Family	Scrophulariaceae
Origin	Morocco
Size, height x spread	1 x 1 metres
Situation	Full sun
Irrigation	Drought tolerant
Temperature	To –15˚C
Evergreen/deciduous	Evergreen
Flowering	Yellow. Spring and summer
Special features	All parts of the plant, except the flowers, are poisonous. Hairs on plants can be irritant to skin.

The verbascum family are stately, structural plants and very useful for our Mediterranean climate. The name verbascum is from the Latin 'barbascum' (barba meaning beard) in reference to the hairy downy stems and leaves. Hag taper is from the Middle Ages when it was believed that witches made love potions from the plant. 'Nigrum' is for the almost black eye of the flower, though now there are many variations, some without the black eye. Mid-green tapered leaves are mainly basal and the yellow flower spikes tower up to 1m or more. Likes an open and sunny position and poor soil suffices. Looks good in gravel, set into paving etc. or grouped in gardens. It self seeds readily into crevices and this 'natural' planting will generally look better than anything we might devise!

Propagation
Spring sown seed and will self sow.

Pruning
None. Dead head after flowering and seeding.

Problems
None.

See also **VERBASCUM BOMBYCIFERUM**.

Verbena Speciosa

VERBENA BONARIENSIS Brazilian
Verbena, Purple Top Vervain,
(Spanish : Verbena Alta, Tapa
Purpura, Hierba de los Hechizos).

HABIT AND CULTIVATION

Category	Perennial
Family	Verbenaceae
Origin	South America
Size, height x spread	1.5 x 0.5 metres
Situation	Full sun
Irrigation	Occasional summer watering
Temperature	To 0°C
Evergreen/deciduous	Evergreen
Flowering	Purple. Summer and autumn
Special features	-

V. bonariensis is one of the tall perennial verbenas which look great in large drifts in mixed borders. It has a basal clump of dark green, toothed leaves from which arise the wiry upright flower stems that carry tufts of purple flowers that sway nicely in the wind. This is a good tough plant that is having a 'fashion revival' at the moment, though it is so good and easy that it deserves to be always in the mode. Plant in normal garden soil, in a sunny and open position and give it some water now and again through summer, though it is almost drought tolerant. It asks for nothing more. Do not fertilise, as this will produce much leafage and few flowers.

Propagation
Autumn stem cuttings.

Pruning
Dead head to promote more flowers.

Problems
None.

Also **VERBENA** x hybrida. Upright perennials, 30cm x 30cm, in a range of dazzling colours, red, pink, blue, mauve, cream, often with a white eye. Can be used as annuals for bedding, pots etc. Prone to mildew.

Also **VERBENA SPECIOSA**. Trailing perennials forming mats of foliage. Good ground cover, path edging, also hanging baskets etc. Ferny leaves with heads of white, blue-lilac, pink or red flowers. 30cm x 50cm.

VIBURNUM TINUS Laurustinus,
(Spanish : Durillo).

HABIT AND CULTIVATION

Category	Shrub
Family	Caprifoliaceae
Origin	Mediterranean
Size, height x spread	3 x 3 metres
Situation	Full sun, partial or dappled shade
Irrigation	Drought tolerant
Temperature	To –5°C
Evergreen/deciduous	Evergreen
Flowering	White. Winter
Special features	Scented. Decorative berries

The Spanish name of 'durillo' aptly reflects the nature of this shrub – the little tough one! Held in great respect for its extreme adaptability and, at the same time, beauty the laurustinus is a great planting for almost any garden. The evergreen glossy leaves always look attractive and the flat heads of pretty white flowers, occasionally tinged with pink, are carried all winter and are delightfully perfumed of honeysuckle. These are followed by purple-black berries, which are also very decorative and held for a long time. It likes an alkaline soil and preferably a sunny position, though it will take some shade. Wind, drought, moderate freezing, dry or salty air are all quite acceptable. Makes an excellent hedging plant.

Propagation
Semi-ripe summer cuttings or autumn sown seed.

Pruning
If the shrub needs pruning, this is best done straight after flowering, though it means loss of berries. Late pruning may result in loss of flowers the following year.

Problems
Too much shade will result in poor flowering and a tendency to mildew and red spider mite.

VITIS VINIFERA Grape Vine, (Spanish : Parra).

HABIT AND CULTIVATION

Category	Perennial climber
Family	Vitaceae
Origin	Mediterranean
Size, height x spread	To 20m
Situation	Full sun
Irrigation	Drought tolerant
Temperature	To –15°C
Evergreen/deciduous	Deciduous
Flowering	Greenish-yellow. Spring
Special features	Edible fruit

The grapevine has been cultivated throughout Europe since ancient times and one of our enduring images of the Mediterranean area is of an ancient and gnarled vine growing over a sunny terrace, providing shade and bunches of juicy grapes. Black or white, seeded or seedless, the choice is yours though it is generally best to opt for what are traditionally grown in your area. The locals have had years of experience at this! It has to be said that the vine-covered terrace, although traditional and charming is a fairly labour intensive planting and rather a messy one too. Litter from the flowers and falling leaves is substantial and, for good crops, spraying and pruning is essential. But for dense summer shade, delicious crops of grapes, raisins and wine – what else can match it?

Propagation
Hardwood cuttings in late spring.

Pruning
The principal is basically the same for low-growing or climbing vines. After cropping shorten back the growths to 3 main leaders, leaving 3 leaf buds on each. A climbing vine should be trained with one single main stem to the height required, then tip out and allow three leaders to develop. Side shoots from these three main stems should be shortened back to 3 leaf buds. An unpruned vine will give you lots of small leaves and little crop and will eventually revert to wild.

Problems
Mainly mildew.

WASHINGTONIA FILIFERA Desert Fan Palm, Californian Cotton Palm, (Spanish : Washingtonia).

HABIT AND CULTIVATION

Category	Tree
Family	Palmae
Origin	California, U.S.A.
Size, height x spread	20 x 5 metres
Situation	Full sun
Irrigation	Drought resistant
Temperature	To –5°C
Evergreen/deciduous	Evergreen
Flowering	Cream. Spring
Special features	-

The desert fan palm is a very popular planting in many parts of the world, mainly because of its relatively fast rate of growth and tolerance to both heat and cooler temperatures, drought and dry air conditions. It develops a stout trunk with the typical fan-shaped leaves, long-stalked and with white filaments. The fruits, which are not edible, are small, rounded and a dark, glossy red. As with lots of other palms this one can be successfully transplanted at almost any size using props to support and tying up the crown of leaves until active growth has started again. Roots can lift paving. Palms establish quicker if planted during the warmer months and, if rapid growth is required, water and fertilise during the growing season but they will live happily on much less, once established.

Propagation
Quick and easy from seed. Germinate best at high temperatures.

Pruning
The old, dying leaves can form a thick thatch around the trunk. These should be removed to improve the look of the palm and also because they can be a fire hazard.

Problems
Invasive roots.

WIGANDIA CARACASANA Purple Nettle, (Spanish : Ortiga Caracus).

HABIT AND CULTIVATION

Category	Shrub
Family	Hydrophyllaceae
Origin	Tropical America
Size, height x spread	4 x 3 metres
Situation	Full sun
Irrigation	Moderate summer watering
Temperature	To 5°C
Evergreen/deciduous	Evergreen
Flowering	Violet-blue. Spring, summer and autumn
Special features	Hairy leaves and stems can be irritant

W. caracasana, as its name would suggest, originates from Caracas. Not too often seen, it is a dramatic and majestic plant, which forms a rather lax growing shrub, with large oval and wavy-edged, toothed leaves, which are covered in fine stinging hairs, giving rise to its common name. Some people have an extreme allergic reaction to them. The five-petalled flowers are held in large upright corymbs, a striking violet-blue and produced over a long season. The whole look of the plant is rather open and giant sized so give it space to spread and develop. Plant it in a fairly rich soil and give moderate amounts of water through the growing season.

Propagation
Easy and quick from spring sown seed, by basal suckers, or semi ripe summer cuttings.

Pruning
Cut down finished flower stems to prevent plant from becoming straggly.

Problems
Whitefly.

WISTERIA SINENSIS Chinese Wisteria, (Spanish : Glicinia).

HABIT AND CULTIVATION

Category	Perennial climber
Family	Leguminosae
Origin	China
Size, height x spread	Up to 30 metres
Situation	Full sun
Irrigation	Occasional summer soaking
Temperature	To –15˚C
Evergreen/deciduous	Deciduous
Flowering	Lilac or white. Spring
Special features	Scented

The wisteria is a well-known climber, generally admired for its magnificence and beauty both in and out of flower. It is perhaps not so well recognised that in our climate it will also perform wonderfully, the plant seemingly being impervious to heat and a degree of dryness. In fact, whereas in Northern Europe it can be a little slow to establish, here it will grow away rapidly from the start and flower very young. It is a beautiful option for a large terrace or free-standing pergola where its drooping sprays of perfumed flowers can be fully appreciated. A wisteria tunnel, as seen in some public gardens, is a truly stunning sight to behold. Remember that this is a huge grower and the weight of an ancient plant is considerable. The very fresh-looking green new growth is by whippy shoots, but the flowers are produced on short lateral spurs. Can also be trained into a very elegant small tree/standard.

Propagation
From cuttings or by layering in summer. Spring sown seeds are easy but flowers can be very variable.

Pruning
Prune after flowering and again in winter if necessary. Cut back to fat flower buds at the base of the spurs.

Problems
None.

YUCCA ALOIFOLIA Spanish Bayonet, (Spanish : Yuca Pinchona, Bayoneta Española).

HABIT AND CULTIVATION

Category	Perennial/shrub/tree
Family	Agavaceae
Origin	Central America
Size, height x spread	5 x 2 metres
Situation	Full sun
Irrigation	Drought tolerant
Temperature	To –5°C
Evergreen/deciduous	Evergreen
Flowering	Cream. Summer
Special features	Dangerously sharp leaf tips

The Spanish bayonet is so called for its vicious leaf tips – situate with care, or cut each tip to avoid accidents! It is a slow growing upright plant with stiff leaves and can become shrub or tree like. The large panicles of creamy coloured flowers, occasionally tinged purple, are very striking. Yuccas generally are a good addition to Mediterranean gardens, their dramatic outlines looking good against a backdrop of white walls, blue skies etc. and perfectly suited to dry gardens. Their structural form also can be shown to great effect in pots or set into paving. Unfussy to soil and liking hot and dry conditions, they are one of our most undemanding plants.

Propagation
From spring sown seed, but easier and quicker by offshoots.

Pruning
Cut out dead flower stalks and dead leaves can be pulled off (wearing gloves) and the trunk is thus formed. If the plant is becoming too tall for its position, lop off the head with a section of trunk. The main plant will then shoot lower down and the lopped section can be replanted in a new position.

Problems
None.

YUCCA GLORIOSA Spanish Dagger, (Spanish : Daga).

HABIT AND CULTIVATION

Category	Perennial/shrub
Family	Agavaceae
Origin	North America
Size, height x spread	2 x 2 metres
Situation	Evergreen
Irrigation	Drought tolerant
Temperature	To −15°C
Evergreen/deciduous	Evergreen
Flowering	Creamy white. Summer and autumn
Special features	-

The Spanish dagger is not quite as dangerous as it sounds, and is a less vicious planting than y. aloifolia. The bluish-green sword-shaped leaves do not carry the sharp tip and this is a smaller grower with, generally, a stout and unbranched trunk with a tufty head of leaves on top. The creamy-white, upright bell-shaped flowers are produced in very long panicles throughout the summer and autumn and are showy and eye-catching – hence 'gloriosa'. Cultivation as y. aloifolia – liking hot and dry conditions and drought tolerant. This yucca is the most cold tolerant of the genus and can be used in coastal situations too. A good container plant.

Propagation
As y. aloifolia.

Pruning
As y. aloifolia.

Problems
None.

Also **YUCCA YEGUA**, a very prettily variegated yucca with green and creamy-white striped leaves. Care and cultivation as above. Liking a touch more water, but still very drought tolerant.

ZANTEDESCHIA AETHIOPICA Arum Lily, Calla Lily, (Spanish : Lirios de Cala, Flor de Cartucho).

HABIT AND CULTIVATION

Category	Perennial
Family	Araceae
Origin	South Africa
Size, height x spread	1 x 0.5 metres
Situation	Dappled or partial shade
Irrigation	Regular watering
Temperature	To –10°C
Evergreen/deciduous	Deciduous at low temperatures and low irrigation levels
Flowering	White spathes, yellow spadix. Spring.
Special features	-

The tuberous perennial calla lily has beautiful fresh-green, large and arrow-shaped leaves creating a lush, tropical look in the garden. The elegant lily flowers are actually large pure white spathes with a central finger like spadix. Plant the rhizomes some 15cm deep and about 50cm apart. It likes some shade and a fairly damp soil and can be grown as a pond border plant, happy in up to 20cm of water. However, it will also survive with seasonal rains, going dormant and disappearing underground in summer to re-appear with new unfurling foliage with the autumn rains. If irrigated throughout the year and temperatures can be maintained at around 8°C, it will stay evergreen. It can also be grown in a pot and the flowers are excellent cut for indoor decoration.

Propagation
From offsets in late winter.

Pruning
Dead head and tidy up dead leaves.

Problems
None.

PLANT CROSS REFERENCE

(Plants have been allocated for sun/shade according to their best suitability. However, for example, many of those listed under sun will also take some degree of shade. Check specific cultivation details.)

GROUNDCOVER - Small, up to 50cm

SUN

Aptenia cordifolia, pink
Arctotis aucalis, cream, yellow, orange, pink, russet
Carpobrotus edulis, yellow, pink
Convolvulus sabatius, blue
Coprosma repens, foliage
Dianthus deltoides, scented, white, pink
Gazania, cream, yellow, orange, russet, pink
Helianthemum, white, yellow, orange, pink, red
Helichrysum petiolare, cream-white
Hypericum calycinum, yellow
Juniperus horizontalis, insignificant
Lampranthus, white, yellow, orange, red, pink, lilac, purple, cerise
Lantana montevidensis, white, yellow, lilac
Lotus berthelotii, gold, copper
Mesembryanthemum criniflorum, white, yellow, orange, pink, red
Oenothera missouriensis, yellow
Osteospermum fruticosum, white, yellow, pink, purple
Pelargonium x fragrans, aromatic, white
Pelargonium tomentosum, aromatic, white
Phlox subulata, white, pink, lilac
Portulaca grandiflora, white, yellow, orange, pink, red
Rosmarinus prostratus, aromatic, blue
Scaevola aemula, blue-white
Sedum spectabile, pink-red
Stachys byzantina, mauve
Thymus vulgaris, aromatic, pink-lilac
Thymus x citridorus, aromatic, pink-lilac
Tradescantia sillamontana, lilac-purple
Tropaeolum majus, yellow, orange, red
Verbena speciosa, white, lilac, pink, red

SHADE

Ajuga retpans, blue
Coprosma repens, foliage
Hypericum calycinum, yellow
Juniperus horizontalis, insignificant

GROUNDCOVER - Large, over 50cm

SUN

Argyranthemum frutescens, white, yellow, pink
Artemisia arborescens, aromatic, yellow
Bougainvillea glabra, purple
Bougainvillea spectabilis, white, yellow, orange, pinks, red, lilac, purple
Euryops pectinatus, yellow
Felicia amelloides, blue
Heliotropium arborescens, scented, lilac-purple
Iris germanica, some scented, all colours
Jasminum azoricum, scented, white
Jasminum sambac, scented, white
Jasminum nudiflorum, yellow
Kniphofia uvaria, orange-yellow
Lavandula angustifolia, aromatic, lavender-purple
Lavandula dentata, aromatic, lavender-blue
Lavandula stoechas, aromatic, purple
Lonicera japonica, scented, cream-white
Nepeta x faassenii, aromatic, lavender-blue
Oenothera speciosa, scented, white
Pelargonium crispum, aromatic, pink
Pelargonium graveolens, aromatic, white
Perovskia atriplicifolia, lavender-blue
Phlomis fruticosa, yellow
Pistacia lentiscus, insignificant
Rosa banksiae, scented, white, yellow
Rosmarinus oficinalis, aromatic, blue, white, lilac
Russelia equisetiformis, red
Salvia leucantha, white-purple

continued

611

Salvia oficinalis, aromatic, purple-blue
Santolina chamaecyparissus, aromatic, yellow
Spartium junceum, scented, yellow
Tecomaria capensis, orange
Teucrium fruticans, aromatic, blue
Trachelospermum jasminoides, scented, white
Verbascum bombyciferum, yellow
Verbascum nigrum, yellow

SHADE

Hebe speciosa, purple
Lonicera japonica, scented, cream-white
Mahonia aquifolium, scented, yellow
Spiraea douglasii, pink

ANNUALS

SUN

Cerinthe major purpurescens, indigo blue
Eschscholzia californica, cream, yellow, orange, bronze, rose, scarlet, lilac, purple
Helianthus annuus, yellow
Mesembryanthemum criniflorum, white, yellow, orange, pink, red
Papaver somniferum, white, pink, lilac, purple, red
Portulaca grandiflora, white, yellow, orange, pink, red
Reseda odorata, scented, white
Tropaeolum majus, yellow, orange, red
Verbena x hybrida, red, pink, purple, mauve, cream

SHADE

Euphorbia marginata, yellow

BIENNIALS

SUN

Echium fastuosum (semi-biennial), blue
Echium wildpretii, coral-pink
Erysimum linifolium (semi-biennial), scented, lilac
Verbascum bombyciferum, yellow

PERENNIALS - Small, up to 1m

SUN

Achillea millefolium, yellow
Agapanthus praecox, blue, white
Ajania pacifica, yellow
Alstroemeria, white, yellow, salmon, pink, lilac, red, purple
Arctotis aucalis, cream, yellow, orange, pink, russet
Argyranthemum frutescens, white, yellow, pink
Asteriscus maritimus, yellow
Asteriscus sericeus, yellow
Belamcanda chinensis, orange-red
Campanula rapunculoides, blue
Canna indica, yellow, pink, orange, red
Centranthus ruber, pink-red, white
Convolvulus sabatius, blue
Coreopsis verticillata, yellow
Cosmos atrosanguineus, scented, black-red
Dianthus deltoides, scented, white, pink
Erysimum linifolium, scented, lilac
Gaillardia pulchella, red, pink, yellow
Gazania, cream, yellow, orange, russet, pink
Gerbera jamesonii, cream, yellow, peach, pink, red
Helianthemum, white, yellow, orange, pink, red
Helichrysum bracteatum, cream-white, yellow, pink, red
Impatiens, New Guinea hybrids, white, pink, salmon, cerise, orange, crimson
Kniphofia uvaria, orange-yellow

continued ▶

613

Limonium latifolium, lavender-blue, blue-white
Linum narbonense, blue
Mirabilis jalapa, scented, white, yellow, pink
Nepeta x faassenii, aromatic, lavender-blue
Nicotiana alata, scented, white
Oenothera speciosa, scented, white
Oenothera missouriensis, yellow
Osteospermum fruticosum, white, pink, yellow, purple
Pelargonium x domesticum, white, pink, lilac, purple, red
Pelargonium crispum, aromatic, pink
Pelargonium x fragrans, aromatic, white
Pelargoium graveolens, aromatic, white
Pelargonium tomentosum, aromatic, white
Pelargonium x zonale, white, pink, lilac, salmon, red
Phlox subulata, white, lilac, pink
Rudbeckia fulgida, yellow
Scabiosa caucasica, white, cream, pink, lavender, violet
Scaevola aemula, blue-white
Sisyrinchium striatum, cream-yellow
Stachys byzantina, mauve
Strelitzia reginae, orange-blue
Tradescantia sillamontana, lilac-purple
Verbascum nigrum, yellow
Verbena x hybrida, red, pink, purple, mauve, cream
Verbena speciosa, white, lilac, pink, red

SHADE

Strelitzia reginae, orange-blue
Zantedeschia aethiopica, white-yellow

PERENNIALS - Large, over 1m

SUN

Alcea rosea, white, yellow, pink, black
Anigozanthos, yellow-green, orange, pink, red
Digitalis purpurea, white, pink, purple, yellow
Echium fastuosum, blue

Hemerocalis, cream, yellow, pink, russet
Iris germanica, some scented, all colours
Leonotis leonurus, orange
Phormium tenax, dull red
Verbena bonariensis, purple
Yucca aloifolia, cream
Yucca gloriosa, cream-white
Yucca yegua, cream-white

SHADE

Acanthus mollis, lilac-purple/white
Alocasia macrorrhiza, yellow-green
Anemone x hybrida, pink, white
Euphorbia characias, green
Hemerocalis, cream, yellow, pink, russet
Monstera deliciosa, cream

BULBS

SUN

Colchicum autumnale, lilac, purple
Crocosmia masonorum, orange-red
Cyclamen hederifolium, scented, white, pink, lilac, purple
Lilium candidum, scented, white
Lilium longiflorum, scented, white

SHADE

Clivia miniata, orange, yellow
Cyclamen hederifolium, scented, white, pink, lilac, purple

GRASSES AND BAMBOOS

SUN

Cortaderia selloana, cream, dusky-pink
Cyperus papyrus, brown-green
Cyperus papyrus 'nanus', brown-green
Nandina domestica, (bamboo look-alike), pink-white
Pennisetum setaceum, copper-red
Pennisetum orientale, coffee
Phyllostachys bambusoides, green-white
Stipa tenacissima, cream
Stipa tenuissima, cream

SUCCULENTS - Small, up to 50cm

SUN

Aloe variegata, pink, scarlet
Aloe vera, yellow
Aptenia cordifolia, pink
Carpobrotus edulis, yellow, pink
Echeveria elegans, pink-red-yellow
Graptopetalum paraguayense, yellow-red
Lampranthus, white, yellow, orange, red, pink, lilac, purple, cerise
Mesembryanthemum criniflorum, white, yellow, orange, pink, red
Portulaca grandiflora, white, yellow, orange, pink, red
Sedum spectabile, pink-red
Sempervivum tectorum, red-purple
Sempervivum arachnoideum, red-purple

SUCCULENTS - Medium, 50cm to 1m

SUN

Aeonium arboreum, yellow
Aeonium arboreum atropurpureum, yellow
Aeonium arboreum 'Schwarzkopf', yellow
Aeonium canariense, yellow

SUCCULENTS - Large, over 1m

SUN

Agave americana, cream
Agave americana medio picta, cream
Agave americana medio picta alba, cream
Agave attenuata, yellow
Aloe arborescens, orange-red
Aloe ferox, orange
Euphorbia candelabrum, orange-red
Opuntia ficus-indica, yellow

SHADE

Euphorbia characias, green

WATER LOVERS

SUN

Cyperus papyrus, brown-green
Cyperus papyrus 'nanus', brown-green

SHADE

Zantedeschia aethiopica, white-yellow

SHRUBS - Small, up to 1m

SUN

Adenanthos drummondii, red
Anisodontea capensis, pink
Artemisia arborescens, aromatic, yellow
Brugmansia meteloides, scented, white
Buxus sempervirens 'suffruticosa', green-white
Capparis spinosa, pink-white
Caryopteris clandonensis, blue
Ceanothus thyrsiflorus var. repens, blue
Convolvulus cneorum, white
Coprosma repens, foliage
Euryops pectinatus, yellow
Felicia amelloides, blue
Genista hispanica, scented, yellow
Genista tinctoria, yellow
Helichrysum petiolare, cream-yellow
Heliotropium arborescens, scented, lilac-purple
Hypericum calycinum, yellow
Lantana montevidensis, white, yellow, lilac
Lavandula angustifolia, aromatic, lavender-purple
Lavandula dentata, aromatic, lavender-blue
Lavandula stoechas, aromatic, purple
Phlomis fruticosa, yellow
Rosmarinus oficinalis, aromatic, blue, white, lilac

Russelia equisetiformis, red
Salvia leucantha, white-purple
Salvia oficinalis, aromatic, purple-blue
Santolina chamaecyparrisus, aromatic, yellow
Thymus vulgaris, aromatic, pink-lilac
Thymus x citriodorus, aromatic, pink-lilac

SHADE

Coprosma repens, foliage
Hypericum calycinum, yellow
Mahonia aquifolium, scented, yellow

SHRUBS - Medium, 1m to 3m

SUN

Abelia floribunda, scented, pink-purple
Abelia grandiflora, white-pink
Abutilon x hybridum, white, yellow, orange, pink, red
Alogyne huegelii, lilac
Aloysia triphylla, scented, white-lilac
Atriplex canescens, blue
Buddleja alternifolia, scented, lilac
Carissa macrocarpa, scented, white
Carpenteria californica, scented, white
Cassia alata, yellow-black
Cestrum 'newellii', burgundy red
Cestrum nocturnum, scented, lime green
Choisya ternata, scented, white
Cistus ladanifer, white-red
Coronilla valentina ssp.glauca, scented, yellow
Cytisus praecox, scented, yellow
Duranta repens, blue, white
Echium fastuosum, blue
Euphorbia pulcherrima, green-insignificant, cream, pink, red bracts
Grevillea rosmarinifolia, pink-cream

continued ▶

Hibiscus rosa-sinensis, white, cream, yellow, orange, pink, red
Iochroma cyaneum, purple
Jasminum nudiflorum, yellow
Kolkwitzia amabilis, pink
Lantana camara, white, cream, yellow, pink, orange, red
Lavatera arborea, pink-purple
Leonotis leonurus, orange
Leptospermum scoparium, white, pink, pink-red
Lonicera nitida, white
Melianthus major, maroon
Myrtus communis, scented, white
Nandina domestica, pink-white
Perovskia atriplicifolia, lavender-blue
Philadelphus coronarius, scented, cream-white
Pyracantha angustifolia, white
Ricinus communis, red
Romneya coulteri, scented, white
Rosa rugosa, scented, white, violet
Spartium junceum, scented, yellow
Streptosolen jamesonii, yellow, orange
Teucrium fruticans, aromatic, blue
Thunbergia rigida, purple
Viburnum tinus, scented, white
Yucca gloriosa, cream-white
Yucca yegua, cream-white

SHADE

Euphorbia characias, green
Fatsia japonica, white
Hebe speciosa, purple
Hydrangea macrophylla, white, pink, blue
Hydrangea quercifolia, cream-pink-white
Justicia carnea, white, pink
Spiraea douglasii, pink

SHRUBS - Large, over 3m

SUN

Arbutus unedo, scented, white
Brugmansia arborea, scented, white
Brugmansia candida, scented, white
Brugmansia sanguinea, yellow-red
Buddleja davidii, scented, white, pink, lilac, purple
Buddleja globosa, scented, golden orange
Callistemon viminalis, red
Ceanothus arboreus, blue
Cotinus coggygria, grey, pink florescence
Cytisus battandieri, scented, yellow
Dodonea viscosa 'purpurea', green-insignificant, pink seed cases
Dombeya wallichii, scented, pink
Erythrina crista-galli, coral
Erythrina coralloides, coral
Fremontodendron californicum, yellow
Hibiscus mutabilis, white, pink, red
Hibiscus syriacus, white, pink, lilac
Jasminum oficinale, scented, white
Lagerstroemia indica, white, pink, lilac, purple
Leptospermum laevigatum, white
Melaleuca armillaris, scented, cream-white-yellow
Metrosideros excelsa, orange-red
Myoporum laetum, white
Nerium oleander, white, apricot, pink, red
Olearia arborescens, white
Pistacia lentiscus, insignificant
Pittosporum tenuifolium, scented, purple
Plumbago capensis, blue, white
Plumeria acutifolia, scented, white-yellow
Polygala myrtifolia, purple
Punica granatum, orange-red
Retama monosperma, scented, white
Tamarix parviflora, pink
Taxus baccata, green
Tecomaria capensis, orange
Thevetia peruviana, scented, yellow, peach

continued ▶

Wigandia caracasana, violet-blue
Yucca aloifolia, cream

SHADE

Camellia japonica, white, cream, pink, red
Ficus benjamina, foliage
Taxus baccata, green

HEDGING - Small, up to 1m

SUN

Artemisia arborescens, aromatic, yellow
Buxus sempervirens 'suffruticosa', green-white
Lavandula angustifolia, aromatic, lavender-purple
Mirabilis jalapa, scented, white, yellow, pink
Rosmarinus oficinalis, aromatic, blue, white, lilac
Santolina chamaecyparissus, aromatic, yellow

SHADE

Mahonia aquifolium, scented, yellow

HEDGING - Large, over 1m

SUN

Abelia floribunda, scented, pink-purple
Abelia grandiflora, white-pink
Bougainvillea glabra, purple
Bougainvillea spectabilis, white, yellow, orange, pinks, red, lilac, purple
Choisya ternata, scented, white
Cupressus arizonica, insignificant
Cupressus macrocarpa, insignificant

Cupressus sempervirens, insignificant
Dodonea viscosa 'purpurea', green-insignificant,
pink seed cases
Duranta repens, blue, white
Hibiscus rosa-sinensis, white, cream, yellow, orange, pink, red
Hibiscus syriacus, white, pink, lilac
Juniperus chinensis, insignificant
Lantana camara, white, cream, yellow, pink, orange, red
Lonicera nitida, white
Melaleuca armillaris, scented, cream-white-yellow
Myoporum laetum, white
Myrtus communis, scented, white
Nerium oleander, white, apricot, pink, red
Opuntia ficus-indica, yellow
Pistacia lentiscus, insignificant
Plumbago capensis, blue, white
Punica granatum, orange-red
Pyracantha angustifolia, white
Rosa rugosa, scented, white, violet
Spartium junceum, scented, yellow
Taxus baccata, green
Teucrium fruticans, aromatic, blue
Viburnum tinus, scented, white

SHADE

Hebe speciosa, purple
Hydrangea macrpphylla, white, pink, blue
Taxus baccata, green

CLIMBERS - Small, up to 4m

SUN

Clianthus puniceus, red
Hardenbergia violacea, lilac-purple
Jasminum mesnyi, scented, soft yellow
Jasminum nudiflorum, yellow
Sollya heterophylla, blue

continued

SHADE

Clerodendrum thomsoniae, scented, red-white
Dipladenia amabilis, pink, white
Hardenbergia violacea, lilac-purple

CLIMBERS - Medium, 4m to 10m

SUN

Allamanda cathartica, yellow
Bignonia capreolata, tangerine
Bignonia jasminoides, white-pink
Clematis armandi, scented, cream (cool root run)
Clematis cirrhosa, cream-white-green (cool root run)
Clematis orientalis, yellow (cool root run)
Cobaea scandens, green-lilac-purple
Dipladenia grandiflora, pink
Ipomoea alba, scented, white
Jasminum azoricum, scented, white
Jasminum sambac, scented, white
Jasminum oficinale, scented, white
Jasminum polyanthemum, scented, white-pink
Lonicera japonica, scented, cream-white
Mandevilla laxa, scented, white
Mina lobata, red-orange-yellow-white
Passiflora caerulea, blue-white
Passiflora edulis, blue-white
Passiflora manicata, red-purple-white
Phaseolus caracalla, scented, white-yellow-purple
Rosa banksiae, scented, white, yellow
Solanum jasminoides, blue, white
Solanum wendlandii, lilac-blue
Tecomaria capensis, orange
Thunbergia grandiflora, lilac-blue
Trachelospermum jasminoides, scented, white

SHADE

Actinidia chinensis, scented, buff
Akebia quinata, scented, purple-mauve
Bignonia capreolata, tangerine
Clematis armandi, scented, cream (cool root run, head in sun)
Clematis cirrhosa, cream-white-green (cool root run, head in sun)
Clematis orientalis, yellow (cool root run, head in sun)
Hoya carnosa, scented, pink-white
Lonicera japonica, scented, cream-white

CLIMBERS - Large, over 10m

SUN

Bignonia ricosoleana, pink
Bignonia venusta, orange
Bougainvillea glabra, purple
Bougainvillea spectabilis, white, yellow, orange, pinks, red, lilac, purple
Campsis grandiflora, orange, apricot-yellow
Clematis montana, white, pink (cool root run)
Hedera helix, yellow-green
Ipomoea indica, blue-purple
Parthenocissus tricuspidata, green
Polygonum aubertii, cream-white
Solandra maxima, golden yellow
Vitis vinifera, green-yellow
Wisteria sinensis, scented, lilac, white

SHADE

Clematis montana, white, pink (cool root run, head in sun)
Hedera canariensis 'variegata', yellow-green
Hedera helix, yellow-green
Parthenocissus tricuspidata, green

CLIMBERS - Self-clingers

SUN

Campsis grandiflora, orange, apricot-yellow
Hedera helix, yellow-green
Parthenocissus tricuspidata, green

SHADE

Hedera canariensis 'variegata', yellow-green
Hedera helix, yellow-green
Parthenocissus tricuspidata, green

TREES - Small, up to 10m

SUN

Acacia longifolia, scented, yellow
Acacia verticillata, scented, yellow
Albizia julibrissin, pink
Arbutus unedo, scented, white
Azara microphylla, scented, yellow
Bauhinia purpurea, scented, purple-pink
Brugmansia arborea, scented, white
Caesalpinia gillesii, yellow-red
Callistemon viminalis, red
Cercis siliquastrum, magenta, white
Delonix regia, red
Dombeya wallichii, scented, pink
Dracaena draco, green-white
Dracaena indivisa, cream-brown
Ensete ventricosum, red-green
Erythrina crista galli, coral
Erythrina coralloides, coral
Feijoa sellowiana, pink-red
Ficus carica, insignificant
Hibiscus syriacus, white, pink, lilac

Lagerstroemia indica, white, pink, lilac, purple
Lavatera arborea, pink-purple
Leptospermum laevigatum, white
Melaleuca armillaris, scented, cream-white-yellow
Metrosideros excelsa, orange-red
Morus alba, greenish
Olea europaea, white-yellow
Parkinsonia aculeata, scented, yellow
Pistacea vera, red, white
Pittosporum tenuifolium, scented, purple
Plumeria acutifolia, scented, white-yellow
Strelitzia nicolai, navy blue-cream
Tamarix parviflora, pink
Thevetia peruviana, scented, peach, yellow
Tipuana tipu, yellow
Wisteria sinensis, scented, lilac, white
Yucca aloifolia, cream

SHADE

Azara microphylla, scented, yellow
Ficus benjamina, foliage

TREES - Medium, 10m to 15m

SUN

Acacia dealbata, scented, yellow
Catalpa bignonioides, scented, white
Ceratonia siliqua, cream
Chorisia speciosa, pink-gold
Eucalyptus ficifolia, red-pink-orange
Jacaranda mimosifolia, lilac-blue
Lagunaria patersonii, pink
Melia azedarach, scented, lilac
Morus negra, greenish
Paulownia tomentosa, scented, lilac
Quercus suber, greenish
Schinus molle, cream-yellow

continued ▶

Spathodea campanulata, orange-red
Taxus baccata, green

SHADE

Schefflera actinophylla, red
Taxus baccata, green

TREES - Large, over 15m

SUN

Ailanthus altissima, yellow-green
Casuarina glauca, red
Cedrus deodara, insignificant
Eucalyptus citriodora, white
Eucalyptus globulus, cream
Eucalyptus gunnii, cream-white
Eucalyptus viminalis, white
Ficus elastica, foliage
Ginkgo biloba, yellow
Grevillea robusta, gold
Magnolia grandiflora, scented, cream-white
Platanus orientalis, green
Populus alba, insignificant
Quercus ilex, insignificant

SHADE

Magnolia grandiflora, scented, cream-white

TREES - Weeping

SUN

Callistemon viminalis, red
Morus pendula, greenish
Nerium oleander, white, pink, red
Parkinsonia aculeata, scented, yellow

TREES - Conifers

SUN

Cedrus deodara, insignificant
Cupressus arizonica, insignificant
Cupressus macrocarpa, insignificant
Cupressus sempervirens, insignificant
Ginkgo biloba, yellow
Juniperus chinensis, insignificant
Juniperus communis, insignificant
Pinus pinea, insignificant

TREES - Palms

SUN

Brahea armata, grey fan
Brahea edulis, green fan
Butia capitata, green feather
Chamaerops humilis, green fan
Cycas revoluta – palm-like, green feather
Phoenix canariensis, green feather
Phoenix dactylifera, grey-green feather
Washingtonia filifera, green fan

INDEX

Latin Names

English Common Names

Spanish Common Names

Notes: _____

_____

_____

_____

_____

_____

_____

_____

_____

_____

_____

_____

Notes: _____

_____

_____

_____

_____

_____

_____

_____

_____

_____

_____

_____